TOMBSTONES

▲

TOMBSTONES

▼

A LAWYER'S TALES
FROM THE TAKEOVER
DECADES

LAWRENCE LEDERMAN

FARRAR, STRAUS AND GIROUX

NEW YORK

Copyright © 1992 by Lawrence Lederman
All rights reserved
Printed in the United States of America
Published simultaneously in Canada by HarperCollins*CanadaLtd*
Designed by Debbie Glasserman
First edition, 1992

Library of Congress Cataloging-in-Publication Data
Lederman, Lawrence.
Tombstones : a lawyer's tales from the takeover decades / Lawrence
Lederman. — 1st ed.
p. cm.
Includes index.
1. Consolidation and merger of corporations—United States.
2. Lawyers—United States. 3. Executives—United States.
I. Title.
KF1477.L43   1991   346.73'06626—dc20   [347.3066626]   91-15580 CIP

*For my mother, Lillian Lederman,
and my father, Jack Lederman,
whose spirits are the inspiration
of my life*

CONTENTS

*It's hard to see the line
if you're standing on it.*

TOMBSTONES

PROLOGUE:
TOMBSTONES

▼

"An offer is really an intangible thing."

On Tuesday morning, June 23, 1987, P. David Herrlinger of Cincinnati called the Dow Jones News Service to announce that he was making a takeover offer on behalf of himself and Stone, Inc., to acquire the Dayton Hudson Corporation, a major midwestern retailer, for $7 billion in cash. His bid of $70 a share offered a stunning premium over the New York Stock Exchange opening price of $53¼, and got prompt attention from Dow Jones. The News Service confirmed Herrlinger's identity from Capital Management, a private investment firm that employed him, and thereafter reported the offer on its national news wire at 9:49 a.m.

No one had heard of P. David Herrlinger or Stone, Inc. Seeking clarification about the offer, the New York Stock Exchange asked Dayton Hudson to comment on its terms, and caught it totally off balance and equally ignorant. The Exchange, anticipating confusion, stopped trading in the stock at 9:53 a.m. The halt covered only trades on the Exchange. Speculative buying and selling began almost immediately in the over-the-counter market and on the Boston Stock Exchange as professional traders sought to get an early position in the imminent takeover.

Meanwhile, Dayton Hudson scrambled for a footing. Shortly after 10 a.m. Dayton Hudson phoned, hooking me into a conference with about seven or eight of its officers in Minneapolis and at least five investment bankers from Goldman, Sachs & Co., some in New York and others in Chicago. As the operator added parties to the call, a dispirited voice confirmed:

"It's an ambush."

"Say who's speaking," another voice demanded.

We were in disarray in four locations in three cities.

"It all seemed easier yesterday," said a voice I recognized as that of a Dayton Hudson executive. He was wryly alluding to our meeting the previous day in Minneapolis to discuss procedures to be followed if the Dart Group, a retail holding company for the Haft family of Maryland, made a takeover bid, anticipated in the $60 per share range. There was no doubt that yesterday's drill, as composed as a Sunday drive with seat belts strapped, wasn't preparation for a $70 cash bid from an unexpected source.

"What do we do now?"

There was no easy answer. But people at the various locations began to talk at once, and the resulting cacophony on the speaker phones sounded as if everyone had suddenly been seized by hiccups. Those talking couldn't hear the way they sounded, and the equipment didn't permit interruption until they stopped of their own accord. Getting in a clear word didn't seem possible. State-of-the-art electronics and stress had produced the modern version of Babel. Finally, we took a roll call and established order.

The question now on the table was: "What do we tell the market?" A prompt answer was necessary. The blackout on the Exchange would ordinarily last until Dayton Hudson issued a statement, but under Exchange policy we had no more than two hours to come up with one, because the Exchange wanted its members to be able to participate in the early trading. As legal counsel, it was my job to decide how to respond: the company should say only what it knew, without speculating on what it didn't know.

What we knew wasn't much: only that Dow Jones confirmed that

P. David Herrlinger was a member of the Stone family, a prominent Cincinnati clan, and Stone, Inc. claimed to hold investments in Wal-Mart, the retailer, and Liz Claiborne, the apparel manufacturer. The only Stone from Cincinnati that we knew was Jimmie Stone, an investor in oil and gas properties. In the over-the-counter market, smart money was trading the Dayton Hudson stock up to $63. It was my move.

"Let's take a half hour and see if we can find any additional facts. Then we'll decide what we can say," I suggested, hoping that something would turn up. Also, it would be easier to think off the phone. About twenty minutes had passed, since we'd begun talking.

We would all resort to our computer terminals to draw on the data bases of *The New York Times* and *The Wall Street Journal*, and call around to our colleagues to see if they knew any more than we did. I set to work and found that there were no investments by Stone, Inc. in any retailers of an amount that would have to be publicly reported, and nothing about the players showed up in either data base. Jimmie Stone couldn't be reached, but his involvement seemed doubtful, since he was primarily involved in oil and gas ventures and was known never to have made a hostile takeover bid. There was no more information.

I tallied what I knew.

Multibillion-dollar bids by individuals were common by June 1987, and the $70 offer acknowledged the widely known interest of the Dart Group at $60 or more and raised the bidding to a level that showed appreciation of takeover strategy.

Against the one right pricing gambit, however, was a series of odd omissions that needed explaining. Bids are usually made by a telephone call to the chairman of the company, followed by a hand-delivered letter, usually before the opening of the Exchange, rarely after trading begins. Herrlinger's bid, as made to the Dow Jones News Service, purporting to come from a well-established family (unlikely to make unorthodox moves), ignored those conventions.

Nothing said Herrlinger's actions had to be predictable. It could be a brilliant strategy; it had served to put us in disarray. But the failure to call management and alert the company to the bid was inexplicable to me. Since the Stone family didn't own any retail businesses, they would need management, if only for transition.

And the cleverness, if it was that, came from our ignorance about Herrlinger, and not from any masterstroke. Had the world changed so much that people whom no one knew, and who didn't seem professionally advised, could raise $7 billion? I didn't think so. Moreover, active trading didn't make the bid real, for in this heated market takeover stocks were eagerly traded on any flimsy information.

All that head scratching led me to believe that the bid wasn't genuine. That wasn't easy to accept: conjectures aren't facts, and the making of a bogus bid was unprecedented.

At about 10:45 a.m. the conference call resumed, with Dayton Hudson calling the roll.

"Has Herrlinger called the company yet?" I asked.

"No," a company officer said, disappointment apparent even in the one-word answer.

The group agreed that Dayton Hudson should keep its public response simple. The prepared release said that the company didn't know Herrlinger and wouldn't comment on proposals made only to the news wires and not to it. That statement would give the trading markets sufficient reason to question the bid, after which the market was on its own, and we'd watch developments.

The release was sent to the news wires at about 11:25 and at 11:49 the stock opened at $59, sharply down from the trading in the over-the-counter market. To cover the story, *The Wall Street Journal* sent a local reporter to interview P. David Herrlinger, who had set up his takeover campaign headquarters in his elegant home. Impeccably dressed in a blue blazer and gray slacks, at ease in a comfortable chair on his rolling lawn, Herrlinger was the perfect picture of old-line money. He took the opportunity of the interview to launch the public relations phase of his offer by telling the *Journal* about himself, his co-bidders, the Cincinnati Stone family, and their interest in acquiring Dayton Hudson. With the *Journal* now aware that the company hadn't been called, its questions to Herrlinger were pointed:

Journal: "Mr. Herrlinger, where will the financing for your offer come from?"

Herrlinger: "That's still undecided."

Journal: "It will take over $7 billion."

Herrlinger: "That's why the financing is very debatable."

Journal: "Is the offer a hoax?"

Herrlinger: "I don't know. It's no more a hoax than anything else . . . An offer is really an intangible thing."

Journal: "Who is Stone, Inc.?"

Herrlinger: "It's not incorporated yet. I'm a vice president."

At about 12:49 p.m. Dow Jones said that the bid might not be bona fide, and shortly thereafter the Stone family disavowed the bid.

What about the effect of the event on the stock market? I called a friend at an investment banking house who I thought could give a thoughtful assessment of the incident. I could hear the clicking of the keys of his Quotron terminal as he punched in the stock symbol to get the price.

"The stock is practically back to where it was when it opened this morning," he said. "I'd guess, based on the trading volume, about $15 to $20 million was lost. Some guys were probably bent out of shape. That's the risk they took."

"People may become more cautious after this," I ventured.

"By tomorrow we'll all forget about it," he said.

"Should we?" I asked.

"There will be a lot of things to do tomorrow." To emphasize the ephemeral effect of Herrlinger's action, he added, "There won't be a tombstone for this deal."

Tombstones are announcements of completed transactions, printed with black borders on the business pages, somewhat in the sparse style of headstones. He was referring, however, to the tombstones that were encased in plastic cubes or imprinted on ashtrays, pen sets, clocks, and the like to commemorate deals meant to be remembered. My office is filled with them, tokens of twenty years of practice.

Looking at the objects around my office, I saw the papers that I'd put aside on the working table opposite my desk, and the message slips of telephone calls I'd allowed to back up. I got back to work, but made room in my day to get reports on Herrlinger.

At about 3:30 p.m. the Dow Jones reported that Herrlinger had been taken to a hospital for psychiatric evaluation. Herrlinger was forty-six years old, a family man with four children. From newspaper stories later that afternoon I learned that Anthony Covatta, his neighbor and a lawyer speaking for the family, tried to provide additional perspective. "You've got a guy who's got some problems that have come on very suddenly. It looks to me like he got into a fantasy mode today. There's not much more to it than that. He's a lovely guy, just as plain as an old shoe . . . This is a terrible thing. A guy who's never owned a pair of Gucci shoes in his life does this."

Covatta's confusion was touching. He was trying to tell us all, and himself as well, that behavior isn't always the arithmetic sum of past actions. Indeed. When is it ever? Herrlinger's life was now a shambles. I felt sorry for him, and for his family and friends.

At the end of the day, I looked at the price of the Dayton Hudson stock. It had opened at 53¼ and closed at 53⅛. The opening and closing prices didn't reflect the day's aberrant behavior. My blood pressure was probably not as resilient. It's people that are fragile, I thought, not the system.

As I looked around my office, the random scatter of the tombstones caught my eye. Their number, over two hundred of them, reminded me that I'd started out a stranger to corporate America and was now participating in its financial restructuring. All the tombstones were dated, pinpointing events otherwise hard to place, and invitingly offered the possibility of a perspective on a world that had changed and transformed me.

I was no longer the person who had graduated from law school determined to be a law professor. Where had the turnings been? The answer was locked in those mementos, which did more than give notice of the life and death of corporations: they chronicled two decades of activity, each a marker of change. But I couldn't make much sense out of them unless they were in chronological order. No surfaces were large enough to arrange them on, except for the floor. Without much effort, I moved four chairs and my working table to one side to give myself room.

Then I sat on the floor, took off my shoes to be comfortable, and began sorting the blocks and other items, arranging the pieces of my professional life in chronological order. At such moments no one should be able to ask you to explain your behavior. Unfortunately for me, one of the uniformed building night watchmen, apparently attracted by the light, came into my office. He was a tall man with thick glasses that made his eyes look uncompromising. Worse, I didn't know him. I stood up, trying to regain my poise, painfully aware of my shoes off to the side. In stocking feet, I felt unequal to him.

"I'm arranging them," I said, relying on the ambiguity to avoid explanation.

I looked back down at the floor at the strange items that I'd started to align in twenty rows and thought: This is an unconscionable mess. I'm going to wind up in the room next door to P. David Herrlinger. No Quotron for him. No computer terminal or telephone for me. But if they let us read the business pages we'd be able to discuss the progress of the deals.

He bent down and looked at some of the cubes, reading a few carefully. "Do you need any help?" he asked.

Clearly he didn't understand what I was doing.

"It's better if I do this myself," I said. "These are mementos of deals I worked on," I quickly explained.

"Do you like what you do?" he asked. Did he want to talk or was he testing my coherence, the way police do at roadblocks for drunken drivers?

"Yes, I like my work," I said.

"Why?" he asked.

"Each day is a surprise," I said. I gave him a hard look to let him know that I wasn't going to be sociable.

"You have some 1977 ones by your right foot. You missed them in setting up the row."

I found the missed cubes, put them in order with the proper flourish that acknowledged his help, and waited until he obligingly left.

I sat down again and continued to arrange the tombstones, stopping every so often to recall some person or incident, and found myself making the needed connections. In these matters, played for high stakes, I'd encountered deceptions more contrived than Herrlinger's, and experienced the satisfaction of separating appearance from reality. Revelation wasn't always so immediate as in the bid for Dayton Hudson. Sometimes it took months, even years, for the tale to unfold. Putting the blocks in place illuminated the past in surprising ways.

Through participation in these deals and seeing their effects, I'd drawn the lessons of my education and my perspective. The markers, lined up like memorials on my floor, displayed the changes over two decades in myself, in the people around me, and in corporate America. But not all aspects were fully illuminated on that evening. Within three months of the Herrlinger incident, the stock markets crashed, and in the next two years, with the end of the decade, some transactions I'd participated in failed or soured. Time and change further rounded out the meaning of the events marked by the tombstones. All that is set out here.

▲
APPRENTICE
▼

APPRENTICE

▼

"There is very little law in the job."

I began practicing law at Cravath, Swaine & Moore. I knew little about practice, less about law firms. Straight from law school, I'd served as a law clerk on the California Supreme Court. The one-year clerkship with the Chief Justice was meant to be a stepping-stone to a career as a law teacher. It offered insight into the workings of the judicial system through participating in the decision-making process of an important court. But I also wanted to learn about corporate law firsthand. The experiences in court and in the law office, like the findings of a field trip, were meant to be brought back to the classroom.

The Cravath firm's antecedents could be traced to 1819. Its lineage, charted out like a family tree, was framed and displayed in the reception area of its offices on the fifty-seventh floor of the Chase Manhattan Building, along with a letter from Abraham Lincoln to the firm, when Cravath had engaged Lincoln as a correspondent attorney in Illinois on a collection matter. In recent times Justice William O. Douglas had practiced there and so had John

J. McCloy, U.S. Military Governor and High Commissioner for Germany. Cravath represented the establishment and was one of the elite law firms. Affiliation with the firm placed you, it seemed, in the top tier of American legal practice. Its history and experience were supposed to rub off, adorning you with its much admired patina.

The firm was known for its master apprentice method of training its associate lawyers, called the "Cravath system." In practice, an associate worked exclusively for one partner for eighteen months to two years, and at the end of the assignment period rotated to another partner until, over an eight-year period, the associate had become a journeyman lawyer ready for partnership. At most other firms, associates worked for a group or several groups of partners and no one person had responsibility for their development. Starting at Cravath, you entered a highly organized and rigid culture.

My first day was the first Monday in November 1967. On that day, I was already out of phase. Almost all the members of the entering class, about forty of them, had started their careers in August, after taking the bar exam, or in September, and the few remaining stragglers had arrived in early October. Reporting for work in November, after finishing my one-year judicial clerkship, I was by far the last to begin.

I was assigned an office, which I was to share. It was a duplicate of sixty other offices for associates, identical down to the last detail of size, furniture, metal filing cabinets, and office equipment. There were to be, according to the rules, no variations. These were sparse, no-nonsense offices, shabby from wear. No diplomas or evidences of admission to the bar or to practice before the courts were ever hung on the walls. That was regarded as gauche, an affectation of doctors or dentists. The redeeming feature of each of the offices was a large window (actually a glass wall) that looked out on lower Manhattan from an unobstructed height. In all the offices, the junior associate sat by the door with his desk against and facing the wall, and the senior associate sat by the window with his desk squarely planted in the center of the room at a right angle to the junior associate's desk, his back to the window and facing the door. The configuration of the furniture rejected the view; its sole purpose was to tell you the occupant's status.

In my case, the senior associate had the office to himself through October without any other desk in the room, and by November he assumed that this office would be his alone, not contemplating a late arrival. Moreover, he'd been at the firm almost eight years and was entitled to his own office, but the firm was overcrowded. On the morning of my arrival they moved a standard-issue desk and filing cabinet into the room, and he found the furniture lodged against the wall, terminating his privacy and any illusion of junior partner status. In his in basket was a copy of my picture and a short biography. As with every newly arrived associate, it had been circulated to all the 160 lawyers (approximately 120 associates and 40 partners) in the firm so that the others also would know something about the new arrival. They were told in typical terse Cravath fashion, bereft of any mention of personal history, that I was a graduate of Brooklyn College, class of 1957, and NYU law school, class of 1966, and since September 1966 had been a law clerk. My address in Staten Island was listed. That was all the others in the firm needed to know. Since almost everyone at Cravath was a graduate of an Ivy League college or law school, it was probably assumed that through that network the relevant information would flow to those interested.

No one knew me. At the time I was one of two lawyers who had attended the City University, and there were few NYU Law School graduates at the firm, only one of whom was recent. My biography and arrival at Cravath spoke volumes about my career (late starter), social class (lower middle), work experience (apprentice grind), speech (probably too New York), and social aspirations (none). These were insights to which they had immediate access, but ones that I wasn't knowledgeable enough to share or even understand; nor could I realize how quickly and decisively I'd been classified.

I introduced myself to my office mate, took my jacket off, hung it up on the hanger behind the door, and rolled up my sleeves to start filling out countless forms waiting for data and signature. While I worked on the forms, my office mate introduced me to the rules and culture of Cravath.

First, the dress code. I was told that in the eight years that my office mate had been at the firm he'd never taken off his jacket, let alone rolled up his sleeves, and he didn't regard my actions as appropriate behavior. Whether or not he relished my discomfort, for I sat there feeling as exposed as if half undressed, he told me that there were some others who did go without their jackets. There could be, he implied, some deviations in dress. No one, however, rolled up their sleeves or wore short-sleeved shirts.

Then protocol. Partners were supposed to be referred to by their last name, "Mr. So-and-so," or as "sir." There were then no women partners. Partners didn't socialize with associates, meaning that they didn't eat lunch with them (unless there was a meeting with a client that the associate had to attend) and didn't meet associates in the evening (unless it was in connection with a firm function). To make the separation complete, partners had their own bathrooms, which associates weren't permitted to use.

And of course there was the work ethic. Work started at 9:30 a.m. and ended when you finished, which was usually late and often included weekend work. If you were busy, it was thought that you were highly regarded by the firm. Therefore, everyone looked busy and worked long hours. With the doors to all offices closed to discourage casual and idle conversation, there was no doubt that this was a hardworking firm. I sensed a note of bitterness.

Finally, the practice of law. I was told by my office mate: "There is very little law in the job." Most deals were a repeat of other deals, and the associate's job was to find the appropriate bound volume where a similar deal had been previously documented and then mark up copies of the papers collected in the volume. Those papers were forms; they were called "precedent" to give them a legal and judicial flavor. Completing the forms was supposed to give you the sense, however tenuous, that the process of filling in the blanks was part of the practice of law. But no matter how slavishly you followed the form, the partner or senior associate for whom you worked would change the words added and the form as well. "Vetting" was the word used to describe the procedure. Each form, vetted innumerable times, was treated as if it were novel, my office mate advised, and the flat tone of his words delivered the full measure of the tedium.

The deals were heavily documented. Such documentation re-

quired administration. Documents had to come in from all over:
other law firms had to produce their share; so did the accountants;
and company officials; and even public officials of various states.
For a closing, all these documents had to come in at the same time,
like acrobats joining in midair. Any failure of precision, and the
closing would be delayed, with the loss of the time value of money
such a delay entails. Nothing is more damning than costing the
client money, and so Cravath associates were taught how to administer deals, with all the rigor and seriousness of basic military
training. When you started at the firm it was assumed that you
would have trouble running a one-car funeral. After a while you
could organize occasions of state.

In financing transactions in which corporations borrowed money,
someone had thought through all the legal aspects a long time ago.
It was hopelessly difficult to separate the substance in the forms
from the compulsive gestures of pinched minds. Your job, however,
was not to deviate; otherwise you were in uncharted waters where
you took foolhardy risks with millions of dollars.

Acquisition transactions were different, I was told. There was
actually give-and-take and discussion with clients. No acquisition
is totally cut-and-dried. Even when all the terms are thought to
have been worked out, the complexity of buying and selling makes
it impossible for any two business people to agree on everything.
And thus the lawyers have a role: in addition to documenting the
deal, they have to find the open points and resolve them in accordance with the elusive logic of the transaction. If that was what
was involved, acquisition transactions seemed rather dry and didn't
spark my interest.

It was hard for me to accept that what I'd walked into offered
such a narrow opportunity for exercising judgment. As a judicial
law clerk I'd participated in making decisions about life and death;
I'd worked on two death penalty cases, sorting facts, applying the
law, and considering the consequences to the defendant and the
system of justice. Here, paper shuffling was treated seriously, and
as a task of great difficulty. My face, I am sure, showed my dismay
as I questioned my decision to work as a corporate lawyer.
Shouldn't I tell the firm that I wanted to be trained as a litigation

lawyer and argue cases in court? Anything seemed preferable to sitting in stuffy offices and marking up forms. But I'd already made my decision, and a change would rupture the Cravath system.

Before hiring an associate, the firm required the applicant to decide whether to be a litigation lawyer or a corporate lawyer. Although that decision determined one's career, Cravath didn't contemplate a sampling of the alternatives. Somehow you were supposed to know what you wanted to do. Many people didn't, I found out later. Choices were made on a variety of preconceptions, many misinformed. Once the decision was made and you started working, the firm rarely entertained a change of mind. My career decision, perhaps more rational than most, was based on my experience as a law clerk for Chief Justice Roger J. Traynor for the year beginning in September 1966.

The California Supreme Court sat in San Francisco and monitored a restless and litigious population, which generated a heavy calendar of cases to be argued. Everything about the courtroom was designed to hear argument, and the courtroom was like a theater. The seven Justices sat behind a bench on a raised platform the height of a stage and the several hundred seats in the court were upholstered, tiered seats for comfortable viewing of the proceedings. Even the acoustics were excellent, but none of that mattered. Despite the structure of the courtroom, Chief Justice Traynor would attempt to limit oral argument in every case and to fit in as many cases as possible during the days in which the court heard argument.

A case began with counsel standing at a podium in the well of the court looking up at the seven Justices, and argument usually commenced with counsel reciting the facts of the case. Traynor, high above counsel, silver-haired and imposing in the black judicial robes of the Chief Justice, would immediately break in and say, "Counsel, we are familiar with the case. Do you have anything to add that is not in your brief?" Counsel would usually say, "If it please the court, I would like to give you a flavor of the facts." Traynor would then say, "Counsel, we believe that we understand the facts." Deferential but firm, counsel would say, "This is a very unusual case, your honor." Counsel would be somewhat vexed at this point and for good reason. Having lost in the court below, he was convinced that the courts didn't understand his case and he wanted an opportunity to see the point of view of the Justices and to change their minds. Moreover, his client was in the courtroom, expecting him to give a star-quality performance.

Traynor would say firmly, "Counsel, we understand your case. Your case is as follows." He would then concisely and accurately, in no more than two sentences, sum up the argument of the case, and firmly ask counsel to sit down.

I was not prepared for what I saw. It was a total departure from anything I'd experienced in law school, where argument was the engine that made the law work. In fact, these same judges appeared in law schools to act as judges of the students' moot court and were congenial and always attentive to the lengthy arguments.

Working for the Chief Justice, I found that courtroom lawyers weren't the only constituency of the court. The court wrote its opinions for the lawyers and the public who used them for guidance in conducting their business and affairs. My classmates told me that in other appellate courts, argument also wasn't considered important. Generally, the better the court, the less important was oral argument by counsel. Even the briefs of counsel, while carefully reviewed, were not always decisive in determining the outcome of the case. Counsel usually took polar positions or adhered strictly to the client's interest, and the court's decisions addressed the middle ground and the public good.

When Cravath required me to make the decision about how I would practice, I chose corporate law, assuming that corporate lawyers gave advice that was tested in the courts and shaped and structured the cases rather than argued them. By my reasoning, corporate lawyers had a critical role in the legal process. But how well founded were my assumptions? My office mate thought that corporate practice was lifeless, offering little chance to give advice about the law. Although shaken, I was reluctant to change my decision on the basis of my first few hours at the firm. I tried to appear resolute, but there was more in store for me that first morning that would test my nerve.

After talking to me and coming to whatever conclusions one does when making a final judgment, my office mate told me that I wouldn't be a partner at Cravath. I don't believe I'd shared the space with him for more than two hours. The effect of such a statement is not quite the same as being told you are terminally ill, but it was damaging enough, especially coming after only two hours on the job.

I was insulated to the extent that I wasn't seeking the brass ring of partnership. I planned to stay for about two years to get practical experience before beginning a teaching career. However, I felt offended. One never likes to be told that there is no future. But he said it all in such a casual way that it was clear that it was said without malice. Most of the Wall Street law firms, including Cravath, worked on an eight-year system of association with the firm leading to partnership. If you weren't elevated to partnership, you were asked to leave. In the end, almost everybody left, most before the final selection occurred, with only five or fewer people remaining out of a group of thirty-five or forty, all graduates of first-rate schools, at the top or near the top of their class. Of the five, one or two and sometimes none would be taken. All selections were supposed to be made on merit, with the best, the firm said, always taken. From that you had to conclude there was always an opportunity to become a partner. In fact, during the six-year period that I was there (beginning in 1968), only two aspirants from the herd of associates were made partners.

For eight years my office mate had never taken his suit jacket off, called everybody "sir," and worked late nights and many weekends, with many of the weekends not worked otherwise ruined by homework. He had everything going for him. He was tall, gracious, and handsome; white and Anglo-Saxon Protestant; and smart, with enough social sense to wear reserved, well-fitting, appropriate clothing. Despite all that in his favor, he'd been asked to leave. Although they could have used him, they didn't need him. For him it was not personal. Everyone in my office mate's entering class except one had been told to leave.

He laid out the practical consequences of his conclusion that I wouldn't be a partner. On all matters that I worked on, I should keep my own files in addition to those of the firm. It was very expensive to keep duplicates, but the firm didn't care, everybody did it, and when I left I would be able to take my files with me. All those copies would represent forms that could be used elsewhere. Despite his irritation at the loss of solitude, my office mate was giving me good, neighborly advice.

My office mate had come for the shine of the firm, and now had to deal with the problems of rejection. On the first day I was seeing the last days. Why would you ever want to start if this was the way it ended? The answer was that being a partner at a firm like Cravath was regarded as the ultimate success for a lawyer, and the firm was looked on as being as much a part of the fabric of America as institutions created by the Rockefellers and J. P. Morgan. Many knew that partnership was, at best, largely elusive and came to Cravath for mobility, to keep their options open, with the hope that the training would allow them to move freely into business or banking or into lesser, but solid law firms. There was also a history of well-regarded law professors who had served a short apprenticeship at Cravath, which was the reason I was attracted to the firm. Leaving, however, sometimes subjected you to the stigma of not having made it at Cravath. There was an opportunity in the third or fourth year (and more rarely later) to exit gracefully into another field, but you had to find the fulcrum point at your own risk.

On the first day, I asked myself again why I had started there. An important reason for me was that Cravath and the law firms like it were the center of corporate financial practice in America, and the partners in these firms were persons anyone involved in financial transactions would encounter and have to understand. It was the first time I'd ever been allowed into an elite organization, and if I left too soon, I would be forever awed by it and cowed by its partners. In its midst, I could learn the firm's strengths and weaknesses, know what the partners knew, and would then be prepared to engage them as adversaries. But that response to myself, important as it was to me later, didn't quite satisfy me, because everything at the firm seemed more routine and less challenging than I thought it would be. I should have understood that the reality of the institution is often not the image that it projects for itself and that it couldn't be understood in a short time. I repeated to myself that I was interested in a teaching career. Even as the thought gave me comfort, I knew that I might not pursue teaching.

My office mate, having compressed over 145 years of the firm's history into personal reality and initiated me into the secret society that was Cravath, took pity on me and offered to take me to lunch. He could see I knew no one and wouldn't for a while, since the doors to all the offices were closed and it was difficult to meet anyone. I agreed to go, although I felt exhausted and depressed from his information and assessment.

After lunch, not knowing what to expect, I went to meet the partners who would control my professional universe and shape my career. On the first Monday I was assigned to work for Francis Fitz Randolph, Jr., and another partner. That was unusual. Ordinarily associates worked for only one partner, unless two partners (older and younger) worked together. These two men didn't work together, and the assignment didn't accord with the Cravath system. Doomed to failure for that reason, it failed for other reasons.

Frank Randolph and I were paired because of my late arrival. The other partners had gotten their quota of associates. Frank had been occupied exclusively as the executor of his father's estate for two years prior to my joining the firm and was winding up the estate when I arrived. The firm, trying to figure out what to do with me, put me with Frank, a gesture that even the firm didn't take seriously. They didn't expect that there would be any kind of bonding between us, or that Frank would be able to pay enough attention to encourage an attachment. Also, from their point of view, Frank's continued involvement with his family's estate entitled him only to half of an associate's time.

Frank's father had been the senior partner and head of J. & W. Seligman & Co., an investment banking firm, and had been a Cravath associate as a young man. Frank had followed uncomfortably in his father's footsteps and achieved partnership status. He was forty-one when I began working for him, and had had a brilliant academic career at Yale College and Columbia Law School, followed by a law clerkship with Charles Clark, a respected federal appellate judge who had been dean of the Yale Law School. No matter, Frank, in mid-life, was everything a Cravath partner shouldn't be. He was undisciplined, eccentric, and often bored with what he was doing. Recently divorced and courting the woman who would become his wife, he was unavailable for evening work. Moreover, after his father's demise he was unquestionably rich and, by Cravath standards, a playboy.

On the first day Frank told me that he had nothing for me to do and that I should come back the next day. It was a bland statement of the situation, honestly put, but without a hint that tomorrow would be different, and totally disconcerting. I didn't think I would have a relationship with this fair-skinned man with blond hair, just turning gray, whose blue eyes looked indifferent.

Feeling the anxiety of no work, I cast around for something to do and went to see the other partner to whom I was assigned, a knowledgeable securities lawyer in the Cravath mold. More than most of his brethren, he looked the part of the Cravath partner: tall, fair-haired, ramrod straight, and always attired in suspenders, called braces. In keeping with the role, he was arrogant and sharp-tongued and reveled in his status. When I reported to him on my first day, he put me on a train to Washington, D.C., to file papers with the Securities and Exchange Commission for one of his clients. First, though, he delivered a spirited lecture about the importance of the job, and its incidental benefits, which included the chance to learn how to get to the SEC and the location of the filing desk. I felt like a pawn in his game.

After I returned from the SEC, my assignment expanded to putting together the file for the transaction and compiling a bound volume of all the papers. There was, of course, a Cravath procedure to be followed. Again, another lecture: this time I would learn a great deal about doing transactions from collating the papers and having them bound. As I took the papers from him, the irritation in my face showed my feelings, which proved to be an effective message, for he never again called on me to work for him and I never volunteered.

On my second day at Cravath, I decided to devote my entire energy to Frank Randolph, rather than fight for reassignment, which my office mate told me was rarely approved. I made the choice after learning that Frank wasn't part of the mainstream of the firm, resigning myself to a boring and short stay in law practice. I misjudged Frank, which was easy to do, because his shrewdness and drive, eclipsed by his charm, were not readily apparent. He had his misgivings about me; I had too much to learn, and he wasn't prepared to teach in an orderly way. Frank, however, needed help, and I needed work.

Frank represented United Fruit, which was trying to sell its communications network in Central America, held by its subsidiary Tropical Radio Telegraph Corporation. The network, a sizable commercial system, was originally developed from ship-to-shore communications between United Fruit's banana boats and its plantations. Licenses and concessions for the network granted by various of the Central American governments were expiring. In view of the high level of hostility toward United Fruit, it believed that none would be renewed or the cost for renewal would be too expensive. Moreover, the Central American governments were looking for a company that would come in and upgrade the facilities, which United Fruit was reluctant to do. United Fruit was eager to sell, and RCA was the interested buyer.

When I left the judicial clerkship, I was the only clerk who went to work on Wall Street. I was told by my fellow law clerks that I would become, if I didn't watch out, a United Fruit fascist bastard. Sooner than anyone expected, I experienced the irony of that statement.

In what was my first corporate meeting, Frank and I met with RCA. Executives of RCA and United Fruit had previously met in New York, without lawyers present, and had agreed on the price, which was to be paid in RCA shares. None of the other terms had been worked out—these were considered details to be left to the lawyers. RCA's lawyers had then prepared the first draft of the purchase agreement, taking the opportunity to formulate these details in their favor. Our meeting convened in the boardroom of RCA. I'd never seen a conference room that large. The RCA group of fourteen was seated on one side of a magnificent wood conference table which was dwarfed by the room. Representing United Fruit were Frank, myself, and a lawyer on staff at United Fruit, who had never sold or bought a business. He was relying on Cravath for guidance. The three of us centered ourselves on the opposite side of the table.

The RCA contingent consisted of middle-aged men dressed in gray or blue. No attempt had been made to explain their individual status, and it took me a while to fathom their various functions.

Although I didn't know it then, such a large group wasn't uncommon. Their team consisted of Robert Werner, the general counsel and a director of RCA, who conducted the meeting; two assistant general counsels, experienced and knowledgeable men, including Eugene Beyer, who subsequently became general counsel; two lawyers from Cahill, Gordon & Reindel (a large Wall Street law firm which did the federal communications and regulatory work for RCA); two independent auditors and two in-house accountants; and two actuaries from Towers & Perrin, an independent actuarial firm. The actuaries were there to comfort the accountants and provide information on the assets of the Tropical Radio Telegraph pension plan. Also present for RCA were three vice presidents from an operating unit of RCA that would run the company to be acquired.

While it was an impressive array of people, I naïvely assumed that with a Cravath partner on our side we matched them. What I didn't know was that Frank had believed that the meeting would be a short preliminary get-together of lawyers to discuss procedures to be followed and wouldn't address substantive issues. Tropical Radio Telegraph's business was regulated by the Federal Communications Commission and a host of foreign governments. Frank Randolph knew relatively little about Tropical Radio Telegraph's business or the regulatory aspects involved in the transaction. The complexity required specialists, whom Frank would have brought or had United Fruit supply if he had been forewarned of RCA's agenda for the meeting. Within three minutes RCA knew they had us outclassed. It took me much longer to understand that we hadn't fielded a team. They wouldn't let us exit gracefully, telling us early in the meeting that they had arranged for lunch.

I watched them play with us. Robert Werner would raise a question about Tropical Radio Telegraph's business, and we couldn't answer it. He would then ask one of his operating people who knew the business and he'd tell us the most likely mode of operation. Werner would then turn to the corporate lawyers and rephrase the question for their use and then it would be rephrased and rolled over and reflected on by the FCC lawyers and the accountants and the actuaries and so on.

I was waiting for our turn to come: that moment when we would show a flash of brilliance and the Cravath colors would fly for everybody to salute. The firm colors hung but didn't flutter. Frank was polite and charming, but not effective. Our preliminary comments on RCA's draft had all been anticipated. Every time we made one, we faced a series of arguments from a string of specialists who told us that they couldn't yield on the point. There was no deferring to any of our points and I came away totally satisfied that they couldn't assent. I didn't understand that a first draft is always an asking position from which people back down. Although they had been aggressive to start, they didn't retreat on anything.

The only respite was at lunch. The seating gave me a sense of the corporate hierarchy. Frank was placed at the table with Robert Werner and the senior officials of RCA and I was seated with RCA's operating people who would run Tropical Radio Telegraph after it was acquired. They knew all about me: about my college and law school, my wife and child, and even the date I'd started at Cravath. They had thoroughly investigated me before the meeting. Their information bled out slowly over lunch. Much as I was offended that they would probe into my life merely because I'd come to a business meeting, their inquiry told me that they were willing to go to great lengths to get very little information, which meant that they were extremely well prepared, and we were not.

Frank beat a retreat after lunch at about 3 p.m., and we went back to the office, where Frank asked me to draw the table: tell him the names of all fourteen people, their organizations, positions, relationship to each other, and contributions to the meeting. In that analysis he also wanted finer assessments, such as whether they were smart or experienced and whether their judgments were reasoned or emotional. Uncomfortable about the poor performance of the day and all that the other side seemed to know about us, I worried that it was a test. As such, it would be difficult to pass.

I sat down next to Frank and did what he asked, drawing the places at the table and telling him the names of all the people, their approximate ages, background information about their schooling or prior employment picked up in conversation, the positions they held, their level of seniority, how they were regarded by all the other people, and how effective they had been. I told him who was smart and who wasn't and who thought he was smarter than he was and who was levelheaded. When he added what he knew as the table began to be fleshed out, I relaxed. We spent well over two hours at it, and Frank relived the meeting to understand the questions asked, his responses, and their reactions. I realized he'd suffered from the pressure of being unprepared during the meeting and wasn't able to follow all that was going on. In my innocence, I'd observed most of what had occurred. We then began to form a strategy for dealing with RCA. In the quiet of his office, he laid out all he knew and what we should try to get for the client. I saw a thoughtful and imaginative mind at work, and to replay the meeting was to become a full participant, with a sense of the adversarial aspects of doing a deal.

At every meeting after that I would always draw the table for Frank and then, when working alone, for myself. It always produces insights, and knowing you will do it keeps you alert. The observations help you to be able to size up, fairly early, whom you are dealing with and to make a decision about where you will be able to come to agreement and over which issues negotiations will be difficult. If you listen, people will tell you the problems they foresee, and sometimes express their reasonable expectations and their worst fears.

United Fruit executives thereafter attended all meetings with RCA. Once the executives articulated their objectives, Frank's talents could work, and his ability became obvious. As a lawyer, Frank Randolph was a trader, which is like being a counterpuncher in boxing. He would look to swap this deal point for that; build up makeweight points (requests for concessions from the other side that he treated as critical) to have bargaining chips that he could later give away; and then go through the trades that were possible given the points. Two of this for one of that. The trading went on until the deal was signed; sometimes even after. The discipline that Frank exhibited was that of a fine, trained mind defining the important and the unimportant. He sought and found a theory of the deal, but never demanded simplicity, allowing the deals to become complex, which made them difficult to document. At the outset of the trading with RCA, there was the question of who gets the profits of the business between signing and closing, which could take as long as seven or eight months because of the regulatory approval needed from government agencies. The amount at stake was sizable. RCA took the position that it was buying the business including the income. Frank's position was they were buying it the way it would be if it were operated in the ordinary course, including the customary payment of dividends. Finally Frank won by pointing out that RCA was not cumulating dividends on its stock in favor of United Fruit between the signing and the closing. Until they owned the company or its stock, they weren't entitled to its income.

Frank was clever in handling the documentation. All lawyers are eager to prepare the papers, but Frank would usually let the other side do the first draft, which freed him to work on more than one or two deals at a time. That reversed the conventional wisdom that it's better to be the draftsman, for it is often thought that the hand that wields the pen controls the nuances of the transaction. Frank would comment, counterpunch as it were, telling me that you have to learn how to read closely as well as write closely.

There were two elements to look for in any draft: one was its accuracy in reflecting the deal, and the other, its omissions. The difficult part was to find what had been left out. Frank would start with "what if" and then go through the structure of the draft and see how it worked. For example, he would ask if United Fruit had to sell its subsidiary under the contract with RCA if it didn't get satisfactory regulatory approval. It might be possible to have to pay damages for failing to sell even though United Fruit wasn't permitted legally to sell. That would not be a happy result. The process of asking questions was like playing pinball. He'd run the ball through the maze and see what lit up and what didn't. He would spin ten or fifteen balls through with me, and the agreement would start to take on shape, then three dimensions and life. When its inadequacies showed, he asked the inevitable question: Could we layer on another level of complexity to account for the omissions? Of course.

The process was very different from what you learn in law school or clerking on an appellate court considering litigated issues. Those situations involved a dispute where the issues were sharply defined. The point here was to craft a deal where there would be no disputes or, if circumstances changed and the bargain became less interesting for one party than another, your client had the leverage.

Accordingly, the problems inherent in any deal were as complex as you wanted to make them. You could be concerned with matters as remote as war, rebellion and insurrection, or the state of the economy, banking moratoriums, or just plain deceit. There were the problems that were readily apparent and those that a fine mind could find. It was important not to be dazzled by your own intellect and reach for remote points or scared by your own shadow and try to cover everything.

Handling any matter required a strong knowledge of substantive law. In litigation there was often the leisure of research, with time to find the law on the disputed issues. A young lawyer can be effective in litigation almost immediately because the skills learned in law school all relate to fact finding, argument, and application of rules to facts. The side of the law for which most people look to lawyers—planning and getting things done—received the least amount of attention in law school. In corporate practice, deals were traded and documented overnight, and you had to know the law or, if you were unsure, take a conservative tack. You could only learn those skills from someone who was experienced and would permit you to participate in the process. The price of the training was apprenticeship, with the apprentice's low status and burdens.

I didn't appreciate the difficulty of using the law as a tool for making agreements until I did some work on my own. Eager to try, I chafed at the bit until Frank let me handle the sale of cable television assets for $5,000, too small a matter for him. What was involved was the simple transfer of assets, which consisted mainly of a cable television antenna in upstate New York, to a buyer who wanted to take over the local cable business. Our client, the seller, sought to be relieved of a performance bond to the telephone company for $35,000. The deal was drawn up as an agreement to deliver the assets conditioned on the release by the telephone company of the $35,000 bond.

In preparing the papers, I didn't require the buyer to "promise" to have the bond released and hold the seller harmless, and when the buyer didn't perform, claiming he was not required to do so under the contract, the seller still owned the company but had no rights against the buyer. I then realized that I had inadvertently given the buyer an option, without charge, and allowed him to change his mind.

I did some legal research to try to justify the papers and wrote a complex and convoluted memo to the effect that the condition for the benefit of the seller was tantamount to a promise by the buyer to perform, trying to make two different concepts the same. After preparing the memo, I realized that I'd never fully understood the concepts.

I took it to Frank, who said, "We can't argue this."

"Why" I asked, still prepared, because of my embarrassment, to defend the point, and angry that the buyer (and his small-town upstate lawyer) had taken advantage of me and my client.

"Because we know the difference between an option where the buyer can buy or not at his whim and a promise to perform," he said, dismissing all my anger. And then he asked a brilliant question: "How would your judge decide this one?"

I frowned. For over a year I had worked cheek by jowl with Justice Traynor in his chambers and understood the decision process. I knew the answer without much thought. My judge would rule against us.

Seeing my face, Frank said, "Let's not waste any more time."

And that was the end of it. And while it was a small matter that went unnoticed, I still smart when I think of it. Thus, I did my first deal alone, learning that I was inept after four years of legal training. The question Frank asked, however, integrated for me my working experience and my training as a law clerk. It was the kind of question you always had to ask yourself, especially at moments of emotional involvement.

Although I had trouble doing one deal at a time, Frank handled four or five at once. He had a facility for moving in and out of a transaction and could shift focus and direction with the agility of a finely trained athlete. Each matter provided a welcome change of attention, and a new problem he could address without losing the threads of all his other problems and matters. He would shut down at a reasonable hour. At 6 or 7 p.m. he would leave me with whatever problems he had and pick them up again in the morning, always unruffled by the fact that there were nagging difficult problems left over from the day before. By the end of the day he was freed from the constraints of the office.

Frank's working on many deals exposed me to most of them and built up a reservoir of experience. Each deal had its own character, and Frank made them unique. I never had the sense of repeating myself, but, as a consequence, I couldn't gauge my level of experience or development.

An adversary unexpectedly did the measuring for me. Frank and I were representing a seller of a pulp mill in Port Hudson, Louisiana, to the Georgia Pacific Corporation. The mill was jointly owned by the Riegel Paper Company and the Inveresk Paper Company, a Scottish company, which was the Cravath client. Riegel Paper was represented by other counsel, who were not as experienced in acquisitions and looked to us to take the lead. Georgia Pacific sent a complex contract to us and we began our negotiations. The contract was like a law school examination: no matter which way you turned there was a trap; and in avoiding one trap you would fall into another. The deal was being handled largely by in-house Georgia Pacific staff lawyers. But the agreement, an acquisition form from Georgia Pacific, had gone through many hands before it had come to us and many minds had twisted and tightened it. Even a mediocre mind, well positioned, can be formidable. We worked at it together until Frank saw it as routine and became involved in other matters. Then it became my deal and I worked on it alone until we came to a bargain.

There was a closing dinner, at which I was reviewed. In the middle of dinner at a fine New York restaurant, Frank asked the lawyer for Georgia Pacific how well we had done negotiating the contract. The lawyer had a round beery face, and his two little eyes bore into Frank. He was judging me, but he concentrated on Frank. He wet his soft, puffy lips, and his tongue came out and caressed them, making them look mushy. "Well," he said, drawing the word out, "I'd say that you did—" Then he hesitated, letting the silence thicken the air. "I'd say you did about 50 percent," he said. "That's not bad; acquisitions are tough. You got a lot of things," he said. "I'd say that. But you missed a lot of things too. I'd have to say that."

Frank didn't say anything, but his fair face became flushed. It was the wrong question, and it had gotten the worst kind of answer. Gritting my teeth, I scowled to hide my pain. There was nothing for me to say. Frank said the only thing one could: "We'll see. We'll see." But it wasn't as if we could seek retribution. We'd closed the transaction and the client had gotten the money. Nothing was left to be done, except to comply with a pulp-sale agreement under which Inveresk would continue to buy its pulp requirements. I went back to the office to reread the agreement, looking for missed points, now knowing there were many. All this brought home to me that there was much to learn.

An opportunity for some satisfaction did come, and sooner than we thought. Inveresk was not doing well in Europe and, as a result of closing down some of its European paper plants, needed less pulp than it had contracted for in the pulp-sale agreement. In a tight position, Inveresk asked Frank whether there was any possibility of renegotiating the contract to reduce the required annual purchases of pulp. With a mischievous eye, Frank looked over the contract to find where the standard contract allowed turning room, a place to force a retrading of terms.

The contract contemplated the purchase of annual tonnage. Inveresk was required to give thirty days' notice before each calendar quarter, stating its purchase requirements for the next quarter, and was then required, during the quarter, to take equal monthly installments of such tonnage.

Frank asked, "What if we say we have no requirements for the quarter?"

I looked at him, not seeing where he was going, but had a ready answer: "You only postpone the problem," I said. "You have to buy fixed annual amounts. The following quarter the tonnage requirements will increase. That's what it comes to. It's a bigger ball to roll up the hill."

"Can we do that?" he asked. "Not buy in a given quarter?"

"Yes, we can," I said. "You were very specific in saying to them that you wanted flexibility from quarter to quarter, although they usually didn't grant that flexibility to others because they want their mills to run without slack periods or down time. You told

them we needed the flexibility because there were seasonal variations and we might want to postpone some of our purchases."

"That was meant to be a small concession. Are they fully on
notice?" he asked.

"Yes," I said, still not knowing where this would lead. "They
are responsible for the consequences of the concession. But post-
ponement doesn't relieve you of your obligations," I reiterated.

Frank had a faint suggestion of a smile on his lips and his eyes
sparkled. "The client tells me that there will be a strike in the Gulf
Coast ports in ninety to a hundred twenty days. That means they
won't be able to make deliveries if the Gulf ports are closed. If
they can't make deliveries, Inveresk doesn't have to buy."

Frank's suggestion of a smile blossomed in full. He let me put
all the pieces together in my mind, and then he recited the
conclusion.

"If we postpone our purchases and lump them in the quarter in
which there is a strike, they won't be able to ship and we won't
have to buy. The client will be in a position of not having to buy
at least six months' worth of pulp."

"That will make them renegotiate," I said.

"At satisfactory levels," he said.

"Do you want to make the call or should I?" he asked.

"You should," I said.

"First I'll have the client send them a telegram that there will
be no purchases of pulp for this quarter." He paused, as if contemplating the telegram. "That will get them to taste their lunch.
Then they'll be prepared for my telephone call."

The incident gave Frank his sought-after satisfaction. For me
there was a deepened understanding of the complexity involved in
deals and the effect of ever-changing circumstances. The surprise
the other side would experience could be my surprise the next time.

Working together, you become close. You share the depression
induced by scorn, even if only from an adversary, and the inse-
curity of not knowing if you have figured it all out. In those moments
when the burdens are shared, you take and give comfort. It is
personal and intimate and crosses the barriers set up between
partner and associate at Cravath. As warm and as personable as

Frank could be, the barriers were always there because he respected them. We shared much and I was fond of him and cared for him, but we weren't friends. I knew little about his personal life, and never during the two years that I worked for him did I see him socially.

At the end of two years Frank told me I would have to begin working for someone else in accordance with the Cravath system. He set me up with an equally eccentric man, but his polar opposite: a man who was the most disciplined, careful, precise, and hard-working lawyer in the firm, William Bly Marshall, whom I sometimes thought of as Captain Bly. The lecture Frank gave me then reminded me of the day I started grade school at age five. My mother told me that they would be calling me Lawrence at school. I'd never heard that name before and had always been called Larry. I asked her why that name and she told me Lawrence was my name. Frank, in the same way, tried to tell me that for the past two years I hadn't been practicing law. Somehow, doing deals (negotiating all the business, as well as the legal points, and letting other lawyers prepare the papers) was not quite the practice of law.

He had me assigned to Marshall to give me the benefit of the traditional Cravath tutelage. Frank could call on Marshall to take me on as his associate because Marshall had represented Frank's father and owed the father a number of favors that the son inherited. I wound up with one of the most difficult men to work for in the firm.

At that point I chose to stay with Cravath and delay going into teaching. I'd experienced the excitement of doing deals, of living by your wits. Frank had made it so. I knew there was much to learn, for at every turn my deficiencies showed themselves. In addition, Frank's deals involved only privately held companies and I didn't know anything about the companies traded in the public markets, a necessary element of my education.

AFTER TWO YEARS at Cravath an associate was entitled to a window seat and a phone with two lines, including a hold button to manipulate them. Those were the prerogatives of a middle-level associate. To anyone at the firm they were the equivalent of battle citations and as noticeable as if they were worn on your breast. The actual timing would depend on when people left the firm, but the advancement was based largely on seniority. The senior associates with six years or more at the firm would usually be given their own offices, but could lose them depending on how crowded the firm was at any given time. As a result, there was a constant shuffling of offices. You would be told on a Thursday or Friday that your office would be changed, your files were moved over the weekend, and on Monday morning you would come into a new space, the same as the last office, but with a new office mate; and the work was supposed to proceed uninterrupted.

In changing offices I met new people, and, through them, others. Over time I got to know the other associates and something about the firm. Cravath was treated like a graduate school by many: they came and went, enriching each other and the firm. Cravath kept the history of all those who entered and left and systematically followed their careers. As one of the few repositories for this kind of arcane information, the firm's records became the major source for the sociologist Erwin O. Smigel, who wrote a book called *The Wall Street Lawyer* in 1963. The book attempted to profile the change in character of the people who became Wall Street lawyers based on background, schools, affiliations, and later jobs. He was able to show that Wall Street lawyers were becoming less homogeneous as a group.

Not captured in the information about the type of people employed was the quality of many of the associates and their relationship to the firm and each other. These were people who had performed at a very high level, often disliked the practice at Cravath, and moved on. They were in many ways the most interesting aspect of the firm. While I was there some of my fellow associates were Phil Trimble, who became a deputy mayor of New York City under Ed Koch and later organized the American expedition that climbed Mount Everest; Carol Bellamy, who became the President of the New York City Council; Oliver Koppell, a brilliant New York state assemblyman; and Tom Hauser, who wrote the book *Missing*, which was made into a successful movie.

Associates not seeking to build a career at Cravath, and often not intending to continue practicing, provided a leavening irrev-

erence. There was always someone who would put the social structure in perspective while challenging the system. For example, one
of the associates tried to bring in his own furniture. The furniture,
a chair and desk, was examined in all seriousness by Mrs. Fordyce,
who had been chief of Cravath protocol as long as anyone could
remember. She ruled definitively that the furniture had partner's
legs, not being perfectly straight and squared off, and couldn't be
used by an associate. To some of the best legal minds in America,
she left open the possibility that you could bring in your own
furniture as long as it had the appropriate legs, regardless of its
other details. Her ruling was a source for great debate. Rolltop
desks could be imagined. No one wanted her to rule again, however.
It was better to debate it without testing it, since we all concluded
that the next decision wouldn't allow variations from standard
issue.

The hierarchical structure of partner, associate, and support
staff didn't accurately describe the pecking order, as suggested by
Mrs. Fordyce's power. In the ranking, associates were professionals, supposed to be served by the staff, and the forms of address
attempted to validate the hierarchy. The staff were required to
refer to associates by their last names and refrain from familiarity,
while associates were free to call staff members by their first names
or even use nicknames. Outwardly, deference was observed, and
the well-mannered formalism hid the tensions from the uninitiated.
Behind the veneer of social conduct, the staff members had remarkable power. You soon discovered that your career depended
on the goodwill of the steno pool and the Xerox room. If you
couldn't produce your work on time, everyone faulted it, no matter
how brilliant it was. If you weren't liked by the staff, if you didn't
observe the proper amount of obsequiousness, your work, when it
was found by a tired messenger, would be dog-eared and have
paragraphs scrambled and pages missing.

At Christmas you were required to give the boys in the Xerox
room and the guys who ran the steno pool a gift, more than a
Christmas card with a cheery sentiment. Nothing less than fine old
whiskey would do, and not just one bottle. The key to success was
to be part of a consortium so that you could deliver a box. Everyone
was always impressed with a box of booze, although the contents

would be counted with great care and the card with the names of the members of the group diligently examined to make sure that the gift wasn't stingy. Those guys knew their vassals and if you didn't comply with appropriate homage, your life would be made miserable.

The partnership was aware of these pressures but didn't care. The work got done, the associates could fend for themselves, and the support staff had an outlet.

For the first two years, associates had to call the steno pool for secretarial assistance. In June we'd meet the girls from Bayonne, the new recruits for the steno pool. Every year Hy Miller, who ran the pool, recruited at Bayonne High School (his hometown) and took the best of the class. The new crop arrived immediately after graduation, between twenty and thirty in number and between seventeen and eighteen years of age. These neophytes spent about two years in training before becoming secretaries. By September, the June recruits were fairly seasoned, so when the new associates needed steno service it was hard for them to distinguish the newly arrived from the more experienced.

At Cravath, great emphasis was placed on dictating directly to a stenographer as the most efficient way to draft letters and documents. Beginning associates usually tried to put off learning the skill because of the embarrassment of haltingly trying to find the right words and sound like a lawyer in front of a young woman. The girls from Bayonne had all been trained at school to display total impassivity. Whether what you dictated was nonsense or poetry, it was met with the same acute indifference. Behind the mask, however, there was always a mind at work, judging and grading you. If a stenographer wanted to be nasty she would fidget when you took time to think, one of the many options on her part that balanced the relationship.

In many respects the careers of the girls from Bayonne paralleled those of the young entering associates. After two years they would become secretaries to two associates and if they stayed long enough would ultimately become a secretary to a partner. Since the partnership was relatively small and stable, few got that far. Most left, using Cravath's peerless prestige for the mobility that it promised. Some married associates, and many left to work for senior associates at their next and more promising jobs in executive suites. If Smigel, in his study of social mobility, had been closer to his subjects, he might have also wanted to follow the careers of the girls from Bayonne, who intermingled with and became part of the lives of the young men from the Ivy League.

There was very little official socializing at Cravath. The one social event of the year was the dinner dance, which was a black-tie affair held in the Grand Ballroom of the Plaza Hotel.

My first office mate was the head of the dinner committee, and he enlisted my services to help him administer it. I got an interesting insight into the workings of the firm, which I hadn't expected. After all the seating arrangements had been made, the managing partner came into our office to review them. This was the first intrusion by the partnership into the event. The managing partner that year was John Hunt, a cheerful, rugged Irishman who didn't particularly enjoy dealing with the day-to-day affairs of the firm. He had, it turned out, a secret list, which he held in a hamlike fist, close to his chest like a poker player not wanting to reveal his cards. The list, reflecting an accumulation of at least fifty years of experience in the firm, specified those partners or their wives who couldn't be seated at the same table with other partners or their wives, and associates who offended certain partners. The list was long enough so that it couldn't be committed to memory and he had to refer to it a number of times, each time with a quick, furtive downward glance, making sure that no other eyes could see.

A number of changes were required in our arrangements, and he asked for all copies of the seating chart, saying that he would change it, have it retyped, and send it back to us for final distribution. There would then be no possibility of reconstructing his list. He then left us, presumably to put his list in the firm's safe for updating immediately after the dinner. Given the tension of the event, every year a number of partners and associates got drunk and offended somebody, and this was brought to the attention of the managing partner. Also, who knows what other slips were made at the party that got reported to him for his list.

For many, the dinner dance, rather than being a social affair, was another test; this time your social skills were measured. The men danced with each of the women at the table and the partners' wives were treated to affable and extremely attentive young men. The partners, too, got their share of attention as they bestowed their grace on the associates' young wives and dates. Working with the dinner committee, I was able to get assigned to Frank's table, and for me at least, the event was a pleasant social evening.

Cravath, I concluded, was organized for the practice of law, and the social aspects, while difficult to live with over an extended period of time, didn't get in the way. I girded myself for another two years, this time with a tough taskmaster.

WILLIAM MARSHALL WAS fifty-five years old when I began working for him in 1970. He had established an excellent academic record at Yale College and at the University of Pennsylvania Law School, from which he graduated in 1940. He began working at Cravath in 1946 after his discharge from the Navy, where he had been a PT boat commander.

Marshall was a chain smoker and had a leathery, lined face that made him look ruggedly handsome. He would sometimes lean his head on his hands and pull his skin tight while concentrating, and you could see briefly the handsome young man who had once been the naval officer. A number of involuntary tics caused him to grimace regularly. They didn't detract from his appearance, but gave the sense of someone who was keeping his emotions under tight control. Anger would rise up in him over some perceived wrong and he would curse. Sometimes he would lash out. There was often a sense of imminent explosion and, at such times, he would be given a wide berth by most people who knew him.

Although Marshall was one of the busiest men in the office, he worked on only one matter at a time. While he might occasionally take calls about other business matters, if he was involved in a deal, he wouldn't interrupt his work, refusing to be distracted by anything else. The client would have to wait. We would often sit in his office for three or four hours working through a problem. He would pose a question to me and I would attempt an answer immediately. That would always annoy him: whatever I said couldn't be right because I'd responded without the kind of deliberation that he went through. Each question or problem had a beginning, middle, and end. Moving from phase to phase, he would parse through all the elements, tease out all the subsidiary questions, carefully define all terms, and laboriously seek an answer. No matter how complex the issue, it would be diced and sliced so thin that it didn't seem to have any complexity at all. A novel question would become mundane.

Each sentence of a document would be reviewed with the same exactitude. If there was a loophole, he would find it. If there was an invalid assumption, it would show. I would sit in his office, impaled in the process, sometimes waiting for him to read slowly and carefully to himself, watching as he worked through each problem with dogged persistence. Other partners in the firm at his age didn't work on drafting papers. They gave advice. Marshall was revered for his judgment and was treated as a gray eminence, but once his advice had been given and it was time to do the papers for the deal, he would do those too. The associate would do the first draft, then Marshall would discard it, begin again, and redraft the document with the associate at his side.

Marshall would never trade a deal like Frank. For Marshall there were business points and legal points. He wanted the businessmen to trade all the business points, leaving him with a complete term sheet so that he could document the transaction. If he found open points, he'd ask the client to trade them out so that the deal could go forward.

In his view there was nothing novel about any transaction. He would always want to start from a precedent, some agreement that had documented a similar deal. In that agreement there was a world of experience for him. His office was filled with several hundred volumes of the documentation for the deals he'd done. He would select all the agreements and parts of agreements that were relevant to the transaction at hand. All work on a new deal started with one of those precedents and from there he would add or subtract on the basis of others. Then he would finally ask whether anything had been left out, meaning had he covered all the points that the client wanted included.

Randolph and Marshall had the same objective, to cover all the issues, circumscribe the risks of the deal so they were all stated as agreed or customary. But they proceeded from opposite directions.

Frank Randolph tortured himself about whether or not he'd covered everything. Marshall always started with a high degree of comfort, but was nervous about the possibility that some precedent might not have been complete. Bad forms were the bane of Marshall's working life. Marshall would always be dismayed when he had to work opposite a lawyer like Frank whose first instinct was to be innovative.

Each looked at the process as drawing a series of concentric circles to circumscribe the risks, with the issues in the inner rings being the most likely risks. They tried to draw as many circles as reasonably necessary, without burdening the deal with too much complexity. Frank's structures were often elliptical, covering issues in the outer rings while sometimes leaving others reasonably near the center uncovered. Marshall's deals were more symmetrical and less complex, unlikely to cover remote or novel risks not near the center (although possibly a problem in time), since he proceeded from precedent.

Marshall's workweek began on Sunday night, when he would call me and others, usually at dinnertime, to discuss the schedule for Monday. He was an indefatigable worker, and worked as late as he had to, often without eating, to get the work done. He would regularly stay at the office until two or three in the morning working with his male secretary, Sy Garrow. Many days he would work around the clock, telling Sy to have a messenger buy him a shirt and a tie and some underwear, and he would begin the next day as if he'd gone home and slept through the night.

Sy Garrow was as much of an institution as Marshall. He would work whatever hours Marshall wanted. Because of his overtime he was handsomely compensated and was reputed to have invested significant amounts of money in Bronx real estate. He appeared to be an instrument of Marshall. Whenever Marshall needed anything, Sy was always there. Also, Sy Garrow was a remarkably skilled secretary. Perfect pages would fly off the typewriter, and he could take dictation as fast as Marshall could speak. It added to Marshall's mystique and power that he could harness such a person and keep him occupied.

Marshall had two or three associates working with him at any given time, but he couldn't delegate to any degree. The associates always worked separately on different deals. Mostly an associate would take comments, field complaints, and gauge the client's annoyance when Marshall was preoccupied with another deal. Marshall allowed the associate to make only small (usually glacial) advances without him. Without this delegation of authority the work would have come to a grinding halt.

Marshall's was actually the largest practice at the firm. It had developed through J. & W. Seligman & Co., the investment banking house run by Frank Randolph, Sr. He represented Seligman and also Blyth, Eastman, Dillon on financing matters. From these two investment banking houses he gained introductions to their clients. Over time their clients became his clients. For example, he represented Honeywell at a time when Honeywell was a leading maker of computers. Cravath also represented its much larger competitor IBM. At a certain point Marshall was asked to drop Honeywell as a client because of conflicts with IBM. That was a major event. The Cravath firm had to screw up the courage of the presiding partner to go into Marshall's office and tell him that he would have to drop one of his clients. For Marshall it was like losing a finger, and he was not easy to live with for days.

Marshall didn't cultivate his eccentricities the way talented people often do. In fact, he suppressed them. Businessmen and their lawyers must relate to each other, he told me. If the lawyer looks strange, he loses trust, and if he acts strange, his word can be questioned. Marshall's furniture was nondescript as well. It looked as though it had been issued by some bureaucracy for temporary use. All this was camouflage. Anyone with a good eye could see how Marshall differed from the norm.

Marshall's time and attention were solely devoted to representing the firm's clients. At one point the managing partner, John Hunt, gave me two weeks' leave in addition to my four weeks of vacation to work on John T. Connor, Jr.'s campaign for the state senate of New Jersey. Two weeks' time off to work on political campaigns had become a routine grant, and a number of associates took advantage of the opportunity. Connor, Jr., was then my office mate. I remember Marshall looking at me over his glasses and asking, "Young John?" John's father, John T. Connor, had been at Cravath and had left to become a business executive. He'd served as

Secretary of Commerce before becoming chairman of Allied Chemical. The senior Connor was a client of the firm, and helping him made sense to Marshall. But young John wasn't a client. When I told him, "Yes, young John," he made it clear that he thought I was wasting the firm's time.

The practice of law wasn't a business for him. He had trouble billing the clients for his services and would run months, sometimes as much as a year behind. Often the presiding partner would have to tell him to bill. Clients grumbled even to me when they hadn't received a bill in a long time. They were worried about the cost and about being able to properly account for it. It was then that he had to face the price of his services, embarrassed by the size of the bills.

Marshall took a joy in his practice that was rarely expressed. One day I was in his office and he got a call from Walter Wriston, then the head of Citibank, who asked him a question about real estate investment trusts. He had heard that Marshall was the leading expert on Wall Street. When he hung up the phone Marshall said to me, "Do you know who that was?" "No," I said. He said, "It was Walter Wriston. He had some questions about REITs. Imagine that." And then he scowled and went back to our discussions.

As a role model he had his limitations, especially when he fought for dominance in his bare-knuckles way. He would tell me our job as lawyers was to control the meetings we attended. You were to listen to everything that was said, accept the good ideas, and firmly reject the bad. We set the agenda and the time schedule. More importantly, we would rule things out of order. If there was a clown at the meeting (defined to mean anyone who wouldn't follow your lead), we were to make sure he wasn't given a chance to speak. Clowns would take everybody's time and destroy the meeting.

At every meeting, Marshall would promptly stake out his claim for control, assert all the power of his client, and if that was not enough, assert the power of his position. Usually Marshall was the oldest person in the room, and his experience was legend. Added to that was the mystique of Cravath and an aura about its partners which facilitated command. Cravath counted itself at the top of the legal profession. The sense of hierarchy didn't start at Cravath.

It was in part built into the system by elitist choices about prep school, college, and law school. On every level of life there was a hierarchy, and whether it truly existed in the practice of law didn't matter. It was in the minds of all the people with whom I worked, however vague their criteria for measurement or analysis. How would you be judged as a lawyer if you left Cravath? was the gnawing question that troubled every associate. Asked often enough, especially in moments of self-doubt, which are many in a long apprenticeship, the answer would deepen those doubts.

Lawyering involves a constant evaluation of yourself and other lawyers. It was assumed that partners at other firms couldn't be as able as the partners at Cravath, and events would usually provide confirming data, if not outright confirmation. What made it tough to be fair-minded was that most lawyers were reasonably knowledgeable and it was difficult to assess where concessions made or denied would make any real difference to the clients. Only on rare occasions would you get any hint of the power of another lawyer, and thus an understanding of Cravath's limitations.

Marshall unwittingly gave me a view of those limits (and his confrontational style) when he became too feisty with William Kaynor, then a middle-level partner at Davis Polk. Kaynor tried to avoid argument at every turn, but Marshall persisted. Marshall wanted certain concessions which Kaynor wouldn't give and Marshall terminated the meeting in a huff, walking out without setting a scheduled time for further meetings. When he talked to me he referred to Kaynor without using his name, saying "what's-his-name" or "what's-his-face." That evening we worked long and hard at being devilishly clever with the papers so that there would be all kinds of barbs and snares for Kaynor, with Marshall smiling in anticipation of Kaynor being caught by them. In the morning we called Kaynor to set a meeting time and Kaynor told Marshall that he was busy and wouldn't be able to meet for at least a week.

The response practically knocked Marshall off his chair, because delay caused by a lawyer's schedule is never tolerated. Marshall would have been prepared to meet at 3 a.m. to begin work if that was the only time that Kaynor could meet. Marshall tried every argument he knew. Kaynor kept saying, "Bill, I'm sorry, but I'm extremely busy. I know that it's hard on your client, but I'm just not going to be able to accommodate you." Only a man of great power could do that: one who was able to control his client and take the heat of not moving rapidly. It was done with finesse and politeness. Stalled, Marshall was devastated. If he complained to his client, the client would know that Marshall had been ineffective. Lawyers were supposed to be able to deal with each other and move things along.

Finally Marshall had to resort to asking me to use whatever goodwill I had with Kaynor's associate to get things moving. In that moment, he recognized me as a participant to whom others reacted independently, rather than someone who was merely an extension of his will. Kaynor's associate was favorably disposed toward me, and I got the deal done working with him. Embarrassing as it was for Marshall, there was no expression of appreciation. But I'd gotten something better than praise; I'd gotten a clearer view of other lawyers. By recognizing that lawyers outside Cravath could match its members' skills and power, I prepared myself to leave when the time came.

In other ways too, I learned more from Marshall than the things he explicitly tried to teach. I realized that the Cravath machine, which looked to the outside like a law factory, was a dedicated lawyer and a bunch of typists who were prepared to spend all night typing. The size of the firm had little to do with the ability to function on complex transactions or produce work on particular deals. Marshall and I would work alone on the largest transactions. If I could do what he could do (which I recognized was awesome), I could do it anywhere. Except for a few specialists, there seemed to be no need for another 150 lawyers to be part of the process.

I'm not sure what would have been the effect on me had I worked for Marshall first. The discipline would have had no context. The approach to problems, always searching for old models, would have been exasperating. Moreover, the attitude that you were an imitator and not a creator would have been too debilitating to overcome if it had been all that I'd experienced. My first office mate worked for Marshall in his early tenure at Cravath and that accounted for, as far as I could see, his feeling that the practice was a process of copying old dusty papers.

With Frank, I'd come to see the excitement of the law, and now

I'd learned its discipline. I could accept the discipline, seeing that it was a necessary element of practice.

WORKING WITH SOMEONE who is experienced and talented trains you, but often leaves you doubting your ability. It's like having a parent whom you can turn to, with the experienced hand always there to pluck you out of water that's too deep. That knowledge (and the comfort of it) often affects and influences your judgment.

The next step was to try to do deals on my own, but the only way to get that opportunity was to work with someone who was a nominal supervisor but would trust my experience. After two years with Marshall, I asked him to arrange for me to work for Samuel C. Butler, who gave his associates free rein. I was postponing my teaching career even longer.

Just before my next phase at Cravath I got another lesson in negotiating, this time from my mother. She visited me at the office before we went to lunch. On leaving the building, she stopped in front of a street vendor selling cloth by the yard. The street was filled with vendors at that hour. This one was practically a permanent fixture. He asked five dollars a yard for his goods. I'd been able to negotiate a four-dollar price for some goods I'd bought for my wife. My mother asked him his price and he told her five dollars a yard, and she appropriately told him she'd pay no more than three dollars. She was in her element.

He responded: "Lady, I can let you have it for four dollars."

"Three dollars," she said.

"How much do you need, lady?"

"Two and a quarter yards," she said, "at three dollars."

"That's my cost, lady. Do you want it?"

She nodded and he began to cut the goods.

"Three dollars," she said, confirming with precise timing her last statement as his scissors cut the goods.

"Lady," he said in exasperation, "I've already cut it."

"That's your problem," she said. "Three dollars, no more."

"Who knows how much it comes to," he said, referring to the novel price per yard requiring an unfamiliar calculation for him, but conceding.

"Six seventy-five. Everything doesn't have to be round numbers or always the same," she said.

"What are you going to do with the two twenty-five you took from me, lady?" he asked, handing her the goods with grudging respect.

"Save it for my children." Then she took my hand and said to me, "See. It's not for millions, but I can do deals too."

SAM BUTLER HAD graduated from the day-to-day practice of law to meeting with clients and dealing with administrative tasks in preparation for heading the firm. He had a younger partner who worked with him and a staff of eight or nine lawyers, a large staff by Cravath standards. He parceled out the work and left the associates largely to themselves to handle the matters. The junior associates worked with the more senior associates. You could talk to Sam Butler if there was a problem. If you presented a problem, he would give you an immediate answer, and then his mind would turn to something else. Like all able administrators, he didn't linger over the problem once the matter was decided. If you wanted to linger, you were left to do it by yourself. If you were dissatisfied with the answer, you could raise it again and he would address it again. He never fretted or worried about whether he'd done the right thing. It was done, and his mind was freed up for other matters.

In 1972, after I'd spent more than four years at Cravath, Sam Butler assigned me to the first sizable transaction that I was to handle largely unsupervised, representing a major group of underwriters in the sale of AT&T's stock in Comsat Corporation. While meant to advance my training in representing public companies, the deal prepared me to leave the firm.

AT&T was Comsat's largest stockholder, but they competed in international transmission of telephonic messages. AT&T used its long line and Comsat beamed signals from earth stations to its satellites and then back down to receiving earth stations. When Comsat was organized by Congress, AT&T was encouraged to invest in Comsat to help it get started. Once Comsat significantly established itself and became a substantial competitor, AT&T was required by the Federal Communications Commission to make a public distribution of the stock it owned in Comsat, thus eliminating ownership by a competitor. Over $150 million of stock was being sold. At the time, this was the largest secondary offering (an offering of a company's stock by a stockholder and not by the company) that had ever been made. To sell the stock to the public we had to prepare a prospectus with a comprehensive description of Comsat's business and the risks inherent in it. The last prospectus dated from the original issuance of the shares when Comsat had been formed, at least ten years before, and the business had significantly changed since its beginnings.

Bruce Wasserstein, who now heads his own investment banking firm, worked with me on the offering. He had been at Cravath a little over a year, making me the senior associate and in charge of the deal. Bruce had worked for Ralph Nader in Washington on an investigation of Comsat the summer before he joined Cravath, and when he heard that there would be a public distribution of Comsat stock, he asked to work on the matter.

Bruce was only on the edge of conforming to the Cravath model in terms of dress and appearance. It didn't take a very trained eye to see that everything was about a half turn off. He walked the halls of Cravath without his jacket on, his shirttails invariably hanging out, wearing soft gummed-sole shoes instead of oxfords. The shoes emphasized his energetic bounce, lending him a boyishness which his pudginess did little to dispel. The eyes were shrewd; and if you missed the eyes, you missed the man. He had an investigator's zeal, which didn't make friends for us at Comsat. He was, however, a good companion and a wonderful ally.

We made innumerable trips to Washington and met with company officials to learn how the satellites were launched, why they remained in synchronous orbit above the United States, and other technical data fundamental to the business. The method of accounting for the satellites troubled us and became a matter of contention. There had been a number of failures in launching satellites, as well as early failures in orbit, with satellites falling into various oceans around the world. The accountants capitalized all the costs attributed to the failed satellites, which meant that they increased the value of the remaining satellites in orbit. It was possible that there would be only one satellite in orbit and ten failed satellites, but the financial statements wouldn't reflect the failures or the tenuousness of the assets and the risk of business failure. Rather than capitalizing these costs, we thought it more sensible if the costs were expensed. That meant charging income for the failures, which would have significantly reduced income and depressed the value of the company.

There was no intention on the part of either the company or the accountants to change the method of accounting, and after some discussion I tried to let the point rest. But Bruce wouldn't let it go. Finally, I called a meeting and had the accountants and company officials come to New York to discuss their financial statements. We spent eight full hours at it, eating lunch in the firm's conference room. By the end of the day the accountants were angry, as were the company officials. Bruce was irritated and I was exhausted. Not one note to the financial statements was changed, and not one number affected. It was clear, however, after the session, that we understood the way the accountants described Comsat's assets and business and that the satellites were the central asset.

In keeping with the importance of the satellites, we had asked the most fundamental questions about them. How well were the satellites performing? Were they moving around in space? Would they fall down? These were simplistic, lay questions, and readily answered. Everything was in working order, we were told, which was confirmed by the various corporate officials responsible for the operation of the satellites. In turn, these answers were reflected in the prospectus circulated to all the directors of Comsat, to senior officials at AT&T, and to all the persons in the various underwriting firms and law firms working on the transaction. A date was set to file the prospectus with the SEC, and the printer was informed that we would be at the printshop the evening immediately preceding the date of filing.

Evenings at the printer's are usually long, routine, and largely boring. There is a lot of mechanical work to be done. The prospectus to be printed has to be fully reread, largely for nonsubstantive matters, to catch typographical errors or dropped words, and changes are made throughout the evening. Page proofs are usually sent to the printer's after the market closes, and the first round of corrections for proofreading are usually distributed in the early evening.

At 9 p.m. the working room was crowded. There were five or six lawyers and business people from AT&T. Each of the three lead underwriters represented almost two hundred other underwriters, domestic and foreign, and each had sent two or three people. There were also a team of accountants, three people from Comsat, and approximately three lawyers from Wilmer, Cutler & Pickering, outside counsel for Comsat. The Comsat team had arrived late because the members had attended the Comsat board meeting that day in Washington to approve the prospectus before it was filed. Page proofs lay on the conference-room table waiting another round of proofreading.

It was at that point that Ellie O'Hara from Wilmer, Cutler told me that she had a rider (a supplemental paragraph) for the prospectus. The rider, I was told, had been prepared by the chairman himself right after Comsat's board meeting. It plainly said that the satellites were degrading and weren't repairable, and no one knew the rate at which they were degrading. Then, in the jargon of prospectuses, it said that no assurance could be given as to the life of satellites, meaning that they could fall to earth at any time. Worse, the next launching by the government wouldn't be for a year, and there was no assurance that such launching would be successful. The last launching had failed.

"Is it true?" I asked. "Are the satellites degrading?" She said that's what the chairman wrote. I told her that we'd spent weeks discussing the satellites and had asked innumerable times about their functioning. Each time, time after time, we'd been assured that the orbiting satellites were perfect. "This is what he wrote," she said. Her face was without any expression of sympathy. "He said we're not to file unless this rider goes in the prospectus." Her voice was firm, as tough as her words. The degrading of the performance of the satellites had been discussed at the board meeting to approve the prospectus and the board concluded that the possibility of satellite failure had to be presented. The information had been kept confidential until the management and the board were sure that there would be a public sale of the stock. From their perspective it was the right thing to do. But with the unexpected information being reported at the last minute, it was disconcerting.

There was no confrontation. The scattered papers in the room looked like the debris of a failed satellite. I did the only thing I could do, which was to tell her I didn't think the underwriters could underwrite the stock or that AT&T could sell it under such a confused set of circumstances. Regardless of the expectations of everyone in the room or the institutions for which they worked, the right thing was to stop the offering. I didn't hesitate and told the group, "We won't be able to proceed."

"What will happen?" Ellie O'Hara asked.

"We'll review the matter in the morning," I said. "I'm going home."

I arrived in my office at 9:30 a.m., the opening of business at Cravath, and found about ten telephone message slips on my desk from various of the underwriters, officials at AT&T, and a Comsat vice president. All were marked "Urgent." I'd met the vice president only once in my many visits to Comsat. He'd treated me as much younger than I was because of my position, a mid-level associate at Cravath. Our conversation had been brief, about the business aspects of Comsat. I had been talking to him about satellites in synchronous orbit when he interrupted and said, "My, you have certainly learned the vocabulary."

"I guess I have," I said.

"You must be good at cocktail parties," he said.

I had no rejoinder and didn't know whether it was a compliment or sarcasm. In any event, I'd been dismissed.

That morning I returned his call first. Comsat was the center of the controversy. If the problem was to be dealt with, it would have to be with Comsat. I got through to him promptly.

"Mr. Lederman?" he asked, hesitantly.

"Yes," I said.

"Lawrence," he said, his voice filled with warmth and friendliness, all expressed in the way he said my name, and I could see, in my mind's eye, his face and could sense the charm he could radiate.

"You've decided not to go forward with the transaction?" he asked.

"Yes."

"There is some mistake," he said. "We'd like to apologize for that rider. We're prepared to change it, rewrite it, so that the deal can go forward."

"Nothing can be changed," I said.

"No?"

The sound of the "no" was hollow. There was a moment of silence and it was clear that he meant "Why not?"

"If it's true, we're going to have to investigate the situation and decide whether we're prepared to take the risk of selling these securities at this time. And if it's not true . . ." I let my voice trail off. There was a moment of silence while I let him understand that there would be no reason to tell us about degrading satellites if it wasn't true. Then I said, "There aren't many ways to say it differently."

"Oh," he said. "This is serious."

"Yes," I said.

"What will happen next?"

"I'm going to have to talk to people responsible for satellite operations—and the underwriters are going to want to do the same thing—and find out what's wrong with the satellites."

"How long will that take?"

"About a week to ten days," I said.

"Will we be able to proceed with the offering?" he asked.

He was seeking my counsel, asking the ultimate question.

"Probably," I said. My voice took on a weighty tone; despite myself, I was inadvertently imitating Marshall's style when he gave his assurances. "It's a matter of getting comfortable with the uncertainty of it. The risks have to be understood and properly described, but all businesses have their risks."

"I feel better, then," he said. I could hear his relief. "Will you set the schedule for us, then, and tell us what you need?" he asked.

"After I talk to my clients," I said. I found enormous satisfaction in saying that.

"Thank you, Lawrence," he said.

I knew then that I could handle deals myself.

Within ten days the offering of the Comsat securities went forward, disclosing the information about the degrading of the satellites in language substantially similar to that in the rider prepared by the chairman. The market absorbed the news without difficulty, and the offering was successfully completed on schedule at about the pricing level originally anticipated.

Shortly thereafter, I decided to leave Cravath. Although I also felt ready to teach, I didn't want to give up the practice of law. To keep faith with myself, despite the long hours of practice, I found a part-time position at NYU Law School, teaching corporate law in the evening. But it wasn't until the end of 1974, more than a year after I decided to leave, that I found a satisfactory position at a law firm. The stock market was finding new lows during the period, and corporate activity of the kind I had been involved with had slowed down considerably. Also, I wanted to join a small firm, one where I could develop my own practice. Small firms weren't interested in taking on new people to whom they would have to make a partnership commitment in a time of economic slowdown. My prospects seemed dreary. But in November 1974, a classmate of mine, knowing that I was looking to leave Cravath, suggested my name to Wachtell, Lipton, Rosen & Katz, a firm of twenty-four lawyers where three of our fellow classmates were partners. I met all twenty-four lawyers over a two-month period before I joined the firm in February 1975.

It was time for me to make my own way. I had taken the advice of the first day to heart and had accumulated my own files, duplicates of the deals on which I'd worked. I had at least fifty cartons of deals to pack. I hoped that the hoarded papers of deals done would make a platform on which I could stand in the next stage of my career.

THE BLACK BOX

▼

"We can never be sure the corporate work will last."

John Francis Hunt, Jr., talkative and ebullient, was telling poor-boy stories. The two of us, in a small, windowless conference room at my new law firm, Wachtell, Lipton, Rosen & Katz, could have been in a booth of a barroom. We were experiencing the glow of good fellowship that sometimes comes only after three rounds of beer. John Hunt waved his hand to embellish a point, a large gesture that drew me into his tale as a friend and peer.

He was a senior partner at Cravath, Swaine & Moore and, on this occasion, IBM's lawyer. If IBM had a corporate problem of any magnitude, they called John Hunt. Facing an antitrust challenge by the federal government in the mid-1970s that could have forced the breakup of IBM, John Hunt worked out various contingency plans for the possible breakup. Short, barrel-chested, beer-bellied, and aggressive, he looked like a workman who could wield a shovel in a ditch more effectively than he could parse a sentence. As if to match his rugged appearance, he was the legal architect for major projects that developed extractive mines requiring the creation of towns, railways, bridges, and the construction of deep-water ports to service them. If you heard his resonant, baritone voice, you could see him as a construction foreman, but if you listened to him, you would hear a man of native shrewdness, a corporate lawyer of great depth and solid accomplishment.

I pulled at my soda can as he told me about Frank Carey, John Opel, and Paul Rizzo, the triumvirate that managed IBM. Tomorrow he would be in the inner chamber at their headquarters in White Plains making his recommendation about the deal we'd been working on together, and they would listen.

They would be advised by the same John Hunt who didn't have enough money after graduation from Columbia Law School to buy a suit to start working at Cravath, a maverick with great drive who had become a success. That level of penury was twenty years before, when he took a job in a brewery as a laborer loading beer kegs on delivery trucks. After two weeks he'd made enough money to begin working as a lawyer. At the time of his admission to the New York bar, he was questioned by one of the members of the Character and Fitness Committee as to why he'd taken the job. With calculated modesty, he explained that he needed a suit; otherwise he couldn't begin work. The old gent examining his qualifications did some fine cross-examination on whether he'd expressed his intentions as to seeking temporary or permanent employment.

"Can you believe that?" he asked. "That was a test of my character."

"The Character Committee is always difficult," I said. "They have relatively little to look at."

"No sense of reality," he said.

John's annoyance was lasting and his common sense firmly grounded. When he became Cravath's managing partner (and took care of such odd matters as making sure that partners were appropriately seated at the dinner dance), he had Cravath adopt a policy of providing loans to all entering associates, so that their characters couldn't be similarly questioned.

I'd been at Wachtell, Lipton, Rosen & Katz for only two months (starting in mid-February 1975) when John Hunt had called to tell me that IBM was making its first acquisition in over ten years. IBM wanted to acquire a small high-tech company appropriately called Neotec, which was publicly traded, and wanted able counsel on the other side of the transaction to dispel claims that IBM had taken advantage of a small company. The transaction was complex and John had recommended my firm to do the job. IBM would pay the costs of the transaction, including our fee. He asked if we would take the matter.

I was flattered to the point of distraction, but before I could say anything, he issued a cautionary note.

"It's a very difficult deal," he said, "hard to discuss on the telephone. You should come down to our offices, if you're interested."

I heard the admonition but ignored it. If it were a wasp, I'd have swatted it bare-handed to extinguish its sting. I told him that I would have to clear the matter with Martin Lipton, the senior partner of the firm, but I thought that we would take it.

Lipton had told me upon my joining the firm that there was no need for me to bring in clients or to seek out business. The firm at nine years of age (consisting of twenty-four lawyers, of whom sixteen were partners) was small enough to be busy in a sluggish economy. Lipton had hired me at the end of 1974, because he felt that there was a need for another corporate lawyer in the firm who could do deals, and asked no more from me. No one contemplated the merger wave which was about to change American business and the practice of law.

The firm was markedly different from Cravath. The reception area of the firm's office on Park Avenue in midtown Manhattan offered the first sharp contrast. It expressed spartan professionalism: too spare and dimly lit to be cozy and too new to reflect any history. The one decorative embellishment, besides a flower centerpiece set on a black granite coffee table, was a new Persian rug, used as a wall hanging, hung about where Cravath had placed the chart of its history. The single suggestion of the energy of the firm came from an overworked young woman who ran the switchboard and acted as a receptionist. To all calls, she responded, "Wachtell Lipton. Please hold," while she juggled calls and visitors.

Beyond the reception area, the disparity with Cravath was even more pronounced. No one wore their suit jackets, and everyone was on a first-name basis. Each associate had his own office. The commodious space suggested privacy, which was an illusion. All office doors were always open, fostering a communal workplace. Everyone treated the office like home, and no one felt any need to knock on doors or to hesitate to cross a threshold. Lawyers would walk into your office, demand attention (almost always bringing cookies and coffee or soda from the small kitchen), and begin talking about what was bothering them, while offering you food, even though you were with someone else or on the phone. The larger your quarters, the more visitors. Communal work habits began at the top, with the founding partners, who had all been classmates at NYU Law School and remained friends.

Without any privacy, everybody knew what everyone else was doing, which meant that knowledge was shared, making the informality more effective than seminars or luncheons arranged for dissemination of information. George Katz, one of the founding partners, embodied this family style. He visited all the offices almost every day, bringing encouragement or news or gossip, a practice which he continued until his premature death in 1989. Always optimistic, George would report on current matters and ask for advice from everyone on thorny legal questions, giving even the new junior associates the sense that their participation was valuable.

I began my affiliation with the firm on a Saturday before my first working Monday to organize my office (this was the first time that as a lawyer I had my own office), and I couldn't locate any of the cartons of papers that I had sent from Cravath. One of the new partners, a law school classmate of mine, had his children with him at the office and his young son went around to all the empty offices, which were many, to find my books and papers. In six years at Cravath I had never seen a child at the office.

For organizations like Cravath, my new firm was the equivalent of a storefront. Joining Wachtell Lipton was viewed by my former colleagues as a retreat from center stage into the dimness of an obscure practice. Proof of their conclusion lay in my failure to take my Cravath secretary with me when I left. Wachtell Lipton had a sufficient number of secretaries and didn't encourage lawyers to bring their own.

But at the time I left Cravath, the outlook for young corporate lawyers there was disheartening. IBM's defense of antitrust cases brought by the government (followed by cases brought by private parties) alleging monopoly practices in the computer industry were consuming much of the firm's energy and manpower. Contrary to the firm's policy of distinguishing between corporate practice and litigation, corporate lawyers were being taken off deal transactions to do depositions for trial preparation of the IBM cases. There were so many depositions that, for a stretch of over six months, Frank Randolph spent his full time coordinating them, largely a routine task and a waste of his talent. Cravath's commitment to the IBM litigation precluded it from accepting takeover matters, and it took the firm many years to make up the ground then lost. Ironically, a number of the lawyers trained in doing deals at Cravath later left to do takeovers elsewhere and became the professional cadre for the merger wave.

In the winter of 1974, however, the pace of corporate law practice everywhere reflected the recessionary economy. During my interview, George Katz had asked me if I could do house closings and matrimonials. Strange as the question was, I had taken it seriously because he was a founding partner.

"Well, I've closed two houses for friends." I paused, trying to come up with something else. Finally I did. "And I handled a custody proceeding," I said, not mentioning that it was also done without fee.

He nodded approvingly, but was he crediting my frankness or my experience?

"Why do you ask?" I queried.

"We can never be sure the corporate work will last," he said. "We want lawyers who can do other things."

To Katz's credit, he was always interested in lawyers doing more than one specialized task, even when the business of the firm didn't require it, for he was the master of many specialties. Still, they had almost lost me then, but Lipton had never intimated any doubt. I relied on Lipton's confidence, which was the genius of the firm.

When I joined the firm as an associate in February it was with the expectation that by year end I would be made a partner, if everything worked out. That is a euphemism for "if everyone likes you and respects you." It was a risk I was willing to take, since I felt at home with these people. I thought, however, that the outcome would be assured if, in addition to doing the work, I could attract desirable clients.

At the time I left Cravath, John Hunt gave me some unsolicited words of advice, since I was entering a different environment from Cravath's with all its institutional clients. I knew him only casually, but he was aware that I was eager to prove myself by finding my own clients. He told me, "Be careful, and don't take poor business. It's unproductive, time-consuming, and doesn't pay."

Although this was practical advice, the problem was that it offered no guidelines for proper judgment. That can only be learned from experience. From the beginning I found myself working on matters that didn't justify the time. I began doing a small amount of business with U.S. Trust Company, largely routine trust indenture work, which I would have avoided doing at Cravath. On the bright side, USAir (then Allegheny Air Lines), which I had on occasion represented while at Cravath, now asked me to do some corporate work, and there were a few other small matters as well. While all the fees just barely covered my salary, it made me feel secure to know that I was carrying my own weight.

When John Hunt approached me, then, I was eager to take on the IBM matter he offered. Attracting Cravath and IBM would be independent verification of my ability. Also, the IBM deal would be important for the firm, a deal with visibility in the marketplace. Fair warning or not that the deal had problems, John Hunt knew that we would take the matter. I asked myself, "Why me?" Although there was no ready answer, I accepted the flattery and the opportunity, and went down to Cravath's offices to see John.

In his own environment, John Hunt was a prince of the law. His office was spacious, with a southern exposure viewing the Battery. Arranged in bookshelves behind him were numerous bound volumes of the deals he'd done, and around him were mementos and tombstones of the various projects he had helped to develop. He sat behind his large desk in a broad, high-back chair that gave him command of the room, and I sat in a small chair on the associate's side, facing him. So positioned, I was again a Cravath associate, or at least that's the arrangement he chose. A shelf pulled out of his desk so that you could lean on it to write, and I was given a pad for note taking. He was going to tell me all the information necessary to get started.

Neotec made a device that could measure the protein content of foods through the use of nondestructive light analysis. "Call it a black box," he said. IBM was primarily interested in the black box to measure the protein content of wheat, although there could be other uses. Wheat was graded and priced worldwide on the basis of its protein content. Analysis of wheat by chemical means was time-consuming. Neotec's black box allowed for rapid measurement and could be coupled to an IBM computer. Then not only would the wheat's protein content be measured, it would also be graded and priced. Used in grain elevators around the country and even around the world, the computer would also keep inventory and shipping schedules. For IBM's computers, the Neotec device could be a seeing eye.

IBM had scoped out at least one market, the world grain market, and there might be other uses for which the black box could be adapted. Intriguing as it was to them, IBM was reluctant at the time to make an acquisition. Buying technology undermined the argument it was using to oppose the government's monopoly charges: that its growth had been largely internal. But a small acquisition could be managed.

John told me that IBM wanted to buy Neotec for $5 million. A purchase at that level wouldn't be considered meaningful by the government. Nonetheless, it was a problem acquisition because Neotec was a failing company, on the edge of bankruptcy, and its debts exceeded the $5 million purchase price. Its million shares of stock, however, were trading at about a dollar a share, and if the company was sold and its debts paid off, the shareholders wouldn't be entitled to anything. It's usually not possible to get the required shareholder approval for a sale of the company without paying shareholders at least a premium over the trading price of the shares.

"That's what we face," he said.

He stood up, as if freeing himself from his chair. Energetic and physical, he found it hard to be seated for very long. He lit a cigarette and walked around me, and I turned my head to follow him as he paced around the room.

"We've checked Neotec's patents and believe that they are challengeable: they won't stand a real test. There's no new art, only know-how, which can be duplicated. We want the black box and the know-how, but aren't willing to pay more than $5 million for it. That's all it's worth to us." He paused to see if I accepted his valuation. My sense was that his challenge to the patent position was mere posturing for the purpose of improving his bargaining position. I didn't commit myself, wanting to hear everything that he had to say, and he continued.

"The company has marketed its black box in supermarkets for customers to check the protein content of cheese and other things." He frowned to let me know that he thought it was an unfortunate use of the technology. "That hasn't been successful, and the company's failing. But if IBM were to acquire the company and give the shareholders relatively little, we'd be sued.

"IBM has approximately $3 billion in cash sitting on its balance sheet. We're a very deep pocket, and no matter what we do we'll probably be sued by the Neotec shareholders for overreaching and stealing the technology."

He returned to his desk, rocked in his commodious swivel chair, and gave me time to absorb all that he'd told me. Putting out his cigarette, he lit another and continued.

"We want to head off any argument that we're overreaching or that Neotec wasn't properly represented. That's why we brought you into the picture." With that statement, he gave me his welcoming smile.

"How do you expect to deliver money to the shareholders, John, if you're not paying enough to cover the debt?" I asked.

"Squeeze the lenders," he said, his face tightening as if it was a physical act and he was doing it himself. "We'd like to see the shareholders get about $2.00 a share. That would give them a premium over the trading price of the stock."

"Two dollars a share is about $2 million of the $5 million," I said, looking at a financial statement. "That doesn't take into account payables, and winding up expenses, including termination of employees. That means that the lenders will take a very substantial discount on their loans."

"Precisely," John said.

"Are the banks secured?" I asked.

"Yes," he said. "They have liens on everything."

"Why would the banks take less than 100 cents on the dollar?" I asked, getting uncomfortable with the situation.

"Because if they were to foreclose there really is nothing for them to take. The assets they would get wouldn't be worth that much and they would probably not get more than $0.30 on the dollar. There is a lot of debt junior to the bank debt as well, and they would probably get nothing."

"If $5 million covers all the debts and that's what you're prepared to pay, the lenders will want the $5 million for themselves," I said, making an obvious but necessary point, risking being tedious.

He stood up and took another turn around the room.

"We won't pay it all to them. If they won't discount the debt, we're prepared to walk away from the deal. We want to make sure that the shareholders get some money, so there are no recriminations or credible accusations."

"Are you really prepared to walk and not do the deal? The technology sounds too interesting." I shook my head to show him that his position wasn't credible.

He found his chair, vigorously rocking, telling me by his action that I was on a sensitive issue.

"Your job is to convince everybody that we'll walk, and not do the deal, unless they take sharp discounts. Your job is to compromise with the lenders and provide a benefit to the shareholders."

"They will all smell the pork cooking." I shook my head again, this time to let him know the degree of difficulty of the undertaking. "For a small amount of additional money, you needn't have such a complicated transaction."

"We're not prepared to pay any more."

John Hunt stopped rocking in his chair and stared fixedly at me to show me his resolve and that of his client. I could tell that he'd worked out the strategy with IBM, based on their determination of a reasonable purchase price, and he'd assured the executives at IBM that they wouldn't have to pay more. Aloof in White Plains, New York, they were all committed to that price, and were prepared to tell the marketplace the same thing, irrespective of how much they desired the black box.

In addition to the bank debt, the company's borrowings were complex. Living from hand to mouth for many years, the company had borrowed against everything it could conceivably claim to be an asset. In all, there were about twenty different arrangements, involving almost a hundred people, artfully put together like a homemade rickety raft to keep the company afloat. Each one of those parties would have to abandon large parts of their rights. Compromises would of course be difficult when the parties realized that IBM would be making the acquisition. The sums involved, minuscule to IBM, were significant to everyone else.

"The company has granted IBM an option to purchase it and its assets," John said. He produced an option contract that contained the definitive arrangements between IBM and Neotec. "This is the deal that the company has agreed to work out. It sets out the level of compromises that have to be achieved with most of the lenders and the agreed-on purchase price for the shares. In no event will IBM be required to pay more than $5 million."

He handed the contract to me across the desk. It was poorly copied and hard to read, copied on IBM's machines because IBM insisted on using only its own machines. John Hunt held up his hand to quiet any protest, thinking that I was bothered by the poor quality of the copy, and told me that IBM's use of its inferior copying machines was something we'd have to live with.

"Who represented the company on this portion of the transaction?" I asked, getting to what was on my mind.

"Local counsel," John said. Neotec was located in Silver Spring, Maryland.

"Let me understand this," I said. "You have already entered into a definitive arrangement with the company and you're asking us to represent the company so that there can be no criticism of IBM." I now understood one of the reasons why I had been called. His native shrewdness was at work. "Isn't it too late to get us on board?" I asked, as if seeking his advice.

He smiled, sat back in his chair, and relaxed. "No," he said. "There's a lot that has to be done."

He wanted to play it out, make me work at making my point, to see if I'd persist.

"To implement the transaction, but not to set it up," I said. "The structure has already been determined, John."

"Implementing is the transaction," he said.

"That may be, but that's not your reason for engaging us."

"There are securities act problems, tax problems, and accounting problems. They are going to need your expertise. Neotec won't be able to do the transaction without your help."

"That may be," I said again. "But you've already struck a deal. You're asking us to work within the framework of the deal. That might not be the best deal for the shareholders."

"If you need some latitude, we'd be prepared to consider what you have to say."

"From the point of view of amending the contract?"

"We're prepared to be flexible."

"How flexible, John?"

"We would like to get the transaction done."

I stood up to show John that I wasn't pinned to my spot, making the office as much mine as his, and walked over to the window to look out. I always enjoyed the harbor view from Cravath, where I could see the changing colors of the water and the boat traffic. A Staten Island ferry plied its way back to the Battery with enviable ease and certainty of purpose. I turned to face John.

"Flexible enough to renegotiate the contract now?"

"No," he said, leaning forward in his chair, forearm and elbow resting on the desk, ready to spring up. "These arrangements have been publicly announced. And we paid Neotec $50,000."

I turned to him. "You didn't get what you bargained for."

"We did. It's in the contract."

"You want to be able to say that the company has been adequately represented. If you want that contract, you don't need us."

"Why would you take the contract away from the company?" John asked.

I walked over to his desk, pleased now that I was standing because

I stood over him, and took the contract in my hand. I thumbed through it, confirming that IBM was not bound to buy the company.

"It's not a contract, John. It's an option on your part. The company has to perform by making its lenders write off the loans. After months of effort, it's probably not going to be able to do it to the degree you demand. It's a straitjacket. And you are Neotec's keeper. But you can walk away whenever you want."

"You're not serious about this," he said.

"It should be a two-way street," I said. "Either we're both bound on reasonable terms or neither of us is bound."

"I told them that you would do this to me," he said, laughing.

"Whom did you tell?"

"The people at IBM. I told them you wouldn't accept an option. If you want, you can set aside the contract," he said. "It's up to you."

"Fine," I said. "Then we'll be prepared to take on the representation of the company."

"Now I'm getting what we bargained for, is that it?" he asked.

"Yes," I said, sitting down, again face to face.

"Good." He laughed. He was full of life and his face lit up with his energy. Even without the contract, he controlled the game. Neotec wanted to sell and IBM would decide whether it wanted to buy. Our economic positions meant that IBM still had an option, and he'd given up nothing. I'd gained some flexibility for the client, but it was more cosmetic than real.

Watching him in action, I discovered why he'd chosen me as counsel. He knew that in my six years of apprenticeship at Cravath I had witnessed innumerable instances of deference to Cravath partners. That training doesn't wear off quickly. Astutely, he saw that his achievements were a substantial part of my aspirations. In a question of judgment, he could expect me to defer to him. He was a master strategist.

"Even if there's no option, I want to get this deal done," he said.

"So do I," I said.

"We're not paying more than $5 million. That price does everybody a favor." He was earnest, making the point that the price hadn't changed, even under these new rules.

"I hear you."

"Believe me," he said. "Squeeze the lenders, not us. We're prepared to walk, Larry."

"I want to meet my client."

"They want to get this done too. It has become too much of a burden, trying to run it without any money," he said, finishing our meeting.

IBM had collected a significant number of documents in White Plains that I needed to review. I was told that I'd be given copies promptly, that the deal had the attention of the chairman and the highest priority. After a week elapsed, I called John Hunt.

"What's taking so long?" I asked.

There was a long pause. Then he said, "Only authorized people can copy papers at IBM. It's a bottleneck. They worry about losing their trade secrets. We have expedited the matter, but it will take at least two or three more days." And then he paused again. "Also, their copying machines are very slow."

"I thought this was a top-priority item."

"It is," he said, "but there's a powerful bureaucracy. Be patient."

The papers came about a week later.

Finally, I got to see my client. Robert Rosenthal was the president and chief executive officer of Neotec. He was a small, energetic man who was an engineer and applied scientist. He had novel and interesting ideas, but had trouble implementing them in this business. For all his energy, each year there was a question about whether the business could survive and he spent the largest part of his time being a salesman, promoting the business. Each year he found people to put up some money to enable the business to limp along. The business also occupied the attention of his immediate family: his wife worked there, as did one of his sons, and although it supported them, the rewards were not much compared with the amount of time and effort expended.

Rosenthal was open and warm, making me feel that I was a part of his family. Liking him, I became troubled by the consequences of the sale of the business. Rosenthal had committed to work for IBM for one year after the sale to facilitate transition. But I knew that his employment at IBM wouldn't last. Entrepreneurial, he had no sense of how to work within a large organization and wasn't used to all the people one had to see before anything was taken seriously. He was a creative man, and IBM found his form of creativity disconcerting. For example, the IBM staff found, in the back of a Neotec filing cabinet, ten to fifteen sketches for instruments related to the Neotec device that measured protein content in various foods. The drawings were not included in the list of assets being sold to IBM, and that made them think Rosenthal was being devious. Rosenthal belittled the sketches, saying that he didn't believe any of them would work and explained that they had been done over a couple of weekends, without any chance to explore their practical capabilities. I explained to John Hunt that the drawings had no value, but Hunt wanted them included in the list of assets sold, to which I agreed. Grinning, Hunt told me to have Rosenthal stop doodling until we got the deal done.

Bankers Trust was Neotec's lead bank, and that's where Rosenthal and I started in our effort to work out the deal. The bank's loan of approximately $2 million was secured by all the assets. If the bank was willing to take a significant discount, then all the other creditors would have to follow. The issue was the credibility of IBM: whether IBM was firm in its resolve not to acquire Neotec if the bank wasn't willing to take a discount. In preparation for the meeting, I spent a fair amount of time doing an analysis of the likely proceeds if the company were liquidated. It wasn't much: probably $0.20 or $0.30 on the dollar. Whatever it was, Bankers Trust could take everything, and none of the other creditors (or the shareholders) would be entitled to anything.

In meeting with a loan officer to announce that his bank won't be paid the money it's owed, you have to forgo embarrassment. Bob Rosenthal had borrowed money from Andy Forester (and not really from the institution called Bankers Trust), who had been willing to take some business risks. Rosenthal was now coming back to tell Forester that everything had gone flat and there was a little something in it for the bank as long as the bank allowed something in it for junior creditors and the shareholders, including Bob Rosenthal. Without the junior class of securities getting something, there would be inordinate delay while the junior securities asserted claims that would have to be adjudicated, and no deal would get done. This is not an easy message to deliver: it contradicts the banker's sense of order. My job was to keep the embarrassment from impeding the deal.

The bank, of course, called IBM and was told that IBM wouldn't buy Neotec unless the bank met Neotec's terms. With that information, the bank took its time, testing IBM's determination, but finally went along. With $2 million set aside for shareholders, and only $3 million available to all other creditors (when $5 million was needed), the bank as a secured creditor insisted on about $0.70 on each dollar of the $2 million it had lent. The other creditors were pared down in accordance with the priority of their claims. Satisfactory compromises took two months of negotiating, involved dozens of people, and were delayed because everybody wanted access to the deep pocket of IBM.

Then it was time for reassessment and renegotiation of the Neotec deal with IBM. IBM was taking only a small portion of the employees of the company, although it was taking all its technology. Rosenthal wanted to find some way to utilize all his employees, even if it meant starting a new business. Finally, we came up with a strategy.

Having torn up IBM's option, we had turning room to try a novel approach. And so I met with John Hunt to renegotiate the deal, beginning by telling him the status of all the creditor compromises, which I thought would satisfy him. Then I told him we needed an additional $250,000. He nodded. We were meeting in the small conference room of our firm. He knew that there was more to our proposal, and he wasn't about to acknowledge what he would do until he heard everything. We'd all been trained to negotiate that way.

"What we'd like, John, is to sell you the business, the trade names, the patents, and the know-how just as you've requested, pay off the debt, and have you license the devices and know-how back to Neotec, royalty free, so that it remains in business."

"Wait a minute," he said. "What am I buying?"

"You're buying the business. You own everything."

"Then I'm not licensing it back. If I license it back to you, you'll compete with me."

"It's not possible for us to compete with you. We don't have the capital or the computers or the marketing ability."

"Then what will you do with the business?"

"You'll be selling to grain elevators, big-ticket items. These are large operations that will require a number of black boxes, all with computers. We want to sell a small, less sensitive device, without a computer, to farmers so they can measure the protein content of their wheat crop and thereby estimate the prices they will be receiving. You will be creating a market for us. And you're not going to want to develop the market that we can sell to."

He sat back and looked at me with his piercing blue eyes.

"What's going to happen with the shareholders?"

"We'll be able to pay out to them the $2.00 a share at capital-gains rates," I said, "and they'll still own their shares in the new business."

"You worked that out?" he asked.

"There are a number of ways we can do it," I said.

"This way no one loses their jobs, do they?" he asked. He didn't wait for an answer. "Where will you get working capital?"

"The bank has agreed to give us working capital," I said.

"After you cut them back?"

"We've found some good business people at the bank," I said. "The extra $250,000 will help also."

"Will they be able to run the business this time?"

"In the wake of your business," I said, "they'll have an excellent chance."

"I like it," he said. "I'll recommend it. Let me look through these papers." There was a stack of papers before him that represented all the compromises of all the creditors. He went through them carefully, asking questions, piecing together the layers of rights and obligations to see that they had been properly compromised, all with the steady care of a knowledgeable lawyer.

"You like it here?" he asked, meaning: Did I like my new firm?

"Yes," I said.

"I like your offices," he said. The offices were new and spacious compared with Cravath's. Being a large organization with leases dating to a time when the firm was smaller, Cravath had to carefully account for the use of all its space. It was almost like the difference between eastern and western cities: starting later, it was easier to plan.

"They've allowed me freedom, which I need. Small firms aren't departmental," I said, telling him how I felt after he showed his receptivity to the firm.

"Good. I'll be seeing Carey, Opel, and Rizzo tomorrow," he said, referring to IBM's leaders. "I'm going to tell them to do the deal."

He smiled broadly and loosened his collar, enjoying the idea of a failing business becoming two functioning businesses. That was something worth promoting, the creative part of being a corporate lawyer. He said, "You did a good job." He paused. "You did as good a job as I could have done."

That was the best compliment I would ever get from him. It was not meant in a vain way. He knew himself, and was pleased. After that he told me poor-boy stories, assuming that the deal would get done, for even a purchasing agent in the bowels of IBM could make a $5 million purchase without spending as much time on the matter as we had.

The next day he went up to White Plains to see Carey, Opel, and Rizzo. They listened to his recommendation and decided not to do the deal. Within a few hours of that meeting, I saw John Hunt in his own office at Cravath. He was ashen and uncomfortable.

"What if we change it?" I asked.

"It doesn't matter," he said. "They decided not to buy the company . . . under any circumstances. They understand all the problems have been worked out. That's not the point. It's a business decision." His manner let me know that he was a Cravath partner, and there was no hint of the camaraderie that we had shared the evening before. The barriers of status between us, which demanded deference, were his personal defense.

"There are a lot of dashed expectations," I said, fighting for my client.

"I know," he said. "But they made their decision."

It was over. I walked out of his offices, called the company, and spent the next few weeks helping them get started again. The compromises we made with the banks and the lenders while trying to do the deal with IBM made it easier for the company to stay in business.

In the weeks that followed, John Hunt never offered an explanation. Despite his momentary embarrassment before me, his client fared well, for IBM was able to withdraw from the deal completely, without incurring any obligations. I first speculated that IBM's decision may have been a rejection of the technology and later came to believe that IBM was not prepared, at that time in its history, to be seen as needing to buy technology. In the end, their action in rejecting the Neotec deal was like the working of the black box itself, an enigma. I took away from the rejection the knowledge that no matter how powerful a lawyer may be, he cannot commit to deliver his client. The lawyer advises and the client decides.

Within two months I got another call from Cravath. This time it was from Richard Simmons, the partner in charge of representing Chemical Bank. The Russians were going to be buying heavy farm equipment in the United States, he told me, and they needed counsel for the transactions. Cravath had been asked to represent the Russians but had a conflict.

"We don't have a lot of experience in that area," I said.

"No one does," he said. "But the people that know you say that you and your firm would be perfect."

"I'll call you back," I said. "Let me clear it at the firm."

I told Lipton about it by phone. He said, "Let's talk."

I went to his office. A large, round conference table served as his desk. There were no papers in sight, for as soon as a matter arrived at his table, he took care of it. While the amount of work that he did was prodigious, he always worked with a clean desk, as if he had no work. To achieve that level of order, he was constantly on the phone or reviewing documents, always occupied, meticulous about all details.

He looked like he'd been born in a dark suit. His clothes closet, one of the young partners had once remarked, was probably one of the darkest places in Manhattan. A large man, heavyset, his bulk diminished you when you sat next to him, especially at the round table without corners to give a sense of physical separation. His thick-lens glasses hid his eyes. When he changed his reading glasses to talk to me, I momentarily saw his eyes, soft and warm.

"Are you busy?" he asked. He knew all the matters I was working on.

"Yes," I said.

"Can you handle this?"

"Yes," I said, satisfied that I could make the effort to fit it in, although it would be an effort.

"Are we doing them a favor?" he asked. I hesitated, knowing where the question was leading. It was a very shrewd question, raising issues of incursions on our independence, even if they were light-years away. He had worked at a small firm for an exceptionally able corporate lawyer, trained in a father-and-son relationship, and then had broken away to be independent. Once having started the firm—ten years before with only seven lawyers—he'd never taken favors, even when he could have used them.

"No," I said. "They are doing us a favor."

"We don't know that, do we?" he asked, offering me a cookie, which I declined. He had a stack on his desk, which fueled his day.

Although he could be gruff, he tried to nurture young lawyers, and understood my need to be independent. Now he was being gentle and careful, letting me see the way he saw the matter, without being judgmental. I had been accepted as a partner in the firm, effective as of the first of the year, and there was no pressure on me to prove myself by taking more business.

"They think they're doing us a favor," I said.

"Do what you want," he said.

"I'll ask them," I said.

"You don't have to," he said. "If you want to represent the Russians, go ahead."

I had to decide whether I would be willing to do Cravath's spill-over business. Lipton had given me complete freedom of choice, which was complete trust, and in that trust I found great confidence in myself. I was satisfied that taking one or two deals from Cravath was not corrupting, and we could turn them down if we felt it was necessary.

I went down to Cravath's offices to see Richard Simmons, prepared to take on the matter. But when I sat down in the small chair opposite his desk, my position in his office gave me the immediate and unshakable sense of being a Cravath associate again, and I changed my mind. I told him we were busy. If Cravath needed help, however, and wanted a favor from us, we were prepared to help them. Otherwise, we'd prefer not to take on the matter because of our heavy work load.

There was silence, for it was obviously a strange statement, made without forewarning. As a shy man presented forcefully with something he hadn't expected, he darted his eyes to look at me and then nervously looked down at his desk as he tried to understand the reason for what had turned out to be a confrontation.

"We thought we were doing you a favor," he said.

"I don't think we'll be able to take the matter, then," I said. "I appreciate your interest." I left his office. The conversation was so short, and my change of mind so abrupt, that I didn't have a chance to fully appreciate what I'd done.

I left him and walked down to the fifty-sixth floor, where there was a firm cashier available to cash personal checks, a convenience that Cravath provided to its employees. About three people were ahead of me on that Friday afternoon. Check cashing had been a Friday routine for me at Cravath. The cashier, whom I'd known for six years, was a small, wizened man who compulsively counted and recounted the cash before he handed it to you. On my turn, I pushed the check under the glass to him and waited while he examined the check and then began to count out the cash. Suddenly, he stopped. He'd recognized my name on the check. He looked up.

"Mr. Lederman," he said. "Good to see you."

"Same here," I said.

He gave me a shy smile. "All is forgiven. Please come back." It was a spontaneous statement of friendship.

I smiled. "It's over," I said. "I won't be coming back." My words were also spontaneous.

On saying that, I realized that in Richard Simmons's office I had finally freed myself of Cravath. It had been almost a year since I had left the firm, but it took that unexpected moment to make me understand. I'd declared myself a peer, whether or not they recognized it, not fully appreciating what I'd gained and how my practice would change.

Cravath called again, within three months, and this time it was for help in a takeover matter. Wachtell Lipton had started to become recognized as expert in mergers and acquisitions. I went to a meeting on the new matter with Lipton, and afterward he asked me if the man that Cravath had sent was a partner in the firm. I told him he was. He seemed surprised and asked me why the firm had sent that man, since he seemed to know relatively little about mergers and acquisitions.

"It's his client," I said, telling him how Cravath worked, and seeing no fault in it.

"That's a funny way to run a law firm," he responded.

Wachtell Lipton was structured in accordance with the expertise of the partners. And seeing that contrast, I realized that the firm was uniquely set up to do deals. Not everything, however, about the structure was practical. The people in the firm were committed to being close and intimate, and as the merger boom came, the structure affected the number of matters the firm could take and how they were handled. The firm would ignore all advice about the necessity of growth. It would watch its competitors set up offices in multiple cities, merge with or acquire other law firms, and grow to upward of a thousand lawyers as Wachtell Lipton remained tightly knit, shunning the hierarchical corporate structure of other firms. Resisting change while being instruments of change for clients and others, everyone at the firm would be surprised at its success. To outsiders the firm looked eccentric in the path it had chosen. And George Katz could rightly say in wonder, "If we didn't exist, no one would believe we could exist."

THIRTEEN YEARS LATER, John Hunt closed the circle for me on the Neotec transaction. I met him by chance in the executive offices of Macmillan, Inc., when he'd stepped out of a conference room into the reception area to be alone with a client to discuss some nettlesome issue. I saw him through the glass doors to the reception area as I emerged from the elevator. I hadn't seen or talked to him in those thirteen years. As I opened the glass door, he finished with his client and turned in time to see me, giving me a warm, affectionate greeting.

We looked each other over for the changes that time brings. He hadn't changed: we could have been meeting a few weeks after I'd left him at his office at Cravath.

"You here on this thing?" he asked, meaning: Was I involved in the restructuring of Macmillan?

"Yes," I said.

Macmillan was in the process of attempting to be divided into two companies—the publishing company and an information services company. In restructuring the company, the board would be declaring a dividend of approximately $1.6 billion. John Hunt was representing the First Boston Corporation, which was making a loan of $400 million for a portion of the dividend, and I was representing the board of directors, overseeing the corporate restructuring.

"What was the name of that company we worked on together?" he asked.

"Neotec," I said.

"That's right," he said. "Neotec." When he said the name, his memory of it seemed to come back to him.

"It's a good thing we didn't do that deal," he said.

"What makes you say that?"

"It wasn't a very good company." He scowled to reflect his view.

"The company was good. The financial structure got out of hand."

"It all turned out for the best," he said. "You got paid, right? And we got paid. So it ended well." Strange statement: it didn't end well. Why bother to tell me that in such an unconvincing way, almost making a parody of our effort?

"That's not the only reason why we do these deals, John." While pleasant, my words had an edge, correcting him firmly, the way I would do with a student, which didn't sit well with him.

"It's over," he said. Still the strong physical man, he illustrated his point with a quick chopping motion of his hand. But something was on his mind, bothersome enough to open the subject for discussion.

"What ever happened to the company?" he asked, loosening up.

"It survived. Rosenthal got it back on an even keel and left about three or four years later. The company was sold in 1980 and is no longer public.

Looking at me the way he did years earlier when he'd told me that IBM wasn't going to do the deal, he hesitated, as if debating with himself. As I watched him, his face became the mask of the poker player with an interesting hole card. All of mine were out, and knowing what I knew, he turned over in his mind what he knew.

"Do you know why IBM didn't do that deal?" he asked. It was an invitation, direct and satisfying, to share the secret, unlock the past.

"No," I said. I thought to myself: This is a man with a first-rate mind and a conscience. Whatever is bothering him, it has rankled him for all these years, and he's still embarrassed. His statement about our both being paid told me that.

Satisfied that I was properly receptive, he said, "IBM had recently been sued by a New England manufacturer for over $200 million. It had to do with some purchases they made of display terminals. The suit had become bothersome. And of course the government antitrust litigation was demanding enormous resources. When I went up there to see Carey, he asked me only one thing: 'Will we be sued?' I told him yes, and he said, 'Let's not do it. It's not worth it to us.' And that was that. He didn't want another lawsuit."

His large shoulders shrugged as he turned away.

Every day helps to illuminate the days before. John Hunt had given me the lesson of Neotec. Carey was too remote: not being personally involved in the deal, he was able to act cavalierly. John confirmed what I knew: it never works if there's no emotional commitment. On my part, IBM's power deceived me. They weren't prepared to use it.

TAKEOVER
ENTREPRENEUR

▼

"Pressure is often more effective than reason."

I was looking at Thomas Mellon Evans in repose. A rare moment. Dozing in the aisle seat opposite mine, he was on his corporate Gulf Stream jet flying to St. Louis for a board meeting of the Missouri Portland Cement Company. His sleep was untroubled, the kind that you would expect from someone without guile. He looked like Santa Claus in a well-tailored blue suit, his pleasant moon face resting on a small, round body.

Appearance belied reality. Awake, he was restless and mercurial, often scowling, engaged in projects that made him too busy on some days to get a haircut, and willing to eat sawdust-tasting sandwiches on his plane in order to pack two days of work into one. On that August 1976 trip to St. Louis he was sixty-seven, and one of the most persistent and voracious acquirers of companies in America. In four decades he'd bought and sold over eighty companies. I thought of him as the "old man," for he was the same age as my father. I called him Tom.

The old man was the first prominent corporate raider that Wachtell Lipton represented. Attracted by the firm's participation in a few takeovers, he came to see Martin Lipton in 1976, who asked me to represent him.

It was no accident that Tom Evans had engaged the firm. The establishment firms were not yet actively involved in takeovers. Such work threatened many of their corporate clients, interfered with their corporate financing activities, and didn't seem lucrative enough to them to be worth the effort. In contrast, we sought to do hostile takeovers. For Wachtell Lipton, then a small group of about twenty-five lawyers with few large corporate clients, hostile corporate takeovers were a way of gaining new clients. Like Tom Evans, the new clients were individual entrepreneurs, creative people pursuing personal visions, often demanding.

Just by working with Tom Evans our reputation as takeover lawyers would be enhanced and others would seek advice. But the contested transactions they wanted to do were more demanding than negotiated ones and more complex. Indeed, there was something sweetly simple about the friendly transactions that I'd learned to do at Cravath. In this new era I had much to learn, but few lawyers were experienced in takeovers, and if I was to master their intricacies, my training would have to come from Lipton and men like Tom Evans and the experience they offered in high-stakes contests. Since the firm was small, I worked on many of the matters largely by myself. Curiously, the stress of learning while doing was lost in the excitement of the work.

The old man woke, asked me a question, listened to the answer, and then fell back to sleep, going into and out of sleep with ease. Never academic, the questions were sparked by neither intellectual curiosity nor restless intelligence. They were practical and precise, always related to matters at hand, posed to solve real problems. In their solutions, he would make money.

Our trip to the Missouri Portland headquarters represented the end of a fourteen-month battle for control of the company. We would be attending Evans's first board meeting of Missouri Portland more than a year after he'd acquired 52 percent of the stock and paid $25 million for it. In all that time, the old man hadn't met any of the directors or the management, unusual even for a hostile takeover. In this case the Missouri Portland directors had locked out their new majority shareholder. To end the protracted battle for control and get access to the boardroom, he'd agreed to appoint only three out of the twelve directors and wait two years before he elected a majority of the board members.

Knowing that we'd be outnumbered at the board meeting, I told him that they would be evaluating him, and if he became difficult, he would have trouble with them in the future. Their control of the boardroom would allow them to ignore him or even be vindictive. Holding his temper was not easy for him. In order to prepare him, I tried to anticipate the kinds of questions that would be asked at the meeting. I'd never been through a situation like this before and felt uncomfortable, as if shadowboxing. The old man looked at me with his eyes twinkling and told me not to worry, he'd be charming, then smiled mischievously, making me feel like a pedantic and ill-prepared schoolteacher faced with a difficult pupil. Of course, he was the teacher and I the pupil.

He was one of the country's richest men and had made the money himself. Although distantly related to the Mellon family, he grew up without personal wealth. After training in economics at Yale, in 1931 he went to work for Gulf Oil, a Mellon-controlled company. In 1936 and 1937 he made about $30,000 on trades of Gulf Oil stock and from that stake built two major American companies— H. K. Porter Company and Crane Co.—reflections of his acumen. Without doubt, he was a financial genius.

We were flying on the corporate jet of H. K. Porter. Tom had acquired control of H. K. Porter in bankruptcy when it was a manufacturer of small steam locomotives. Buying businesses that were losing money, and finding value where others failed, was part of his style. In 1937, he bought Porter's defaulted bonds, which were converted in bankruptcy to the common stock of the company, and with a majority of the bonds, he got control of the company. Under his guidance, it turned profitable and became a major New York Stock Exchange company. Control of Crane Co., his other corporate vehicle, was acquired in 1959, when he bought about 15 percent of the company in the open market. At the time the company was a poorly performing manufacturer and distributor of plumbing products.

The two companies, initially in different businesses, made many parallel investments. Porter owned a steel company, Connors Steel, and Crane owned Colorado Fuel & Iron. The two companies acquired cement companies; Porter took on Missouri Portland Cement, and Crane acquired Medusa Cement. Both companies were in the manufacturing, distribution, and warehousing businesses for various valves and pipes and other metal-bending items. For all the similarities that developed over time, the old man kept the two separate. Each had its own corporate jets, its own offices, personnel, and managerial staffs. His personality, however, was imprinted on both. They were equivalent to the right and left halves of his brain and he was their central nervous system, their only means of communicating. Separate enterprises usually reflect different facets of a personality, but his singular personality was mirrored in each of them.

The old man had relaxed on the plane, and I took some comfort from that. But still uneasy because I didn't know what to expect of him at the board meeting, I turned to talk to Edward P. Evans (called Ned), the second of Tom's three sons, who was then thirty-four years old and president of H. K. Porter. Ned, a graduate of Yale College and Harvard Business School, was usually patient and calm under stress, even in the face of his father's impatience. Our small talk revealed that Ned wouldn't speculate about what his father might do, for he knew the old man would do what he wanted and there was nothing we could change. Expressing his stoicism by turning to his business reading, he left me with my concerns.

I held myself available to answer the old man's questions and tried to assess from them how he would handle the board meeting, but I couldn't anticipate his strategy. I told myself that I was prepared for anything, but knew, as we approached the Midwest and the moment of reckoning, that I was not.

After landing at the private jet airport in St. Louis, the three of us squeezed into a run-down cab for the fifteen-minute ride to the company in Clayton, a St. Louis suburb. Not having a limousine waiting was typical of the old man. He didn't pamper himself: if it was utilitarian, it would serve. It was hot in the cab and I could feel my clothes beginning to stick to me. The heat didn't seem to bother the old man or affect his energy. He barked orders at the cabdriver, telling him to turn off his radio since we wanted to talk.

At the Missouri Portland offices, along with John Kountz, the general counsel of H. K. Porter, who had arrived separately from Pittsburgh, we were ushered into the boardroom and introduced to all the members of the board. Ordinarily, it's hard to keep the names and the faces straight, especially after only a cursory introduction, but this time it was different. I'd sued each of them in the fight for control and I was eager to assign faces to names at last. Relatively old men, they didn't seem to embody, individually or collectively, the indomitable spirit that had fought to keep the company independent.

Coffee in cardboard cups and doughnuts on paper plates had been set out for us. As with most well-run industrial companies that didn't deal with the retail public, no frills were to be seen. The austerity was mirrored by the people in the room, with few smiles in evidence. Everybody was on good behavior, however. While holding coffee cups, we exchanged pleasantries: largely banal remarks about the weather. Tom, at least, talked about his horses. He was soon to have a Kentucky Derby winner with his horse Pleasant Colony. His charm was abundant, but the social mixing was as tentative as that at a prom, where everyone feels a little ungainly.

While the businessmen tried to chat, I met our legal adversaries for the first time, the corporate lawyers from Davis, Polk & Wardwell: William Tucker, a senior partner of the firm, about sixty years old, and his associate. Tucker, a large good-spirited man, tried to make me feel at home, taking seriously the role of host since he and his client controlled the boardroom. In the end, the good manners had a telling effect: they made me feel the nastiness of displacing his clients.

Soon the social adhesives wore thin. People grouped around those they knew, and the old man and Ned wound up on one side of the room, while the directors were on the other, finding the polar extremes. The professionals banded in the middle. The start of the meeting was welcome.

Moss Alexander, the president of Missouri Portland, called the meeting to order, as if it were an ordinary meeting, one of the many since the business had been founded by his family in 1907. He'd been a director for twenty years, holding the longest tenure of any director in the room, and had presided over the board for many years, as had his father before him. This was a place of many triumphs for him. That history must have buoyed his confidence, for he appeared tall and commanding seated at the head of the board table. Once he began the meeting, showing perfect authority over its rituals, he looked comfortable with his continued control of the board and fell into a routine.

MOST OF THE old man's Missouri Portland shares had been acquired in a hostile tender offer, which is an offer to buy shares made directly to the public through an advertisement in national newspapers (and through a printed offer) without first seeking management's approval. Accustomed to shrugging off other people's disfavor, he didn't mind management's opposition or the opprobrium associated with hostile takeovers. Further, he delighted in this process which did away with any pretense of friendliness. By making an offer directly to the shareholders, he gained the advantage of being able to select companies on the basis of his own analysis of their performance and assets and to buy those not otherwise for sale. Moreover, he could acquire control for prices set by him, remove management to whom he had no obligations, and put the assets to better use or sell them at a profit to someone else who would operate them.

He didn't follow the conventional rules with respect to buying companies, and began his career out of phase with the merger cycles in American business. The first great merger wave began before his time, at the turn of the century, producing such business giants as U.S. Steel and International Harvester. The second wave began in the 1960s and produced conglomerate companies such as ITT, large holding companies managing diverse and unrelated businesses. It was assumed that professional management could operate any business, and diversity was supposed to supply financial balance to offset the effects of business cycles. By 1960, controlling both Porter and Crane, Tom Evans looked like a conglomerateur. But he was following his own economic principles. He didn't worry about modifying the effects of business cycles. Interested always in hard assets—minerals, basic steel, industrial products, and commodities such as cement—he bought companies with assets that were inflation-proof. These kinds of companies would keep their value, would require little marketing or advertising of their products, and were not subject to fashion or taste. As to price, he looked to buy at less than the carrying value (or "book value") of the assets on the financial statements. But to buy at such prices he often had to consider marginally profitable companies or those losing money because they weren't efficient enough to meet competition. These businesses were often neglected, with high costs and low productivity. Operating them profitably meant pruning deadwood by selling nonperforming businesses, laying off people who were expensive and not fully productive, and generally cutting costs sharply.

When he bought companies, he therefore changed them, which is necessarily disruptive, and his actions were often regarded as ruthless. After he'd closed down—over a five-year period ending in 1973—five facilities of Crane and Porter in New Jersey, including John A. Roebling & Sons, the steelmaker for the Brooklyn Bridge, and laid off over 3,400 people, Congressman Frank Thompson, Jr., from New Jersey called him the corporate equivalent of Jaws. The impression of Tom Evans in the business community was that he was an American original: a nineteenth-century buccaneer capitalist, unencumbered by altruism. Spooked by his reputation, the Missouri Portland board had stiffened their resistance to his takeover bid.

Compounding his difficulty with the board was his discomfort with negotiating. He didn't like adjusting differences and wasn't a good listener. Intransigence seemed inherent in his style: when alternatives were offered, most often they were rejected. Buying or selling for him was strictly a matter of setting the price, without emotional attachment to any business or its parts. In the takeover battle, he characteristically didn't try to negotiate a settlement, which prolonged the fight.

The quality of Missouri Portland, which excited him and kept him fighting for control, could be seen in its thoughtful business design. Each of its three cement plants, as well as its distribution terminals, was located on a major river to facilitate shipment by water, making transportation inexpensive. And the plants were low-cost producers of cement, using relatively cheap coal as fuel, with raw materials obtained from nearby quarries owned by the company. With these advantages, Missouri Portland maintained a dominant market share within its geographic area.

In August 1975, at the time of the old man's first purchase of a block of stock at $24 a share, Missouri Portland's book value was over $28 a share, and the replacement cost of its assets was approximately $129 a share. Replacement cost was what it would take to build those facilities at that time. In actuality it would have been nearly impossible to duplicate such well-planned facilities. Tom Evans had found value for H. K. Porter.

Unlike many of his other acquisitions, this one was an efficiently functioning business with able management, which he was buying at bargain prices. This was possible because the stock market was depressed (as it was for most of that decade) and the everyday trading prices of the Missouri Portland shares didn't reflect the value of control of the company. The old man was entering (and introducing me to) a new era, the acquisition of undervalued companies, often well managed. He knew a truth that would eventually fuel an explosion of mergers and acquisitions in this country: it's cheaper to buy going companies than to build them.

Tom Evans's presence in the boardroom also meant a new era for the company. By asserting the rights of majority ownership, the old man was turning the passive public stock into an assertive force, diminishing management's power. In trying to take any action, he would cause a confrontation with the board because they shared management's vision of the company.

At the board meeting, with Moss Alexander presiding, the board members clung to their procedures, the housekeeping details that made up the routine of their meetings. They called the roll to determine if there was a quorum, asked for approval of the minutes of the previous meeting, followed *Robert's Rules of Order* with respect to the procedures for making motions, seconding motions, and voting on them, and had a detailed agenda which they followed meticulously. The board meeting was to continue from 10 a.m. until noon, at which time they would all have lunch together.

It was one of those meetings where within the first few minutes you believed it was going to be endless. Everybody was extraordinarily polite and no one was prepared to be assertive or to advance the meeting. Strangely, the old man sat there with a smile on his moon face, an uncharacteristic pose, and it made me suspect that peace wasn't going to last long. All the others in the room knew that the agenda was pedestrian, and had nothing to do with the monumental fact that the new owner was on the premises. They were all working at making the meeting deadly dull, hoping that this meeting would signal the kinds that they would experience for at least two years: quiet, polite, noncontentious, and without substance. They may have even believed that their majority of the board positions would ensure that.

They didn't know Tom. His mind didn't tolerate the insipid, and he wasn't about to be lulled to sleep. He would allow about a half hour to pass before he said anything.

The old man had realized that the battle for control would alienate the directors, but for him, it was part of the cost of doing the deal. He hadn't expected, however, to find himself in a minority position on the board while holding a majority of the stock. This unfortunate circumstance was the result of the way he'd conducted the tender offer.

The tender offer for control turned out to be more costly than he had anticipated. He had H. K. Porter make the tender offer for 48 percent of the stock, initially at $24, then raised it to $26 a share to ward off competition. The old man chose the 48 percent figure so that he would be seeking less than majority control (and thus not look voracious), although with that stock position he could demand a majority of the board. Unfortunately, the tender for less than a majority turned out to be a major tactical error.

When Porter closed its tender offer he had them buy all the shares that had been tendered, which put Porter's ownership at 54 percent. Missouri Portland claimed that if Tom wasn't seeking majority control, then he shouldn't have bought more shares than he'd been seeking. They accused him of misleading the public and claimed to have caught him in a typical maneuver: the change-of-intention gambit, trying to look like a sheep while being a wolf. The old man contended that since the excess shares were tendered he was doing everyone a favor by buying them at $26 per share, a significant premium over the market.

Possession was the law for him. If he held the shares it would be hard to take them away. If they tried, it would take time to do so. He knew that the process of the law is slow. Missouri Portland would see the power of his majority block and settle. But the Missouri Portland directors were incensed by his tactics and felt that Tom Evans's lack of candor was a fatal defect. Angrily, they locked him out, wouldn't count his shares as validly owned, and thus turned the tables on him by using the slow process of the law against him.

There had never been a situation in a public company where someone had purchased over a majority of the outstanding shares of the company and then hadn't been allowed to enter the corporate premises and exercise control. The Missouri Portland directors were doing to the old man what he did to everybody else, stalling and trying to tire him out. He came to our firm at a moment of deadlock.

I told Tom Evans that he had to be patient, that the court case could take as long as a year. He wasn't willing or able to accept the advice.

He told me, "I don't have to wait for them. I can sell my stock. If I sell my stock, what are they going to do?" He was satisfied with the alternative, as if a sale was an easy answer, when it was no answer, since he didn't want to sell the stock.

"They're going to claim it was illegally acquired," I said, following through on his argument.

"You mean I can't sell my stock?" he asked, boldly challenging me.

"You're not going to get a reasonable price for the block if there's a dispute over whether you properly acquired it." I'd sidestepped a collision.

"I can't wait." That was why he'd come for advice, to avoid delay. He was used to having people listen to him, and getting his way. The members of his staff, who were highly competent, were like amoebas: they would incorporate his position and reshape themselves. That daily obedience had not prepared him to accept intransigence in others for very long.

"You have little choice," I said.

"The problem," he said, "is that they have nothing to lose. If we sue them personally and threatened their personal assets," he said, "then they'd have something to lose. Pressure is often more effective than reason."

He understood the art of corporate warfare.

We sued the Missouri Portland directors personally, and within a short time I was called by their lawyers at Davis Polk and asked if the old man wanted to settle. He allowed me to negotiate for him, grumbling thereafter at the proposed settlement, under which he would have to wait two years to get control of the board. Settling was attractive to him, however, because he could then sit in on board meetings.

Surprisingly, the Davis Polk litigators wouldn't meet to discuss the drafts of the settlement. Rather, they sent typed comments by courier. The battle had been so difficult and prolonged that they seemed to have become almost as emotionally involved as the Missouri Portland directors. That was a new experience for me. Since we didn't meet, and they were meticulous, the process dragged on. The old man expressed his impatience, which I had to absorb but couldn't do anything about.

Finally, the last barrier was Missouri Portland's insistence that H. K. Porter guarantee that the minority shares (the other 46 percent that he didn't own) wouldn't be acquired by Porter at a price less than $26. While it was of great concern to the Missouri Portland directors, Tom didn't like setting a floor on the stock price for the public, but assumed, like them, that the company would grow more valuable over time. To get the matter done with, he agreed that if he bought any additional shares they would be purchased for at least $26 a share. Almost as an afterthought, he had me add in the agreement that securities valued at $26 a share could be used instead of cash, which turned out to be a critical addition.

With the settlement complete, we set out for the first board meeting. I knew that the old man still wasn't resigned to waiting two years to get control, but it appeared that the only way out of his minority position on the board was to buy the whole company. Such a purchase didn't seem possible. He didn't have ready funds to buy out the other shareholders because of H. K. Porter's other commitments. Given limited funds, he didn't have any cards to play. Nevertheless, I reminded myself of his determination to seize control and guessed that he would probably make his move at the board meeting.

MOSS ALEXANDER WAS talking about capital expenditures for two new barges to ship cement produced in the plants to the distribution terminals. He was proceeding to allocate the capital of the company for the next fiscal year. At last, something of substance.

The management had obviously held off deciding on some of these capital items until the old man had joined the board, giving him an opportunity to pass on the expenditures. It was the first suggestion that the board would entertain his point of view, although they didn't seem to be seeking it. There was an anticipatory stillness as paper shuffling and chair scraping diminished.

The old man didn't address the issue on the table. Seemingly distracted, he asked, "Why do we own a furniture company?" His voice was not loud, but it was demanding, as always, and came out as harsh because the question was irrelevant.

Missouri Portland owned a small institutional furniture company that was worth less than $2.5 million and was barely holding its own. A relatively recent acquisition, it had troubled the old man because it didn't fit with the business or make any operating sense. But why bother to argue over something so small when they had given him a chance to discuss the capital budget?

"It's a good financial investment," Weldon Rogers replied. He was the chief financial officer and the youngest of the Missouri directors, but powerful because he was financially sophisticated. The question had flushed out that buying the furniture business was Rogers's decision. Weldon Rogers was fair-skinned and had a hint of red in his hair. You could see that he had a temper.

"It takes away from management's time," the old man answered, not minding the flush in Rogers's cheeks. "And it's too small and marginal to matter," he added, taking the ground Rogers could have used.

"It'll contribute to our earnings," Rogers said sharply. He was reminding everyone in the room why they had bought the business, assuring them it was right, and keeping his group cohesive.

"Not enough to justify the time," the old man retorted. "The next thing you know we'll be buying a brassiere company because you say it's a good financial move. Cement is our business, not rags or furniture. What do we know about those businesses?" His voice had risen slightly to counter Rogers's temper, letting his scorn come through. He was driving a wedge between Rogers, the professional manager, and the old men on the board like himself who knew and appreciated the cement business. For him, Rogers's attempt to diversify the business was an aberrant move.

"There's no point in stripping assets from the company," Rogers snapped. That was a rallying cry to the others on the board, telling them, in effect, that Tom Evans would even sell the chairs they sat on to turn a profit.

"We'll put the money back in the business," the old man said. He paused, and then decisively made his point. "Where it belongs."

"Do you think we should sell it, Tom?" Moss asked, intervening, showing his concern over the confrontation.

"Yes," he said.

Moss said in a conciliatory tone, "A number of us have also thought that it doesn't make any sense for us to own a furniture company." He looked around at his fellow board members, making eye contact with each, as if polling them on their position. "You're right," he said. "Cement is our business. We should sell it."

"We ought to spend more money on barges," Tom said, not giving anyone a moment to contemplate the change he'd just effected in the company. His voice had lowered. The tone wasn't as sharp but it was still commanding. Also, he'd shifted in his seat and turned away from Weldon Rogers, in that move dismissing him, concentrating solely on Moss Alexander.

"That was our plan, Tom," Moss said.

Tom said, "Not enough. We have to transport all our cement by river, and we're not fully capable of using our production capacity and meeting our delivery schedules."

"That makes a lot of sense," Moss said, not sounding as sure as his words.

"We should invest more money in the plants," Tom lectured, almost as if from a pulpit. "The dividend we pay out is too high. Some of it should go back into the business."

Now, with the full message starkly stated, Moss Alexander looked at him forlornly. Moss Alexander and his family had a relatively large stock position and a cut in the dividend would sharply decrease their income. Although he could oppose it now, a dividend cut seemed inevitable, making Moss Alexander squirm. The old man's image as a takeover entrepreneur had confused them, for they hadn't seen him as interested in operations, willing to improve plant and equipment. They were familiar with his recent takeover of Anaconda, a mining company, and that battle seemed to define his abilities and interests. Showing no interest in running Anaconda, Crane (the old man's other company) had acquired about 18½ percent of Anaconda's stock in an exchange offer for Crane's debentures (which were becoming known as "junk bonds"), giving Crane a control block, which the old man promptly sold to Atlantic Richfield. Crane, in a six-month contest, had made an $80 million profit, much more than the total value of Missouri Portland.

In 1975 the purchase of control of Anaconda for debentures and the subsequent sale was one of the all-time successes in arbitraging control of a company. It pointed the way for all the other takeover entrepreneurs who followed, such as Carl Icahn, Irwin Jacobs, T. Boone Pickens, and Asher Edelman. The Anaconda takeover also signaled the beginning of the third and longest merger wave in the twentieth century. Even then the Missouri board members could recognize the takeover as innovative and could conclude that Tom Evans wasn't interested in building businesses, just in dismantling or selling them.

The old man's total concentration on the business and economics of Missouri Portland panicked Moss Alexander and then the board. Although Moss Alexander sat at the head of the board table, he wasn't presiding. Anyone could see that there would be no restraining the old man, who couldn't be stroked or petted into docility. The old man had to be dealt with on business terms. What no one anticipated before this moment was that the board and management would all be looking to him for business direction.

A role reversal had occurred. Tom was taking the long view, and they, contrary to their own prior business judgments, were interested in the short term because their tenure expired in less than two years. With that change of status and their sense that he'd want to cut the dividend when he got total control, the management felt that it would be best for them and the other shareholders who relied on the dividend income if the old man bought out the public shareholders. In fact, where control has passed, it's quite common for the board to seek to have the public shares purchased. The principal reason is that minority positions have depressed trading values because there is little chance of a takeover premium and the stocks do not appreciate as well as those where there is no controlling stockholder.

It was no surprise when Moss Alexander asked, "Tom, why don't you buy the rest of the company?"

He said, "I haven't thought about it."

"Why don't you think about it?"

"I don't have enough cash at H. K. Porter to do it," Tom said. "I also don't want to put additional debt on H. K. Porter's balance sheet." He reminded them that the profit he'd made on the sale of Anaconda was Crane's and not money that H. K. Porter could spend. It was as if his left pocket was full, his right pocket empty, and he couldn't switch money between pockets. Although unusual, the situation existed because there were different public shareholders in each of his companies. He smiled and let them understand the difficulty of the problem they had presented to him.

There was a long silence. He could be comfortable not saying anything, letting everyone contemplate what they faced if he didn't buy out the public shares, all the time waiting as if he were thinking of his alternatives. In that moment I almost believed that he would let the opportunity pass. His timing, however, was impeccable. Just as I shifted in my chair, he floated a novel idea in a soft voice. "If you are interested," the old man said, "we could use the debt of Missouri Portland to acquire the stock."

Ned Evans looked over at me to see if it was possible. Highly unusual, it hadn't been done before. I nodded to show him that it could be done, telling him only later that it was one of the questions that the old man had casually asked me on the flight to Missouri. The effect of the maneuver was that a major public company, Missouri Portland, would be completely buying out the public ownership for its own bonds. If the debt swapped for its common stock was worth at least $26 a share, there was no reason why it couldn't be done. It was something the board wouldn't have seriously considered before this meeting.

Tom said, "I'm prepared to use a $30 debenture [which was a note for the $30] of Missouri Portland and put a 10 percent interest rate on it. We'll have it listed for trading on the New York Stock Exchange. That would permit you and the public to sell the debenture and get at least $26 and maybe $30 [or whatever the trading value of the security was after it was issued] or hold it and get $30 [at maturity] at 10 percent interest [until maturity]."

"Would you seriously consider that?" Moss Alexander asked.

"Yes," the old man said.

Missouri Portland was paying an annual dividend of $2.50 a share, which was not tax-deductible to the company. The $30 debenture at 10 percent interest would pay the shareholder $3.00 rather than $2.50, but the company would be getting a tax deduction, which meant that the company would be paying only $1.50 a share. In other words, shareholders like Moss Alexander got more and the company paid less, which was possible when the government, through deductible interest, subsidized the acquisition. Missouri Portland's buying its common stock for its debt was a bootstrap transaction, with the company buying itself. The old man was initiating one of the first leveraged buyouts for subordinated debt, later commonly known as junk bonds.

Bill Tucker whispered in Moss Alexander's ear. Moss nodded and then addressed the old man:

"We'll need an opinion from an independent investment banker that the debentures are worth at least $26 and that the deal is fair. That may not be easy to do, Tom." Moss, while indicating that the task was formidable, was smiling, encouraging the old man. Such an opinion was necessary before the Missouri Portland board of directors could recommend the transaction to its shareholders.

"I'll take care of it," the old man said, "as soon as I get back to New York."

AFTER THE MEETING broke up, Tom was in a hurry to return to New York to follow through. Knowing that he wouldn't truly control the company until he bought out the management, he acted as if he'd mesmerized them, and needed to get the deal done before the spell was broken. There was no convincing him that it was appropriate to have lunch with them. There were sandwiches on the plane, he told me, and that would save time. In the rush of ending the meeting, I got Tom to agree to take Bill Tucker and his associate back to New York on the H. K. Porter jet. Taking them with us would give me the opportunity to talk to Tucker to set in motion with him the arrangements for implementing the exchange of Missouri Portland debentures for public stock.

We set out for the airport in two separate cabs: Tom, Ned, and I in one, Tucker and his associate in the other, and we arrived first. After the old man sat down in his seat and buckled himself in, I stepped outside to make some telephone calls while we waited for Bill Tucker. I was on a public phone in the hangar when the old man came out of the plane looking for me.

"Let's go," he said.

"We're waiting for Bill Tucker," I said.

"He's not here. I don't want to wait any longer," he said.

"I'm in the middle of a call," I said, "and we can't go without Tucker."

"He's not here," he insisted.

"His driver probably took a wrong turn. He'll get here."

The entrance to the private jetport of the St. Louis Airport was hard to locate, but I stressed to Tom that the driver would soon find it. Tom Evans didn't care. Every fiber of his being seemed inflamed by the irritation of waiting.

"Wheels up in five minutes," he snapped.

"That may not be enough time."

"I'm leaving, with or without him," he said.

"I won't go without him. I have to work with him, and it's not right. We told him we would take him," I said, thinking the commitment would end the discussion.

"You told him we would take him. I'm leaving in five minutes."

"Then you're going without me."

He stopped, looked at me. His moon face showed little emotion while he calculated his next move. I had expected him to erupt in full fury. Instead, he turned back to the plane without a word. I finished my call to my office and stood by the public telephone looking out at the airplane, not prepared to board it. If I boarded, he might leave without Tucker, and so I stood by the telephone and waited.

Soon, however, I grew restless and stepped outside to look for Tucker. I could see the planes taxiing in the distance, preparing for takeoff. I watched the other planes leaving and arriving and let myself become involved in the activity of the airport. The sun's stark reflection from the concrete runway hurt my eyes, and waves of heat, visible and shimmering, baked me. I suddenly ached. I expected the plane to start its engines to pipe cool air to the passengers and then to taxi away from me into the broad field leading to the runway. I avoided looking at it, as if by so doing I could make it stand still.

Let him leave, I told myself. That was the proper attitude, indifference. Without concern, I could easily wait, even in the heat. But I was angry and couldn't express it, which made waiting all the more difficult. Finally, Tucker arrived. As endless as it felt, I'd waited only ten minutes. The cab pulled out to the field near the plane and I walked to meet him. If Tom makes any remarks, I said, let them slide, don't take him on, since the old man and I had already had it out.

We boarded the plane. The old man, immersed in his papers, said nothing to us. I sat down, buckled myself in, and looked at him. He was as relaxed as he had been on the way going out. It was as if the incident had never happened. I was upset from the confrontation and wet from the heat. Not until the plane was in the air, well along toward New York, was I able to relax.

THE KEY TO the deal now was the engagement of an investment banker, who could value the debentures and render an opinion on the fairness of the exchange of debentures for stock.

Tom called Goldman, Sachs & Co. and asked them to act for Missouri Portland. A representative of Goldman Sachs had recently been to his office looking for investment banking business. The old man felt that if they were looking for business, they would do anything he asked. He had a jaundiced view of investment bankers.

To his surprise, Goldman Sachs turned him down, telling him that they were too busy to take the matter.

When I heard the reason Goldman Sachs had given him I said, "Large investment banking firms are rarely too busy to take on a matter. There must be something else bothering them." He agreed that the reason didn't make sense. I felt the transaction was too sensitive to rely on such a superficial statement. If there was litigation, Goldman Sachs's records would be checked, which made it necessary to pin down the real reason for declining the invitation. With the old man involved, there was always a possibility of litigation, and I didn't want to be in a position of being surprised in the discovery process when private records were inspected.

After some telephone calls, I found the person at Goldman Sachs that the old man had talked to and discovered that Goldman had concluded that the firm shouldn't take on the matter because they believed that they couldn't "render an opinion that Tom Evans's junk would trade at the $26 level." The old man's reputation as an aggressive corporate raider who would take every advantage had probably made them skeptical of the value. In a memorandum to their files they reflected that decision and consistently referred to the bonds that Missouri Portland would be exchanging as "junk." While the term "junk" was gaining currency for bonds that weren't investment grade (not rated as such by rating agencies such as Moody's and Standard & Poor's), it was a characterization, at that time, which severely denigrated the value of the debentures to the uninitiated, including the courts. I told Tom that we had to tell whomever else we asked to act as an independent banker about Goldman Sachs's negative reaction. The stockholders also would have to be told.

Goldman's action also raised the possibility that the old man might not be able to get someone else to act favorably. He made a few telephone calls and told me that he'd found some people at Lazard Frères & Co., a prominent investment banking firm, who seemed interested in the business. He sent Ned and me to Lazard to work out the arrangements. Investment bankers usually charged a percentage of the value of the transaction, from ½ of 1 percent to 1 percent (from $125,000 to $250,000, in this case) depending on the services performed. Bankers often helped select target companies (as appropriate acquisition candidates) or helped defend against a takeover raid by finding other bidders to buy the company at a price higher than the takeover offer. In this case, however, the investment banker's role would be limited to valuation (making an appropriate study of the company's earnings and assets to fix a value on the Missouri Portland bonds), and thus Tom was looking to pay the low end of the fee range.

Before we went to Lazard's offices, we discussed the fee negotiation. Tom felt that we should pay the fee only after we got the favorable opinion. I told him that, given the one misstep, it would be wrong to put ourselves in a position where Lazard's independence could be questioned or, worse, where it could be said that we had coerced the opinion. Therefore, he had to pay the fee irrespective of whether they rendered a favorable opinion. He was irritated by my advice. It ran counter to his business sense, which was: if you don't control them through the payment of the fee, they control you.

The Lazard Frères partners were Frank Pizzitola and Peter Jaquith. They had their sense of the dignity of Lazard and weren't about to let it appear that Lazard could be influenced by the fee or the opportunity for future business. Tom Evans's reputation as a knowledgeable and voracious acquirer of companies had followed us into the room, as if he were present and about to control the meeting. In response, the two men were stiff-necked and wary.

The conference room was bleak, with no thought of comfort reflected in its furnishings. There was one table that looked as if it had been bought fifty years before and had never been moved from its original position. The chairs looked like the original chairs, aged by the compulsive restlessness of hundreds of obsessed men.

It was my job to tell the Lazard partners all the facts and assure them that they weren't being asked to compromise themselves. I told them about how Goldman Sachs had refused to render the opinion. The protocol of the meeting called for their deciding whether to take the engagement before we discussed the fee. They proceeded to ask all the relevant questions to the point of tedium. They were letting us know that they intended to be uncompromising. We all fidgeted in our chairs, aging them further.

Ned's stance was that he had an engagement to offer, but he didn't have to offer it to them. His diffident manner left no doubt that he could easily find other, equally qualified, independent investment bankers. Accordingly, Ned asked about Lazard's experience—how they handled such matters, the kinds of approaches they would take to test the value, and so on.

They, of course, had more practice, and after forty-five minutes Ned had run out of steam, while they still had further questions. It was clear he wasn't going to get an answer. Finally I attempted to direct the discussion to end the meeting.

I said, "We believe the debentures are worth at least $26 a share."

"Yes," they said. They were acknowledging our belief, nothing more.

"Is there anything that we've said that leads you to a different conclusion?" I asked.

"We haven't begun our review," Peter Jaquith said.

"We know that," I said. "But sometimes it's easy to see that you may not be able to confirm our opinion." I was now close to the point.

"That's true," Peter Jaquith said.

"Well, is this one of those cases?"

"Whatever we say now may have no bearing on what our ultimate opinion may be."

"I see," I said. They would say nothing, which was the correct posture, and allow no concessions.

Ned stood up, for they had made their point.

"We'd like you to do the job," he said.

Everybody smiled.

"What will your fee be?" Ned asked.

As quick as a shot, Peter Jaquith said, "Two hundred fifty thousand dollars." Without a pause he said, "The payment is for the opinion, whether or not favorable."

Ned sat down. "Two hundred fifty thousand dollars? That's a lot of money. There are a lot of bankers who would do it for less."

"This is a difficult opinion to render," Jaquith said.

Then Ned stood up again. "Let us think it over," he said.

▾

WHEN WE RETURNED, the old man called me into his office. He'd already worked himself into a state of annoyance, letting me feel its force as he told me that he didn't like the position we'd gotten ourselves into with the investment bankers.

His office was spartan, with his desk the focal point. Near his desk was a TV screen flashing stock quotations and news from the Dow Jones wire. He gave the market activity most of his attention, even when you were talking to him. A conference room adjoining his office was rarely used. Ned Evans's office, much smaller but in the spartan style of his father's, was nearby.

"They have us over a barrel," he said. "We don't know what they're going to say." His deep voice seemed larger than his body.

"There isn't much choice," I said.

"And they're charging us too much money. They've made this into a high-risk situation. It's something that a kid in business school can do."

He turned away from me to watch his TV screen with the latest stock quotes, not looking at me while I talked, and I had the impression that he didn't care about what I said. That made my speech pedantic.

"Their opinion is necessary to do the transaction. The debentures have to be priced by someone who is independent, not by us, and it's only reasonable for the Missouri Portland board to require an opinion of independent bankers that the transaction is fair to their shareholders."

"Don't lecture me," he said, letting me know he was not seeking advice.

"I may be repeating the obvious," I said, "but it seems to bear repeating." I'd become testy.

He looked at me now.

"Listen," he said. "The problem is that we have to disclose Goldman Sachs's nonopinion. All I did was make a telephone call."

The meeting at Lazard had gotten him to reflect. If his request for an opinion by Goldman Sachs didn't have to be disclosed, then the whole process would be much more relaxed. Without disclosure no one would be in a position of having their judgment tested against

Goldman Sachs's judgment, though of course there was a question whether Goldman Sachs had made the kind of analysis that could be reasonably characterized as an opinion.

My view was that Goldman Sachs's position had to be disclosed. Everything the old man did received publicity and was carefully examined. The perceptions that others had of him, with all possible subjective distortions, were a reality that affected reactions to him.

"The disclosure of Goldman Sachs's position is the problem," I acknowledged. "You're right."

"I know I'm right. I don't want to do it," he said. His eyes were now small and threatening, totally focused on me.

"It has to be done," I said, meeting his stare.

"Is it illegal?" he asked, knowing that was not the issue.

"No, it's not illegal," I said.

"I'll take the risk," he said.

"You don't know the risk you're taking," I said. I saw the possibility of an investigation by the Securities and Exchange Commission, which would be disruptive.

"I've been taking these kinds of risks from before you were out of diapers. I know the risks I can take," he said.

I hadn't presented the issue properly to him. My role as counsel was to persuade him. How much easier my job would be, I thought, if I could just read a rule to him that told him what he had to do.

"You have to look at this situation the way others will look at it," I said, changing my tone, suppressing the hard edge, as I tried to suggest for the first time that he should understand the effect of his reputation.

"What do you mean?" he asked, responding to the softness in my voice.

"The Missouri Portland board will find out about Goldman Sachs. They'll have to report it to their stockholders. There are no secrets. You could be damned for trying to cover up. People are willing to believe that it's the kind of thing you would do."

"If the importance of the Goldman Sachs nonopinion is exaggerated, I could lose the deal," he said, rejecting my contention with a bellow. "I don't want to be at that board's mercy ever again."

"No matter how they find out about it, the opinion's importance will be exaggerated anyway. Everybody will be afraid that you'll outsmart them. They will be very cautious and suspicious. Your success has done that to you," I said. I tried to take on a conciliatory tone, seeing him on the edge of erupting. "You won't lose the deal. Let's understand what we are talking about. We're talking about money. It may mean that you'll have to pay another dollar on the debentures and make them $31."

"That's a million dollars. If your advice is going to cost me a million dollars, I don't need you." He was angry. "I don't want it disclosed."

"If you don't disclose, you'll likely lose the deal," I said. "That's the risk you take."

"I make the decisions. No disclosure . . . I won't lose the deal," he snorted. "I don't need you for disclosure."

He was fierce, totally self-possessed, not seeing that the same misconceptions of him that had disarmed the Missouri directors and given him his deal could also undermine him and lose it for him. There was no reasoning with him. As was his practice, he was using pressure, where reason wasn't working, to manipulate me.

"You'll have to get yourself another lawyer," I said, and walked out of his office.

Crossing Park Avenue I felt the discomfort of a young first-year partner who had just lost a large client. I would have to explain it all to Lipton. Lipton would listen, ask astute questions, and draw out all the facts. I didn't want to make it a long story, but I didn't know where to begin the explanation, and could see that the process would be painful. Everything turned on the meaning of a short telephone conversation. I had to be careful not to be perceived as overly high-minded and arrogant, and involuntarily winced at the complexity of getting appearances to reflect reality. Although I was sure Lipton would back me, as he always did, my discomfort swelled like a bruise that was beginning to throb. I groused to myself: dealing with the clients can be more difficult than confronting adversaries, for there at least you could express anger and even enmity.

When I got back to my office, the old man called me. "Okay," he said, "let's do it your way."

From that, I had learned something more about him. The old man fought only when there was something at stake. He'd waited for me at the airport because there was nothing to win, except a few minutes. In this case we had tested the limits in the only way that counted for each of us: for him, over money; for me, over the exercise of judgment. I'd found that he was prepared to reassess even his view of the way others saw him if that was necessary to get his deal done. Although difficult to contend with, he was an exceptional man.

He made his deals. Missouri Portland was completed without having to raise the price. I learned from them. The lessons learned on offense taught defense. As major corporations entered the lists to become corporate acquirers or acted to defend themselves against takeovers, they looked to those lawyers who were familiar with complex adversarial transactions. As a result, Wachtell Lipton's major corporate practice began to develop. But the firm was small and had to learn how to do intricate deals against much larger competitors.

▲

JOURNEYMAN

▼

WINDOW INTO
CORPORATE
AMERICA

▼

"We told them we loved them.
That was very important.
We were paying a big price.
They had to understand that we loved them."

Behind Imperial American Energy's grand name was a small Denver-based company that had fared badly in the cyclical oil and gas industry. In September 1977, its marginal oil-drilling business had been in bankruptcy for over five years operating under the stewardship of a trustee. And just as it emerged from under the trustee's protective umbrella, Consolidated Oil and Gas, another relatively small Denver oil company with an imposing name, made a hostile tender offer to acquire a majority of Imperial American's shares. The same rising oil prices that had lifted Imperial American out of bankruptcy, unburdened of the full weight of its debt, had induced Consolidated Oil to become a corporate raider.

Both companies, minor players in a major industry, began battling like titans, and got as much attention. For Wachtell Lipton, taking engagements as they came meant being available to both raiders and target companies. In this case we represented the target, Imperial American.

To a student of the game, Consolidated Oil's tender offer was hastily put together, its precipitousness everywhere evident. So recent had been Imperial American's exit from the bankruptcy courthouse that the shareholders, formerly limited partners in various oil-drilling funds, hadn't yet received their stock certificates in the mail from the court, and the newly appointed board members hadn't held their first meeting. Consolidated Oil was trying to make up in speed and surprise what it lacked in financial strength. In an industry of lumbering giants there were still opportunities for the nimble.

Besides agility, attempting a takeover requires craft and the willingness to take risks. Initial planning usually starts with a small group committed to secrecy, but mounting an attack, even against another small company, calls for a substantial team, including public relations firms, commercial banks (and their staffs), accountants, and printers. All these people leave telltale signs, though to cover their tracks they use code names. Not surprisingly, the paraphernalia of intrigue also signals a coming contest. Extensive rehearsals and thoughtful anticipation of all likely defenses are practically impossible for a raider to achieve before its intentions become known. In going forward quickly, Consolidated Oil knew that it wasn't fully prepared.

It launched its tender offer on a Monday morning in mid-September 1977 with a notice in *The Wall Street Journal*, achieving the objective of taking Imperial American totally by surprise. The offer advised shareholders that they had ten days to tender their shares to receive $17 in cash per share. The share price of $17 was a substantial premium over the pre-tender bid prices of $9 to $10 for the newly minted Imperial American shares. So far, so good.

But seeking only a majority of the shares, a commitment of $22 million for about 1.3 million shares, qualified the offer as weak and signaled that Consolidated Oil was financially stretched. Any counterbid for all of the 2.5 million outstanding shares, even at the same price, would top the offer. The real strength of Consolidated Oil's offer came from its short duration. In ten days it's hard to defend against even a lackluster bid. Also, few shareholders would want to be left in a minority position when majority control passed to Consolidated Oil, and unless a better alternative developed in the brief offering period, shareholders would be forced to tender.

In this contest, Consolidated Oil controlled the timing and had the advantage. Three years later, in 1980, the minimum tender offer period would be extended by law to twenty business days, about twenty-six calendar days, reducing the element of surprise and allowing more time for defense. The tactics and strategy of the offense were largely worked out in the era when tender offers could run their full course in ten calendar days. Defensive strategy flowered only after 1980.

The importance Consolidated Oil had placed on speed and surprise led to its launching the tender offer without having first acquired a significant number of Imperial American shares. That was a costly decision. The well-advised raider usually begins by stealthily buying up to 5 percent of the target's stock in the open market. Amounts up to that level don't have to be publicly reported. Purchases at market, without the payment of the tender offer premium price, reduce the overall cost and provide substantial gains if the target finds another bidder for the company, a White Knight.

But Consolidated Oil couldn't have bought any Imperial American shares during the planning process without calling attention to its hostile motives. Imperial American, although a small company, had approximately 25,000 shareholders, all with relatively small stock positions. The company was an affiliate of King Resources, which had sold interests to "widows and orphans" and then itself had become bankrupt. Any concerted trading activity to accumulate a large share position would have been noticeable. Further, since there were relatively few shares available until the new certificates were in the hands of all the shareholders, it was impossible to buy any blocks. In such an imperfect market situation, any extended buying activity would have also significantly driven up the price of the shares.

More was at risk in going forward than merely forfeiting a possible profit. By mounting a takeover, Consolidated Oil had put its own independence on the line. Entering the hostile arena, it sanctioned takeovers and gave up the moral right to protest against attacks on itself. As a practical matter, its ability to fund a tender offer indicated that it could raise cash to help cover the cost of a takeover of itself. For good reason it would thereafter show up on computer screens as a potential target.

Despite the risks, in the mid-1970s tender offers were no longer unusual. Consolidated Oil was one of many companies willing to attack another. Before 1975, most aggressive acquirers were individuals like Tom Evans. In the corporate world, hostile offers were frowned upon, and very few were willing to endure the social disfavor. After 1975, with the stock market prices of most companies at a low, reflected by the Dow Jones Industrial Average, which hovered around 800, the merger and acquisition market became active. Everyone came to see that it was easier to buy than build, and almost all companies began to consider growth by acquisition a legitimate and even necessary technique. Economics changed social attitudes. Then takeover activity fueled itself. Even target companies made raids, as defensive measures, to achieve a size that made them a more complex and less interesting target. If Consolidated Oil acquired Imperial American, it would take on significant debt and likely become less attractive to others. That put additional incentives in place for winning.

I liked Consolidated Oil's side of the game. Given a choice, I preferred representing raiders. Besides enjoying the planning, as an outsider I was attracted to the entrepreneurial clients, interesting men with a sense of themselves who were trying to make their mark and didn't mind challenging and dismantling rigid corporate empires. Moreover, I had no affinity for the corporate hierarchy that seemed indigenous to most established corporations. But representing the target company Imperial American wasn't a big step to take. The managers of Consolidated Oil, while aggressive, weren't like Tom Evans. For the most part, acquirers were now established corporations, with large staffs ordered in ranking bureaucracies, little different from the people they were out to acquire.

These new acquirers changed the character of the work. Indeed, I sometimes found that I was participating in war games. Many companies simulated or went through takeover routines, playing mock battles, carrying through all the variations of thrust and parry. In effect, they were planning an invasion, often one that was one or two or more years away, more remote than most of their long-term plans. Takeover activity was a diversion for them, frequently separate from the life of the operating businesses. These corporations sought the experience and encouraged the game, for little else in business galvanized people and brought them together as cohesively as organizing an attack that would require speed, surprise, and precision timing. It also prepared them to defend themselves, without acknowledging their target status. Corporate staffs, otherwise keenly protective of their free time, would work in the evenings and even on weekends energized by strike-force apparatus such as beepers, security clearances, and "eyes only" memoranda.

Even when the acquisition got off the planning board, the game aspect of the raider's side sometimes elevated keeping score and beating your opponent above thinking about what the fighting was over. Among corporate executives making or contemplating their first hostile acquisition there was often a locker-room mentality. I found that all the mystery and excitement of sex, of breaking down resistance, of scoring and conquest, were associated with a takeover. Manliness was at stake, and measured. In order to learn the ropes, executives talked to friends who had made acquisitions.

"Was it hostile?"

"Initially."

"What made them come around?"

"There was no choice. Somebody would take them over."

"They didn't mind dealing with you, even though you were the one that put them in play?"

"We told them that we loved them. That was very important. We were paying a big price. They had to understand that we loved them."

"We're looking at some acquisitions. We're on some White Knight lists, but we're preparing to do a hostile."

"Sometimes that's the only way to get what you want."

For some it was a rite of passage, and with it came acceptability. Even more, respect: the takeover told of cunning and daring and the power to take what you wanted. Even those companies that didn't do hostile acquisitions contemplated them. Often they threatened to launch one to coerce a company to negotiate with them.

That is the buyer's side. While it's multifaceted, it's limited to taking. There is another side, that of the seller determined to get the highest price.

While the buyer chooses, the seller must attract and hold the buyer's interest. "Being a seller is like being a high-priced whore. You hang out in expensive bars. You have to pretend that it's not for sale, except perhaps to them because with them it would be a perfect combination. You stare, and let them look, but never get too forward. Of course, you deliver when they meet your price." Jack Seabrook, former chairman of IU International, told me that view of the seller's side. What he was saying was that no matter how well the boys in the corporate locker room had learned the moves, the rituals of a mating dance were only the beginning. The boys at Consolidated Oil would soon learn how difficult it would be to capture the prey.

Once Consolidated Oil initiated its bid, it expected a fight, even from the trustee of Imperial American. The trustee had been appointed the new chairman of the board, and Consolidated Oil expected that he would want to retain his position. But faced with the Consolidated Oil tender offer the trustee had an unpredictable response. The trustee's charge, all through the bankruptcy, had been to find value for the security holders, and he saw this situation as a continuation of his role. Accordingly, he was prepared to negotiate with Consolidated Oil. He promptly hired Goldman, Sachs & Co. to advise him.

At Goldman Sachs, Peter Sachs, after hearing out the trustee's desire to sell the company, nevertheless decided to oppose the bid and keep Consolidated Oil at arm's length. Peter Sachs was then a vice president in the mergers and acquisitions department and a shrewd observer of changes in the marketplace. Only three days before the Consolidated Oil tender offer, he had visited the trustee and offered Goldman Sachs's services to defend against possible hostile takeovers. The trustee hadn't believed that the services would be necessary. Peter recalls leaving the trustee's office and flying back to New York the next day, only to get a message on his arrival that he should turn around and meet the trustee in Denver because there was some peculiar movement in the company's stock.

The following business day, Consolidated Oil commenced its tender offer. Peter's prescience had gotten him the engagement.

Peter's assessment of the selling opportunities was that Imperial American's distress from the unsolicited attack would induce other bidders to come forward as effectively as Jack Seabrook's method of posturing and hanging out in fancy bars. Peter saw the urgency of the tender offer as creating a climate conducive to an auction and began preparing to organize and call one for the sale of the company in Denver, a center for the oil and gas industry, where the company was headquartered. Consolidated Oil was to get the fight it anticipated but not for the expected reasons.

Peter Sachs recommended that my firm be brought in to represent Imperial American. We were described to the senior management as experienced, using the metaphor of the surgical operating room. "When you're spread out on the table, everything has to be done quickly and you don't want someone learning on the job." Expert efforts would be needed to fend off the raider while Goldman Sachs sought other buyers who would be courted as White Knights.

Goldman Sachs didn't want to stop the tender offer, just slow it down enough to encourage counteroffers to facilitate the auction. My first task, then, was to delay the offer's expiration so that there would be more time to process bids. That meant a challenge in the Denver federal court, claiming that the tender offer was false and misleading, requiring corrective disclosure. If we could convince the judge of the validity of our contentions, he would make Consolidated Oil start over again, which in effect granted a delay.

The offer, precipitously put together, wasn't artful, leaving a lot of room to maneuver. But we were seeking an injunction, extraordinary relief from the court. Our claims had to show unequivocally that shareholders would be detrimentally misled. We had to point to clear mistakes, obvious on the face of the tender offer. Allegations that needed factual substantiation would get bogged down in the presentation of evidence through witnesses, taking days to prove. The longer it took to validate the assertions, the more legitimate the Consolidated Oil offer would seem to the court. Making the task more difficult was that, in our experience, showing the court one mistake wouldn't do. No tender offer is perfect, and the court could reasonably overlook a mistake, unless it was remarkably egregious. We had to find at least three to give the cumulative sense of error and lack of care. Also, three would give the judge a choice to see whether he fancied all or some as the reason for starting the offer over again. Furthermore, we had to find the errors promptly; otherwise they wouldn't look serious. High drama needs fresh tears.

The litigators did the arguing. My job was to help gather their material. There was a bag of tricks that I worked from, knowing that none would be likely to be persuasive in the New York courts most familiar with takeovers. Generally, the knowledgeable courts honored the minimum ten days and wouldn't intervene to create a different time schedule. In Denver this would be a case of first impression.

George Katz, our lead litigator on the matter, flew out to Denver by himself to work on the court papers with the Denver lawyers at Holland & Hart. They were essential to the effort because they were familiar with local litigation practice and knew their way around the courts. Their offices became our work stations, complete and well equipped, without overhead. Also, they gave us as much help as we needed. The breadth of local legal talent all over the country allowed us to compete with the larger New York firms. Our position as experts, heading a large team effort, freed us from billing on an hourly basis, the traditional arrangement. Hourly compensation was recognizably not adequate. We discovered that a small expert group could command premiums for expertise and premiums for favorable outcome. We began to bill like investment bankers, on the basis of the size and complexity of the matter. Since we were specialized, many local lawyers didn't feel threatened that we would compete for their clients' business and sought the firm's expertise. All this encouraged us to keep the firm small.

As luck would have it, we got Judge Fred M. Winner for our case. He was an activist judge, familiar with the history of Imperial American in bankruptcy, and wanted to see an auction develop. George Katz and the judge found an immediate affinity. "We need to delay the tender offer to help the shareholders, your honor. Some shareholders haven't even gotten their stock certificates, which has created confusion. Some may not be able to tender. An unfair situation has developed." George approached the problem in lawyerly fashion, finding injustice. He was, however, arguing for delay by indirection.

"Is your concern with making sure that all shareholders will be able to tender to Consolidated Oil?" the judge asked, letting George know that he wasn't naïve and wanted frankness.

"Well, not exactly. We'd like the time to develop some competition," George responded, right to the point, confirming what the judge knew, that there would be a sale of the company. The judge appreciated the difficulty involved in selling a company in about a week. Two of the ten days had already elapsed.

The obstacle that even a sympathetic judge faced was finding sufficient reason to stop the offer. Our claims, cobbled in more haste than Consolidated Oil's offer, weren't very persuasive. They were variations of alleged failures to disclose Consolidated Oil's plans for treatment of the minority shareholders, and omissions of descriptions of the majority's obligations to the minority shareholders, which we claimed made the offer coercive and designed to stampede shareholders. Each was almost embarrassing to argue and taken together didn't seem to have enough weight to tip the scale in our favor. Judge Winner found his own reasons. He worked from the following facts. Consolidated Oil had indicated, in accordance with standard tender offer practice, that it could withdraw its tender if the offer was challenged in court. We were, on behalf of Imperial American, objecting to the offer as misleading. Our challenge, Judge Winner found, satisfied that condition of the offer, which meant that the offer could be withdrawn. Judge Winner then concluded that it wasn't clear whether there was an offer outstanding, since it could now be withdrawn at any time on any whim of Consolidated Oil, which made it illusory and confusing. On that basis, he justified judicial intervention and granted an injunction.

Even we, as desirous of getting a favorable order as anyone, hadn't thought seriously of pressing such a circular argument. If the offer didn't exist, why stop it? Since we hadn't raised the question, we fortunately didn't have to answer it. Let it be understood that no court since has ever accepted that decision as persuasive. No matter, the tender offer had to start again, and on the third day, we got a new ten days. All of us felt renewed, and the amazing result confirmed our expertise.

What looked like a compassionate decision of the court to us looked wrongheaded to Consolidated Oil. But it would be foolish to appeal to correct the wrong decision. An appeal would only take up more time and thus be self-defeating. Consolidated Oil had to accept the wound and begin its tender offer again, having lost the speed for which it had already paid dearly. It recommitted itself because it believed that another buyer wouldn't be easy to find in the next ten days.

In the next three years the courts all over the country would come to see that if you interrupted a tender offer for intuitive reasons of fairness, you discouraged the process. Without the assurance of surprise and speed, tender offers wouldn't be made. The courts would let market forces work, without interference. Victories like this were numbered.

In preparation for the auction, Peter Sachs sent out brochures by overnight mail, reporting on Imperial American's oil and gas reserves to all the major oil companies (and many minors) and told them to be in Denver the following week to submit bids. About a hundred companies were contacted. The brochure, widely circulated as an invitation, contained only publicly available information, but set out the process. This was still the early days of takeovers and we were making up the rules for the procedures as we went along. Fairness that could withstand judicial scrutiny was our guide. All bidders would be given an opportunity to speak to the management of the company and to review engineering reports in a data room set up for the purpose. About thirty-five prospective bidders showed up. Management had the best view of the potential for finding additional oil reserves. With their cooperation the company became more salable, and the White Knight was advantaged to some degree over the raider, who remained an outsider throughout. It would take another ten years before hostile bidders could claim access to information given to all other potential purchasers.

After making their assessments, potential bidders were told that they could submit sealed bids which would be kept secret. Only the highest bid would be announced. All were asked to make their bids for cash and structure them as tender offers to compete with

Consolidated Oil's tender. The urgency of the situation was duly stressed because a winning White Knight would have to be chosen before the expiration of Consolidated Oil's tender offer.

In making the rules as we went along, we didn't anticipate all the possible moves by the players. After reviewing the data, Petro-Lewis, a Denver-based oil company, ignored the auction process we had so carefully detailed and made a tender offer for Imperial American. By offering $17 for all shares and getting a head start by commencing the tender offer early, Petro-Lewis was attempting to discourage all other parties from bidding. It was a disconcerting gambit but didn't stop the auction. (After that tactic by Petro-Lewis, we would revise the auction rules to require all parties that had received data to agree not to make hostile tender offers competing with the auction process.)

Peter Sachs and I decided to use a conference room at Holland & Hart for the auction. We sat at the center of the table, opposite the door, so we could face the bidders as they came in. Our schedule covered a two-day period, allowing up to half an hour for questions by the prospective buyers and an exchange of last-minute information. The buyers who contacted us first were given the opportunity to see us first.

Bidders entered the conference room with their investment bankers and lawyers and made feeble gestures at asking questions. Our expectation was that after the half-hour session they would submit their bid in a sealed envelope. The early bidders showed great reluctance to do anything that would tip their hand, saying they hadn't made up their minds and wanted to know the deadline for submitting bids. What we hadn't anticipated was that everyone felt that their bid would be opened and disclosed to the next bidders. Those who had eagerly contacted us first wanted to see us last. As the day wore on, the later bidders, after going through the preliminary questions to show serious intent, asked us to tell them the high bid.

We quickly caught on to the dynamics, and to each one we promptly reiterated the rules: no one would be told any other person's bid. Bids could be submitted at the last minute, but that meant waiting around Denver instead of doing other productive work. That caused the cynical to ask a lot more questions so that they could carefully scrutinize us to see if trust was warranted.

We assumed that there would be a small range of prices in the bidding. All Imperial American's wells were mature and the oil reserves were known with a high degree of precision. There was little romance in this company. The only questions, in terms of valuation, were how long it would take to extract the oil and gas and what were the expected prices for oil and gas. Everybody had the same information. The winning bid probably wouldn't be much above the other bids, and we were likely to face the accusation that the winning bidder had been tipped. It wasn't a happy situation.

Sitting in the bare Denver conference room for two full days watching representatives of oil companies and their investment bankers and lawyers come on center stage and then depart, I got a good view of the professionals involved in mergers and acquisitions. The investment bankers were from firms like Lehman Brothers, Morgan Stanley, First Boston Corporation, Kidder Peabody, all recognizable as old-line Wall Street firms. The background of the bankers was as traditional, and with as little variation, as the clothing they wore. The style they affected, however, didn't tell all.

Peter, whose grand-uncle was a founder of Goldman Sachs, looked like he'd been a banker from birth, or at least since he had gotten out of school, but his career hadn't followed a conventional path. After graduating from Harvard College, he spent eight years racing formula cars in Europe and selling high-performance and antique cars in Europe and in the States. He didn't join Goldman Sachs until he was over thirty years of age, and on entry, people at the firm met a well-mannered, suave young man with an aristocratic bearing. Wary of him because of his unusual activities after college and the instant credibility his name afforded, his elders put him to work at tedious tasks with long hours, trying to scrub off the gloss of pride. Finally, they gave him his own deals and let his ambition drive him. Many of his opponents were equally driven, their lives not anywhere near as crisply tailored as their conventional suits.

Most of the takeover law firms, however, weren't part of the Wall Street elite, and many of the lawyers advising participants in the Imperial American auction sharply contrasted with the bankers' regular lawyers. The firm of Skadden, Arps, Slate, Meagher

& Flom, already our firm's main adversary, was headed by Joe Flom, who, slight and stooped, looked like a tailor, concentrating more on your cuffs and sleeves than on your face. One of his assistants and my counterpart on a number of my early transactions, and many since, was Morris Kramer, who was known to wear velvet suits, had shoulder-length hair, and a high-pitched voice with a pronounced Brooklyn accent. But looks and speech can be deceiving, as I well knew growing up in Brooklyn: these were accomplished and knowledgeable men. If there was common ground between the bankers and lawyers involved in takeovers, it was that all were ambitious, intensely competitive, and not rattled by the stakes involved.

Finding commonality, however, didn't explain the sharp differences. Why the involvement of the traditional investment banking firms in takeovers, while their law firms weren't involved? Concern for clients on the part of the law firms couldn't be a sufficient reason, since the bankers were able to overcome that concern. What made them different? I concluded that the banking firms were much more directly fee-driven.

It was no accident that I'd first met Peter Sachs in our offices in 1976, the year before, while mediating a fee dispute. We were representing a corporation contemplating an acquisition of a reluctant seller. The corporate client understood that the acquisition might only be possible on a hostile basis, but it was loath to resort to that. Goldman Sachs was competing with Smith Barney for the investment banking business, but Goldman Sachs would only act as the banker for the corporation if the transaction became a negotiated one. Goldman Sachs had always taken the position that it wouldn't initiate hostile takeovers and would only act as a banker on the defense side. Smith Barney was advising the corporation to commence a hostile tender offer without first contacting the target company's management, thus retaining the elements of surprise and speed. The strategy excluded Goldman Sachs. John Adams Morgan, a grandson of J. P. Morgan (and a lineal descendant of John Adams), was doing the counseling on behalf of Smith Barney, where he was in charge of corporate finance and mergers. Built like a rail splitter, with wide shoulders and thick chest, he looked as if the hostile taking of share certificates was second nature. More so because those shoulders and thick neck supported a powerful, bald head with the fierce Morgan family nose.

Goldman Sachs, in reaction, had positioned itself so that Smith Barney was excluded if the target agreed to negotiate. The fee issue, all or nothing depending on the initial strategic decisions of the client, had to be resolved before the deal could go forward. Even the client was immobilized by the conflict between the Sachses and the Morgans. No one was embarrassed to fight directly over money, and the warfare was open and slightly acrimonious, although socially everyone showed the best manners. Each had their own lawyers from equally well-regarded Wall Street firms ready to protect the fee, but not to work on the deal. Large sums were involved (a percentage of the purchase price which could amount to as much as $5 million), and this kind of aggressiveness seemed bred in the bone and accepted by their lawyers. Mediation between these two groups was necessary to get the deal going, which I took a hand in doing. Finally, they entered into a treaty that provided for intelligent fee splitting, allowing us all to cooperate. While not a very propitious way to meet, it was the beginning of a long relationship.

From that incident I saw that the banking firms were oriented to doing transactions that brought in fee income and were sensitive to changes in the market. Looking further, I came to see that in those firms most partners were well off financially and retired in their early fifties, except for the very few that led the firms. Important responsibilities were necessarily given to young people, all ready to embrace change. In the law firms, however, changes in the marketplace had to filter through to the top-tier lawyers, who were tradition-bound, much older than their banking counterparts, and remote from the market. Also, lawyers billed on an hourly basis, making one kind of work not much more profitable than another. As a consequence, law firms rarely developed new specialties. And lawyers didn't move around from firm to firm as much as business people. Accordingly, there was limited ability to move or to grow into new areas of the law. I was in that room because the market had created a need and my firm was young enough to commit itself to the new area. Our being oriented to resolve disputes in favor of doing the deal is what attracted Peter Sachs. Already I could see that the opportunities were vast.

In the middle of the second day of taking bids, we met Gaines Godfrey, the chief financial officer for Mesa Petroleum, T. Boone Pickens's company. Gaines Godfrey was a combination of Texas oilman and eastern financial analyst. He unabashedly displayed the mixture in his outfit, a business suit and cowboy boots. He'd come to the meeting himself, but, sitting opposite Peter and me, he kept looking around the room, uneasy with the situation. There was nothing in the room to see other than a bare conference table and a couple of stark wooden chairs opposite us. Watching him for a few moments, Peter was compelled to ask, "Is something on your mind?"

"What's the highest bid?" he asked. There were no other preliminaries. The directness was without guile, but it was nonetheless tiresome after two days of the same question. Moreover, the bidding ran between $18 and $19 a share, bunched around $18.50, which now guaranteed accusations of bid shopping.

"We're not giving out that information," Peter responded, without expressing any irritation. "This is a blind bidding procedure. You'll have to make your bid on the basis of your own estimate of value." Peter was very proper. "Of course, your bid won't be revealed either," Peter added, and smiled.

Again, Gaines Godfrey looked around the room, as if verifying that nothing had changed, obviously disappointed. Something was on his mind. He scanned the room a second time and finally asked, "What's Goldman's fee going to be?"

Peter told him, without hesitation, that the fee would be about ⅞ of 1 percent of the aggregate purchase price. The target company paid all fees, which meant that the buyer absorbed them as part of the purchase price. Looking further around the room, he signaled that another question was forming. "What's your fee?" he asked me. He understood that we wouldn't be billing merely on the basis of time spent. Word travels fast in the marketplace. Calculation of our fee was more complicated since it was still keyed to some extent on estimated time, plus premiums for intensity of effort and success. I had an estimate, which I'd given to Imperial American, and told him.

"You'll have to excuse me for a minute," Gaines Godfrey said, and left the room. He had the same look on his face as a man who had an unexpected and urgent call of nature. He closed the door sharply behind him to assure privacy.

When he came back into the room, he told us that his bid was $20.73. From the odd number, it was almost certain that he'd recalculated his bid, deducting the fees. To follow his mental processes, we did the arithmetic. With 2.5 million shares, the aggregate price for the company was $51,825,000. Not an odd-numbered result like the per-share price, which made it almost certain that, with some rounding on his aggregate price, he'd deducted our fees.

Peter said to him, "Stocks are traded in hat sizes, Mr. Godfrey." Peter was being playful.

"What does that mean?" Gaines Godfrey asked.

"Stocks are traded in eighths," Peter explained. "You should round up your bid." Peter wasn't giving any indication that the bid was off the charts.

"Round down," Gaines Godfrey said.

"If that's the way you want to play it, we're prepared to leave it at $20.73," Peter said. And then added, "Suit yourself," as if rounding down made a substantial detrimental difference.

That gave Gaines Godfrey pause. He scrutinized Peter, trying to evaluate the statement. "Leave it at $20.73," he said.

Turning to procedure, we then asked him if Mesa Petroleum was prepared to make a tender offer. He said, "Boone Pickens won't make a tender offer. We want to buy assets." Pickens had made a tender offer, about a year before, for a company called Aztech Oil and had lost out to other bidders in the contest. Gaines Godfrey insisted that Pickens had sworn off tender offers after his bad experience. He wanted to enter into a traditional asset form of arrangement for buying oil properties. An asset purchase would take sixty days or more, while a tender offer would take only ten days. In an asset purchase, the company sold all its assets to the buyer and then distributed the proceeds to its shareholders in liquidation of the company. The terms of the agreement and the sale and liquidation required a shareholder meeting for approval, which was the time-consuming process. The greater the time period before closing, the greater the risk of nonconsummation. Again we warned him that the terms would be taken into account, and that could affect the likelihood of acceptance of his bid, but he wouldn't reconsider. A tender offer was out of the question. His price was substantially higher than the $17 tender offer by Petro-Lewis so the shareholders would refrain from tendering during the sixty or so days required for the Pickens deal to get the $20.73.

At the end of the second day, we still hadn't gotten all the bids from those who wanted to bid at the last minute. Peter visited Petro-Lewis at their offices at 7 p.m. (although they were a hostile bidder) and was told that they would increase their tender to $19 a share, and at 10 p.m. Fred Hamilton of Hamilton Petroleum called Peter and me and asked us to come to his office down the street from our hotel. He then put in a bid of about $19, sure that he was the last bidder.

The Mesa Petroleum bid was the highest by far. The auction had produced a price beyond anyone's expectation, even on a property where the value should have been in a narrow band. Corporate auctions became, for that reason, the method of choice for selling companies.

We had no alternative but to go along with Gaines Godfrey's terms and proceed to do the transaction as a sale of assets. We then turned to Pickens and asked him to be prepared to promptly enter into an agreement, but Pickens wanted to do an investigative study of the company, expressed as doing due diligence, before signing. His investigative work would take about a week. The Petro-Lewis tender offer (which topped the Consolidated Oil bid) would attract tenders unless we could discourage them. We felt constrained to announce Pickens's offer, although he wasn't bound at that price, and stated in the press announcement that a definitive agreement would be entered into the following week. At the time of the announcement of the $20.73 price per share, tenders of shares to Petro-Lewis were withdrawn in favor of the Pickens deal.

At the end of the week, the date set for signing, Pickens asked for an additional two to three days' extension. He was still doing his investigative work. The failure to sign was unsettling, but Pickens had us pinned by his high price. Although disappointed, we publicly announced the extension in as positive terms as we could manage. The slippage in the schedule made the two months to completion of the deal seem even more risky and longer than before. If in the next two or three days Pickens decided not to do the transaction, there would be very significant questions about the value of the company's assets. We'd be asked: What had he seen? The fact that he'd been willing to pay more than anyone else would no longer be a comfort. Was Pickens having second thoughts about the price, which any reasonable person would? We had more questions than we had answers.

And then, almost immediately after the failure to sign at the deadline, one of the other bidders rebid. Petro-Lewis called the trustee and Peter Sachs and told them that it was now prepared to pay $20 a share for all outstanding shares. Petro-Lewis saw Pickens's delay as a breach of his agreement, permitting another round of bidding. In fact, the extension we'd granted Pickens didn't legally bind Imperial American. Pickens wasn't bound to follow through on his offer and the extension wasn't meant to be an option tying up the company. While priced at less than Pickens's bid, the Petro-Lewis offer looked more satisfactory, since Petro-Lewis would be immediately bound and would conclude the transaction promptly, at least two months before Pickens. Without hesitation, Peter and I told the trustee that he could accept the Petro-Lewis bid. The arrangement was endorsed within hours and announced only a day after the first deadline for Pickens's investigation had expired.

Pickens publicly protested and expressed his annoyance loudly to the newspapers. His bid was at least $2 million higher, he told the press, and he didn't understand how the board could reject it. Talking to the press, however, made no difference. He could mount a challenge to Petro-Lewis only by commencing a tender offer. When Pickens didn't act to compete, Petro-Lewis acquired the company at $20 a share.

Pickens's failure meant that in the future the fainthearted couldn't participate as White Knights. Two or three days in a data room and a day with management was all the time the process would allow to evaluate complex business enterprises. The next time no one would wait for an anticipated signing. Either the deal would be done immediately after the close of the auction or there would be another round of bidding. And that was the last time that Boone Pickens refused to make a tender offer. He too had to accept the changes in the marketplace. Indeed, no one could resist them, and either you embraced them or you ceased to be a player, sidelined indefinitely.

THE
COUNTERREVOLUTION

▼

The office was the war zone.
The home front was within commuting distance.
Each day, no matter how late, everyone went home and tried
to explain what they couldn't understand because
it was happening too fast, without historical examples.

The aggressive bidding for Imperial American in 1977 was only an early swell in the takeover wave. A year later it became apparent that almost all companies trading publicly were takeover targets, not only those poorly managed. In truth, the most attractive companies were well run, performing profitably, and had good market shares in their industry. When both Pan Am and Eastern Airlines sought to acquire National Airlines in 1978, their rallying cry was that they were failing enterprises and needed to acquire a profitable company to keep them aloft. Representing National, I was awed by the frankness of its suitors. In admitting their motives to the federal regulators at the Civil Aeronautics Board, they had turned the reasons for takeovers inside out and showed the seams. Being a good airline didn't save National, and Pan Am acquired it. Few companies thereafter were required to be as candid, but everyone knew: good companies and management attracted takeover bids.

Bankruptcy had conditioned Imperial American for sale. Expecting a liquidation, no one had any emotional attachment to the business. Most businesses, however, become part of the lives of the people working in them. And in defending against takeovers, I experienced the profound effect of the imminent loss of career. There were few effective defenses against a cash tender offer. In ten days organizations were dismembered and the lives of senior management profoundly changed. In the seventies, corporate take-overs carried harsh dislocations. Even as I told management what to expect, they educated me about their feelings.

In the first and second days of the tender offer, senior management would require their underlings to pledge their loyalty to them in a clasping of hands all for one, one for all. That was the early, tentative optimism. I have never seen so many businessmen touch each other as in the beginning of a tender offer, radiating warmth, camaraderie, and reassurance. Taboos about expressing feelings were set aside, overcome by the threat of loss of position, the imminent collapse of an ordered world. No one would acknowledge that those in senior management positions were terminal cases. Senior managers convinced themselves that if anyone acquired the company, they and middle management would all walk out, leaving the company an empty hulk. What was the company without its management? The raiders were initially scorned as incapable of understanding or running the business. Reason would set in, the managers told themselves, and the banks lending the money to the raider would see that the business, built on delicate relationships, would fall apart without the management. At dinner everyone would drink too much and loudly mock the raider. Even as I had dinner with them, and introduced the forbidding prospects, the investment bankers were evaluating the company, preparing to sell it away from them. We ran two tracks (with the target company's bankers trying to sell the company while its lawyers exhausted legal options to keep the company from being sold), for there was no time to do otherwise.

Sometimes management's lack of understanding continued into the third day. But usually by the third and fourth days, they realized that the only people who would be replaced were those at the top, and the implications of that thought were eye-opening. By the fifth and sixth days, senior management recognized what their employees would soon see, that the employees wouldn't leave, that the business wouldn't waste away, and that loyalty was purchased like everything else in business.

Sometimes, those below were as quick as their seniors to understand what was happening. There were incentives for them to see the looming change and the benefits. If the top level left, there would be opportunities for those below. There could even be a larger, more stable organization offering growth. By the seventh and eighth days all the management, except the most senior members, were waiting expectantly for the new employer.

Management and local counsel usually sensed early that they were over their heads, wanted help, but needed instruction before they could even accept advice. The first hurdle was making local counsel understand, along with the management, that the company would be lost. Not until 1980 did leveraged buyouts become a reasonable defensive technique, and it wasn't until 1985 that defensive strategies, like poison pills and leveraged recapitalizations, were developed and validated by the courts.

"Why will this attack succeed?" some gruff chief executive would usually ask me.

"About 15 percent of your shares have traded in the first day of the offer. Each day more shares will change hands. The shares are being bought by market professionals, called arbitrageurs, who intend to tender them. The institutional shareholders also act like arbitrageurs, seeking a quick profit. By the end of the week the arbitrageurs and the institutions will hold a majority of the company's shares. The loyal shareholders will be in the minority."

The reality of the trading volume and the change of ownership of the shares was frequently convincing. The market mechanism was personified by Ivan Boesky, the demon arbitrageur. Boesky was thin and bony, cadaverous-looking. His bloodlessness made him appear infinitely greedy, and his fierce, focused eyes looked intent only on immediate profit. You could say with complete confidence, "He's buying up your company. He has a horizon of only a couple of days, and unless the bidder is blocked by the courts or you find a White Knight, your company will be taken away."

Despite the logic, management resisted, emotionally not prepared for the consequences. The company served more than its stockholders. It was expected to fulfill such public purposes as providing jobs, advancing equal opportunity, enhancing the economic growth of the community. Although it was a private enterprise, it was imbued with the public interest. What would the community be if the business was moved? Management hoped that the courts, tied to the status quo, would help them.

When the local lawyer acknowledged that there was little likelihood of any judge stopping the offer for the benefit of the local community's economy, a whole series of other myths and fictions then had to be attacked, to get realism into the executive suite. "Even if they get a majority of the shares, we'll control the board for two years. Won't that stop them?" I had to tell them of how Tom Evans, with only three out of twelve directors, devastated the Missouri Portland board. No board would want to stand up to a majority shareholder. Each day the CEO and senior management were confronted with outcomes different from what they had expected, all contrary to conventional wisdom, as the relentless countdown to the end of the offer continued. The amount of information they had to know was more than they could absorb in a few days, and it all became experienced as pressure.

It was strange even for me, a takeover tactician. All my life I'd lived under the assumption that working for a corporation offered security.

My father questioned me: "You mean to say you can just put an ad in the paper and take over a company?"

"If you can get the money."

"What happens to the people?"

"The new owner decides that."

"And this is good?" he asked.

"If it's bad, I defend against it."

"Of course," he said wryly.

In the boardroom, the directors were concerned with their own personal liability. The easiest and safest course of action for them was to sell the company to the highest bidder, rather than trying to thwart the shareholders' desire for a premium price. If the board of directors didn't use reasonable business judgment in the shareholders' interest, each member could be personally liable. None wanted to be involved in protracted shareholder litigation involving staggering sums. A more intangible influence on the deliberations of board members was the language the raiders used to give moral weight to their takeover activities. Management was characterized as entrenched, slothful, and inefficient. Defending against a takeover was resisting "putting the corporate assets to a higher and better use." Even as the CEO was trying to see if he could hold his organization together and remain independent, the board would lose patience with that as unrealistic. Nothing can ameliorate the despair and pressure resulting from finding that your friends on the board have abandoned you.

As the illusions dissolved, there was the last misconception, that the company would find a White Knight, someone who needed or respected the management. The investment bankers would proffer the White Knight list as early as they felt the CEO was emotionally prepared to receive it. The list was handled gingerly, as if it unlocked access to a safe haven. On careful examination, however, everyone came to see that it was merely a list of buyers known to be interested in making an acquisition in the industry, much like the list of companies called on to bid for Imperial American. Names weren't eliminated because the people weren't nice. I have seen many CEOs go over a White Knight list and discover that the proffered saviors were more obnoxious than the raider.

Even when the company was acquired by a benign White Knight, senior management usually lost their jobs. For many the jobs had taken years of effort to achieve, including the sacrifice of climbing slowly through the corporate hierarchy, secure in the assumption that each rung of the ladder would be available. Salary and stock-option arrangements never contemplated that the corporate ladder would be pulled away. The knowledge acquired by many of these executives was largely limited to the industry in which their company was involved. There would be few opportunities for them elsewhere. A senior manager's job also carried with it a position in the community and often defined social standing. Much of that would be severely attenuated or lost with the job.

To cushion the blow, we would redo management's employment contracts, have the board of directors vest their stock options and try to get them severance payouts of from two to five times their annual salary. These arrangements became known as golden parachutes. They were seen by the public as defensive measures, but in fact they facilitated the takeover. It was the board's way of easing management out. In the early years, large payouts weren't common, because takeovers weren't anticipated as part of corporate life. Later, management was better prepared and the payouts became larger, until corrective tax legislation imposed some limitations.

I rarely saw the families of senior managers, and no one talked about the effects on them. The office was the war zone. The home front was within commuting distance. Each day, no matter how late, everyone went home and tried to explain what they couldn't fully understand because it was happening too fast, without historical examples. I'm sure that, for many, losing their job was a form of inadequacy not explainable to their family or friends, especially when only days before they had prophesied with bravado that they would win.

In the endgame, managements turned to getting the highest possible sales price for the company. The reasons, in addition to the obvious one of getting the most for their own stock, were varied. A few did it to keep from experiencing anarchy. For others, paternalism was a strong motive, to provide for the troops. And many, whatever their other motives, wanted to spite the raider. It was a form of vindication, an attempt to find some victory in crushing personal defeat. Competing against an opponent helped many to lose themselves in the process and avoid being immobilized by personal anguish. Spirited battles ensued. They would show everybody what their company was really worth. Whatever happened to them, they could say that they got one hell of a price.

There had to be a corrective. Change came at the end of 1978 —about a year after the bid for Imperial American—in a surprising way.

Houdaille (pronounced: who-die), a small conglomerate, became a target because it moved its corporate headquarters. It was a diversified manufacturer of engineered sealing devices, industrial pumps, lubrication systems, banding and clamping devices, and energy-absorbing devices. The location of the corporate headquarters wasn't particularly essential to any of the businesses, but change in any company was noticed by the frenzied merger market.

Gerry Saltarelli, who ran Houdaille, moved the offices from Buffalo, New York, to Fort Lauderdale, Florida, just as he and his senior management were reaching retirement age. Saltarelli was an important member of the Buffalo community, but he, along with his senior management, wanted a warmer climate and a more favorable tax structure. Also, each year the Buffalo papers published his salary, not that outstanding by national standards, but enough in Buffalo to call significant attention to him, which he disliked. Seeking less notoriety and more peace, he was an unlikely instrument of change.

Moving to Florida signaled the marketplace that senior management was bent on retiring in a few years. To the merger world that meant management wouldn't oppose a sale of the company. Actually, the inferences drawn were stronger than that. In Wall Street's logic, embracing retirement was equivalent to putting the company up for sale. The company's name began to appear on public lists of targets in trade papers and journals, and there was heavy speculative trading in its stock. Although Saltarelli had initially thought that he could run Houdaille for several years in Florida and then turn it over to a younger management, while retaining a board position and a consulting arrangement, the prospect of a takeover made implementation of that plan unlikely. At first he tried to bolster the company's defenses, which got me involved. There were no defenses, however, that could stop speculative trading. Rising prices for the company made him assess what he could realize on a sale. And once he'd traveled that mental distance, a sale began to seem like an opportunity. All the shareholders would be better off. The company could be placed in strong hands, and the stock he owned and his stock options would be worth much more in a sale. He could retire more comfortably than he'd anticipated.

Although a tender offer by someone always seemed imminent, especially with active trading in Houdaille's stock, no hostile bidder appeared. What discouraged the circling predators was that the company's businesses were all relatively small (although in the aggregate large) and were in second- and third-tier positions in their markets. In addition, all were mature, with little prospect for growth. To attract buyers and control the process, Saltarelli asked

Goldman Sachs to put the company up for sale officially. Goldman Sachs announced its engagement to sell the company (designing it as an invitation to bidders) and showed the company's financial information to at least thirty prospective purchasers in the United States and Europe.

The high bidder was a relatively unknown investment group called Kohlberg, Kravis & Roberts, recently formed in May 1976 to buy companies. The trading price of the Houdaille stock (which also was about the carrying value of its assets on financial books) was around $20 per share, adjusted for speculative trading, and the high bid was $40 for all shares, a remarkable premium. The aggregate purchase price was about $350 million, making the transaction sizable by any standard. Although the group was unknown, their histories were readily available. Jerome Kohlberg was the senior member of the bidding group: he'd been head of the corporate finance department at Bear Stearns, a major investment banking firm. He was gracious, soft-spoken, and exceedingly well mannered. His steel-wire-framed glasses with small lenses emphasized the large size of his bald head. Nothing about him suggested that he was a risk taker. George Roberts had worked with Kohlberg at Bear Stearns. Henry Kravis's name was familiar because his father, Ray Kravis of Oklahoma, was a well-known petroleum engineer. Ray Kravis had rendered the reserve reports for Imperial American.

Kohlberg, Kravis & Roberts (who called themselves KKR) had no significant assets of their own. Their initial capital amounted to $120,000. They intended to purchase the company largely with debt, putting up only $25 million in common equity, less than 10 percent of the purchase price. The equity was coming from a group of investors whose money was managed by KKR. The balance would be put up by banks and insurance companies, whose loans would be secured by the company's assets. Nothing could disguise that it was a bootstrap acquisition, that the company was buying itself.

Bootstrap acquisitions were not unknown at the time KKR made the bid. They were also known as management buyouts. But those transactions were relatively small, measured in tens of millions of dollars, none approaching a hundred million or more. KKR's first deal in 1977 was the buyout of a company called AJ Industries. The acquisition price of $25.6 million made it a relatively large deal. The KKR partners supplied equity of $1.7 million. Most bootstrap acquisitions before the Houdaille deal relied on the book value of the assets as limiting the amount of the borrowings. The KKR bid for Houdaille changed all that. KKR was offering to buy the business at practically twice the carrying value of the assets on the books of the company. For the lenders, it wasn't the value of the assets that counted, but the ability of the company to produce cash that could service the debt. In technical terms, the lenders were no longer relying on the balance sheet but on the cash-flow statement. That change opened the way for a revolution.

Saltarelli had second thoughts about selling out to KKR under such circumstances. He wasn't prepared to abandon his healthy and liquid company and watch it become heavily laden with debt. It might easily fail, and many people who had spent their working lives at the company would lose their jobs. In all the time that he'd run the company, its long-term debt had never exceeded $50 million: now debt would be increased at least sixfold. Saltarelli had always been reluctant to borrow against the company's assets. He'd lived through the Depression and worried that in an economic downturn, heavy debt could topple the company.

There were, however, other considerations. Younger management, the next generation, wanted KKR to be able to do the deal, since such management would be given an opportunity to take equity at the favorable insider's price paid by KKR, plus free stock options, and wind up with 10 to 15 percent of the company, an undreamed-of percentage for a public company. They believed that they could run the company and pay down the debt. They had never experienced in their lives a market crash, or even a sharp change in business cycles, and were emotionally attuned to living on credit. All the economic incentives were in place to have the deal go. Saltarelli, however, kept hesitating because the specter of business failure was very real to him. In the debate that followed, leveraged buyouts were being examined, much the way they would be thereafter in boardrooms all over America, in terms of whether management was emotionally prepared to live with significant debt.

Age often decided the issue. KKR's timing was fortunate, because the members of the new managerial class were born after the Depression.

There had to be some test, some way to show whether or not the debt burden was truly bearable. Kohlberg met with Saltarelli. He was in his fifties, the right age to talk to Saltarelli. He too had experienced economic hard times, and was close enough to the Depression to understand its emotional impact. Years later Kohlberg would break with his younger partners, Kravis and Roberts, over the choices of companies selected to bear significant leverage. Age made the difference there also. Saltarelli appreciated Kohlberg's tact and knowledge and experience. Kohlberg said, "Look, let's not assume we're always in an inflationary economy where we earn more money every year. Let's assume that there's a downturn in the economy to see if these businesses can withstand 10 and 15 percent declines and still pay off the debt." Saltarelli felt that would be a good test, and ran financial models on that basis.

In the process Saltarelli discovered something he hadn't known about his company: it was a cash cow, providing a stable and predictable annual amount of cash. With the high interest cost and a new level of depreciation reflecting the purchase price, the company wouldn't pay income taxes for a number of years. That provided more cushion than he'd anticipated. Every year, year in and year out, the company could produce enough cash to cover the debt, even when the business experienced a decline.

When Saltarelli asked me if I thought it would work, I was fully receptive to the transaction. I'd seen it work, in part, in Tom Evans's acquisition of Missouri Portland Cement, which had been purchased from borrowings in a bootstrap fashion. I encouraged him to do it, being in tune with the younger management. Saltarelli, after getting over his initial hesitation, allowed the transaction to go forward. In effect, the younger generation was taking up the debt and paying out the older generation and the stockholders.

Nonetheless, Kohlberg wanted Saltarelli to stay on and head the management team. Prudential, the principal lender, needed the assurance of seasoned management. But Saltarelli wanted to retire and therefore visited Prudential to assure executives at the insurance company that the younger management was well capable of taking over. He was then offered a position on the board of directors, which he also declined. Saltarelli didn't want to be in a position where he would be perceived as being able to second-guess management and thus dampen their enthusiasm for this new undertaking. By stepping aside, giving up what had been a large part of his life, Saltarelli helped launch a new era.

Transactions like this don't go unnoticed. Within a short time the market realized that it had witnessed a remarkable phenomenon: a leveraged buyout transaction could be structured to compete with and pay more than corporate bidders and still offer management between 10 and 20 percent of the company. Almost overnight, other buyout groups were formed (about two hundred firms were doing leveraged acquisitions by the mid-1980s) and the leveraged buyout became a practical option to management faced with the prospect of selling the company to a third party. Indeed, most management thereafter considered a leveraged buyout the most attractive defense option. If you teamed up with buyout groups that didn't have operating management, you could be your own White Knight.

In a sense, the development of leveraged buyouts, called LBOs, was a counterrevolution. The justification for the raids was that an aggressive entrepreneurial group would be able to replace overly complacent or incompetent management and put the assets to "a higher and better use." The argument for the buyout groups was that the current management, given proper incentives and disciplined by the debt burden, could do the same. In fact, what made the acquisitions interesting for both groups was that purchases were being made with borrowed funds. The conflicting positions were never fully explored. Those willing to pay the highest price won. Often it was the current management, using the company's earning power and assets to have the company buy itself.

In the end you didn't have to accept either theory. Leveraged buyouts created a new universe of buyers in the marketplace, increasing demand for the sale of companies. This demand increased the prices offered and the number of transactions contemplated and completed. The free transferability of property was being encouraged, facilitated by borrowed money. These deals brought with them vast opportunities for success and huge risks of crushing failures. It was change that was being fostered. Change of such prodigious proportions transforms all aspects of society. Administering it all, the corporate lawyers learned how to reshape corporate capital structures with complex layers of debt, clearing the way for more change.

THE LIMITS
OF VISION

▼

*"Businessmen are doomed to have their most
interesting exploits reported and
measured by accountants."*

Jack Seabrook, the chairman of
IU International, was between planes at La Guardia Airport, and
between deals. I was returning from the Midwest, my bag filled
with papers for a corporate takeover, intent on getting back to the
office. Jack was headed for the Air Canada gate on his way to
Toronto when our paths crossed by chance. Always elegantly
dressed, he wore a striking black cashmere coat, lined in purple
silk and topped with a rich black velvet collar. His white hair and
tall figure set off the finery. He looked regal. Greeting him, I admired the coat.

"It's Bishop Fulton Sheen's coat," he told me. Setting his feet
carefully in place as he faced me, he was as poised as a dancer
about to begin a demanding turn. From such equilibrium comes
deftness. And with his next words he drew me into his circle. "The
bishop and I had the same tailor," he said, and grinned. "The very
day the bishop died, I saw the coat chalk-marked for cutting on
the tailor's bench. No ordinary coat, it was tasteful and decidedly

worldly. And the proportions were right. What a waste!" He paused to let me see his dilemma and appreciate the delicate decision point. "I told the tailor to erase the bishop's chalk marks and fit me up. What else could I do?" Jack smiled broadly at me, pleased with his audacity.

I hadn't known him in his younger days, but at sixty-two his acumen and guile were married to engaging charm, all at the service of his business interests. The company he headed, IU International, was a huge conglomerate, traded on the New York Stock Exchange, with over $2.5 billion in revenues. Twenty years before, in 1959, when Jack became the chief executive, the company had less than $100 million in revenues and owned utilities in Canada that the Canadian government would be seeking to repatriate, giving control back to Canadians. In the 1960s, Jack had enlarged and diversified the company through numerous acquisitions, preparing for the eventual loss of the utility business in Canada. He'd followed the economic credo of the period that the whole was worth more than the sum of the parts. His entrepreneurial spirit was that of the generation following Tom Evans.

The company's range of businesses was stunning: land transportation, through trucking companies serving most principal U.S. markets; utilities, providing gas and electric utility services in Canada, and water and sewerage services in the United States; manufacturing, involving the fabrication of valves and flow-control systems; mining, extracting silver and gold; distribution services, supplying paper products and institutional food products; and an agribusiness, producing sugar and macadamia nuts. The company was diversified, not only in terms of its investments in various industries but also with respect to its labor-intensive and capital-intensive segments. Financial architecture enabled the labor-intensive sector to provide capital to the manufacturing units, allowing the company to act in part as its own bank. The company's headquarters were in Philadelphia, and Jack had a farm, Seabrook Farms, in nearby New Jersey. His ownership position, while large in dollar value, was small in percentage terms.

It was January 1980, and Jack had begun to change the company, for conglomerate companies had gone out of economic fashion. In the previous decade large conglomerate companies had been found to perform poorly. Conglomeration entailed large administrative costs and didn't bring entrepreneurial drive to the individual units. Economic reevaluation had depressed stock prices of conglomerates. The parts were now worth more than the whole. The market preferred "pure plays," companies in a single line of business. And by 1980 the merger wave had developed a fierce undertow, forcing conglomerates to make a choice: either realize new profits for their shareholders by selling off businesses acquired in the 1960s or risk being dismantled by corporate raiders in search of those same profits. Jack had begun pruning peripheral businesses. He'd recently spun off Gotaas Larsen Shipping Corporation to IU's shareholders (a transaction I had worked on), and it now traded separately on the Exchange. Jack remained the chairman of that company and would hold the position after he turned over the chairmanship of IU in the next five years.

His trip to Canada was in response to renewed pressure from the Canadian government to relinquish control of IU's electric and gas utility in Alberta. The Canadian government wanted IU to sell some of its subsidiary's shares to Canadians and reduce American ownership to below 50 percent. IU's holdings had declined from about 88 percent in 1972 to approximately 58 percent in 1980. Although Jack had been reducing IU's position by degrees, he'd resisted giving up control for a long time. But now the pressures of the takeover marketplace were forcing him to sell the utility business to harvest value for the shareholders. He would be visiting investment bankers in Toronto and told me that he would see me in a few weeks.

An idea was germinating. Jack always took his time and played with all aspects of a deal before he was willing to discuss it. Once the project was fully formed in his mind, he'd see me. Implementing the plan wouldn't be easy. This transaction, involving Canadian properties, would have, at the very least, cross-border complications. But doing another deal with Jack would be a treat, for Jack never approached problems from obvious directions. His general counsel once told me that if Jack wanted to inspect a building with an open front door, you could expect that he'd want to enter through the back and begin with the basement. Considering his novel turn of mind, the deal would likely be a first of its kind, even trendsetting.

About a month later Jack called me to set a meeting at my office and told me he'd be bringing three other people. He fixed the time at noon so that we'd be able to have a working lunch and he'd be free later in the afternoon to visit his daughter, a practicing lawyer in New York, and to do some shopping. Jack was wearing a dark blue pin-striped, double-breasted suit with a natty dark blue tie with light blue polka dots that he told me expressed sincerity. For him, his dress asserted his state of mind. It let everyone present know that we were at a revelatory stage in the deal and Jack would be completely open and forthcoming.

With him was Bill Goldstein, a senior tax partner at a prominent Philadelphia law firm, who had represented Jack since 1962 and knew his thinking as well as anyone. He was about my age and I had come to think of him as cousin Bill. He was the cousin of Dan Neff, an associate in the firm close to me, and through Dan I was familiar with Bill's career and achievements. He had done a stint with the Treasury Department at a senior level and was one of the most knowledgeable tax lawyers in America. Also accompanying Jack was Bob Calman, the chief financial officer of IU. His openness and apple-cheeked good humor made him instantly likable. An astute financial executive, he had an uncanny way of translating knotty problems into measurable dollars-and-cents issues. The third person was a senior partner from an Ontario, Canada, law firm, a smart commercial lawyer. To Jack's credit, he always surrounded himself with knowledgeable people. Many chief executive officers have weak staffs and fawning advisers who constantly confirm their worth. The people close to Jack were mature, had a sense of their own worth and a balanced assessment of their involvement. They didn't need Jack and could be effective foils.

On my side of the table I had Peter Canellos, my tax partner. He was not only expert but also sensible and would be in a position to evaluate Bill Goldstein's tax structure. Attending all meetings also was Ilan Reich, a young corporate associate who had been at the firm less than a year and was then working with me full-time. The firm was growing and I had started to work with one or two newly hired corporate associates. I would have them work exclusively with me on all my matters for a year or two. I was developing my own version of the tutorial process that I had learned at Cravath. By contrast, the other entering corporate lawyers in the firm worked in a pool arrangement, available for different transactions (or aspects of transactions) for the various other partners. From my description of Jack, Ilan shared my sense of anticipation.

"The most interesting way to describe this deal is probably to begin backwards," Jack said, and paused. "Like life, it's always satisfying to know how things will turn out. But let me start at the beginning. That way, you'll see how it's supposed to develop." Jack was acknowledging his penchant for oblique approaches. That introduction promised an adventure.

IU, Jack told us, planned to start an exchange offer in Canada, exchanging the stock of its subsidiary Canadian Utility with IU's Canadian shareholders for IU common stock. The exchange would only be made in Canada. In the proposed swap of stock, IU's ownership of Canadian Utility would be reduced from 58 to 48 percent. Pressure from the Canadian government, Jack said, to relinquish majority control was intense. Various Canadian tax concessions would be granted to IU if the reduction was effected. For Jack, however, the proposed swap of stock in Canada was the official scenario, not the way he would like the matter to come out.

What he thought might happen, Jack told us, was that once he announced an exchange offer and indicated that IU was prepared to reduce its ownership below a majority, there might be bids from a number of Canadian companies for IU's whole majority interest in Canadian Utility. That would give him an opportunity to negotiate for the sale of control, affording IU a chance to get a large premium price for its 58 percent interest. Jack anticipated that he could get a price equivalent to twice the utility's book value at a time when most utilities sold at their book value. In addition to getting an excellent price, Jack also had another objective. He wanted the sale to be free of United States taxes. To accomplish that result, the Canadian acquirer had first to buy IU stock in the market and then swap the stock for the Canadian Utility shares. For the deal to work, the Canadian acquirer had to agree to the two-step process, using only IU stock as its currency.

Bill Goldstein advised us that there was a provision in the tax code which said that if you exchanged shares of a subsidiary company for shares held by a holder of more than 10 percent of the parent company's outstanding shares, the swap would be tax-free. That there were no holders of more than 10 percent of IU's stock didn't bother Bill. In his view, you got the same tax-free result if the Canadian bought more than 10 percent of IU's stock in the open market and then swapped the stock for the Canadian Utility stock. Bill anticipated that the Canadian acquirer, eager to close the deal, would make a tender offer for IU's stock at an agreed-upon premium price, and IU thereafter would swap its Canadian Utility stock.

Bob Calman energetically put the general description we'd heard into concrete terms: "IU's stock is trading about $12 a share," he said. "The tender offer by the Canadian should be made at about $17 a share for about 16 million shares, which is a little less than half of the 35 million outstanding IU shares. If you do the multiplication, the Canadian acquirer is paying about $275 million for the IU shares. Once the shares are swapped for our Canadian Utility stock, IU would have a gain of approximately $90 million on the sale of the subsidiary. In addition, after the swap IU's earnings per share would go up from approximately $1.91 to $2.91 per share. The reason for the increase in earnings per share is that Canadian Utility hasn't been earning as much as IU's other businesses and IU would, after the sale, have significantly fewer shares."

Bob Calman bounced in his chair, delighted with the outcome. "It's as if we sell our majority interest in Canadian Utility for $275 million and buy back and cancel about half our stock, 16 million shares. And IU doesn't pay any tax. After the sale the IU stock should remain at $17 a share or possibly even go higher." He paused to let us contemplate this outcome. "With earnings at $1.91 and the stock at $12, IU trades at a multiple of earnings a little better than six times. The quality of the company after the sale will be at least as good and probably better. With the same multiple of earnings per share, IU's stock should trade around $18." Pleased, he nodded his head before giving his prediction: "In my view, the stock should do better than $18."

"This is a great deal for our shareholders," Jack Seabrook said. "The IU stock they sell gets a premium and the stock they keep is worth 50 percent more. The fly in the ointment," Jack added, "is that the U.S. tax cost is approximately $70 million; and if there is a Canadian tax cost [ordinarily about $20 million], there wouldn't be any gain on the sale. This transaction doesn't bring cash into the company. If we get hit with tax bills, we'd have to sell additional assets to raise the cash, which would significantly reduce our earnings. The transaction doesn't make any sense if we have to pay the taxes."

"Has anyone tried this before?" I asked.

"No," Bob Calman said. "We're plowing new ground."

"How comfortable are you, Jack, about getting Canadian tax relief?" I asked.

"The Canadians want us to sell control and should give us the concession we want," Jack said. "But nothing is certain."

"How comfortable are you on the U.S. tax side?" I asked Bill Goldstein.

"Pretty comfortable," Bill Goldstein said. "The record will show that we weren't seeking to sell Canadian Utility for cash. If we tell the buyer that we won't take cash and will only take IU's stock in exchange, then we fit directly under the rules. Our case is that the company wasn't for sale unless someone swapped stock for it."

"You're still telling the Canadian buyer that you want $17 for the IU stock. Isn't that equivalent to saying you're selling the Canadian Utility stock for cash?" I asked, testing the limits of the tax position. It looked tenuous to me, like a cash sale, but tax lawyers regard the world differently from the rest of us.

"It's not the same as a cash sale," Bill Goldstein said. "The company isn't for sale unless there is a swap for IU stock. That's the distinguishing element."

"Of course, if there are no bidders for the whole company," Bob Calman said, "then we go through with the exchange offer and reduce our position to 48 percent."

"We're fishing in the Canadian pond," Jack said. "And the risk is that there won't be a buyer for our majority interest. But I'm willing to take that risk, because if I don't do a tax-free swap, I can't temporize with the Canadian government and I'll have to reduce our ownership interest."

"That's why Bill can say to the IRS that Canadian Utility is not for sale for cash," Bob Calman said.

"How does the tax side look to you, Peter?" I asked my partner.

"Literally read, the law covers the transaction and the deal should be tax-free to IU," Peter told me. "Generally, the tax law is read strictly. But the government will probably object. The Internal Revenue Service will argue that the tax law was meant to accommodate only 10 percent holders that held their stock for a significant period prior to a swap."

"There's nothing in the legislative history," Bill Goldstein said, "that negates acquiring an ownership interest immediately before the swap. We expect that the government will challenge us. But we think we have the better case."

Jack had heard all the arguments before and was satisfied with the tax case. He wanted to know from me whether some unexpected third party could make a tender offer for IU and kill his anticipated deal. The likelihood and consequences of hostile takeovers now had to be factored into the planning of all transactions.

"It's a risk," I said. "If a Canadian makes a tender offer at $17 for half your shares, which IU encourages, someone may be induced to make a tender offer for the whole of IU at that price."

"Is there any way to stop an ambush?" Jack asked.

"We should tell shareholders that $17 per share isn't a sales price for the entire company but a value put on the shares for the sake of the Exchange. Specifically," I said, "$17 per share yields only a fair price for your 58 percent interest in Canadian Utility. That approach would give you the right to fight off a tender offer and show that a price of $17 is inadequate for the whole company."

"If the transaction goes through, the stock will be worth more than $17," Jack said, "and we'll tell the shareholders all that."

"That's your best defense," I said. "But having a good defense doesn't mean that someone won't try anyway."

"If we don't take this risk, the IU stock will languish at $12 a share and then we'll truly be vulnerable. It's a risk we have to take," Jack said determinedly. "But what about the Canadian acquirer of IU deciding to buy the whole of IU at $17?" Jack asked me. "It's pretty tempting. For $275 million he only gets the Canadian Utility company. For another $275 million he gets the whole of IU."

"We'd have a contract with the Canadian acquirer," I answered. "The acquirer would be bound to buy no more than 16 million shares, and bound to exchange them only for the Canadian Utility stock. That's how the agreement would work."

"What about regulatory delays?" Jack asked me.

One of my tasks was to steer the transaction through the regulatory maze of government scrutiny, including processing by the Securities and Exchange Commission. Jack was particularly sensitive because the SEC in an investigation had accused him of misappropriating IU shareholders' money. Jack had denied any wrongdoing but settled all differences with IU by paying it $225,000. The SEC proved to be relentless, and Jack bears the distinction of being the first American to have his Swiss bank records broken into by the SEC (in which, incidentally, the agency found nothing of note). Jack was concerned that the SEC would needlessly delay the transaction.

"We won't need their clearance," I told him, "and they won't interfere, not in a legitimate commercial transaction."

Satisfied, he turned to the Canadian lawyer and asked whether there were any problems in Canada.

"The tender offer would have to be registered with the Ontario Securities Commission," he said, "but that wouldn't hold up the transaction."

"Then we go fishing," Jack said, "and see what we find in the Canadian waters."

In April 1980, IU cast out its line by publicly announcing that it was considering a plan to exchange approximately two million of its Canadian Utility shares for common stock of IU held by Canadians. Consistent with Jack's dual plan, the announced purpose was to facilitate increased ownership by Canadians in Canadian Utility. Jack's assessment of the Canadian market and the response to IU's announcement proved to be correct. Shortly after the announcement IU was contacted by Atco Limited and Calgary Power;

both companies were interested in acquiring IU's 58 percent interest in the Canadian Utility stock. Serious negotiations with the two followed immediately after the first contact.

It was just like Jack to run the two negotiations concurrently so that each party would know that they were merely a contender. Competing deals meant no respite for any of us. We'd finish one meeting and immediately start another with a whole new set of problems and personalities. One deal had become two. Calgary Power's deal was more complicated than Atco's. It was willing to pay cash in the United States to American holders of IU stock but wanted to offer Calgary Power shares to IU's Canadian holders. Calgary Power disliked risk and saw demons everywhere, creating pockets of complexity that made putting the papers together difficult. Jack, however, didn't mind complexity; he enjoyed the twists and turns and kept encouraging them. His encouragement served a sound economic purpose, for Calgary Power had the capacity to pay more than Atco, although it wasn't prepared to reach as far as Atco. Jack spent a lot of time with Calgary Power trying to induce management to keep enhancing their bid. Atco's transaction was basically a leveraged buyout of Canadian Utility, relying largely on Utility's assets to raise the cash purchase price. Jack, not fully comfortable with the leveraging, kept putting them off, which had the effect of getting them to keep raising the price.

Jack was the kind of player who was obsessive and would quickly forget or ignore the time of day or night once negotiations began. He was prepared to go around the clock and begin again the next day without rest, and expected nothing less from me. One evening at 2 a.m. I was working at the downtown law offices of Fried Frank, the firm representing Calgary Power, when Jack called. He'd just finished dickering with Atco and had gotten them to raise their bid again, this time to $17 a share for the IU stock, which is where he thought the price ought to be. "Finish up negotiations with Calgary Power," he told me, "and then begin contract discussions with Atco." He didn't want me to cut short my discussions with Calgary Power's lawyers or to leave abruptly, because he felt he might be able to get Calgary to raise again and wanted to keep the contest going.

"Jack," I said, "it'll be three in the morning before I can finish with Calgary Power."

"Atco will be waiting for you," he said.

"Who's waiting at this hour?" I asked.

"The lawyers at Shearman & Sterling," he said. "They're in the old Citibank building, on Wall Street, a block or two from where you are."

"Who at Shearman & Sterling?" I asked. It was a 400-person law firm, at least. I felt that at such an hour they wouldn't be able to line up anybody of enough seniority to work on the matter. By demanding a specific name, I felt that I'd be able to hold off further negotiations until a reasonable hour in the morning, affording myself and Ilan a decent night's sleep.

Without hesitation, he gave me the name of a young partner working on the project at Shearman & Sterling and his home telephone number. "Call him up," Jack said, "and tell him to meet you at his offices when you're ready. He's waiting for your call." I wasn't surprised to find, on calling the young partner, that he was as much annoyed as we were and thoroughly unenthusiastic. But he wouldn't take responsibility for postponing the meeting. He'd been told to be at the Shearman & Sterling offices whenever I got there with Ilan.

We arrived at 3:30 a.m., walking through dark, deserted streets. The offices were closed, and only the night watchman was there to meet us. Our reason for beginning a meeting at that hour didn't seem credible to him. He said: "I've seen meetings go to this hour, but I've never seen meetings start at this hour." I had to agree with him. Despite his skepticism, he allowed us to use a phone and we called the Shearman & Sterling partner from the watchman's desk. The partner told us he'd be at his offices in about forty-five minutes to an hour, reluctantly admitting to not quite being out of bed yet, but he promised that he'd soon begin showering and shaving and generally getting himself in order.

Waiting for anyone at that hour when a long day has sapped your energy is a form of torture. I figured that his procrastination meant that he'd be arriving at his office at about 6:00 a.m. or later, which was beyond my patience. Also, my fatigue was palpable. My evening's stubble was tearing at my collar, irritating my neck, and my clothing felt gritty, like sandpaper. I knew that we'd be totally at a disadvantage when he finally arrived in his own good time, freshly showered and rested.

Ilan had been working for the firm about seven months at the time, and I told him that he'd have to hold the fort when the partner arrived by taking all his comments on the papers. In the meantime, I was going home for some sleep, a shower, and a change of clothes and would rejoin him at about ten or eleven o'clock. At that time he'd be able to go home and get some sleep, and we'd be able to spell each other and continue the negotiations. It was too late now to get anyone else in the office to work on the deal since most people were fully committed, and to get immersed in the middle of this imbroglio would be extremely difficult. I had confidence that Ilan would hold up his end.

When I returned I was somewhat refreshed, and Atco's lawyers hadn't gotten very far. They had been as reluctant as we were to begin any discussions early in the morning. At that hour they didn't have contact with their client or the client's Canadian lawyers, so they didn't begin looking at the papers until 9 a.m. Ilan rejoined the group about 4 p.m. and negotiations went into the evening. By that time we'd worked out most of the difficult aspects of the deal, and I was wondering whether Jack had been in further discussions with Calgary Power and would want us to start another session after we'd finished with Atco. Much to my delight, negotiations had broken down with Calgary Power, and Jack, late in the day, was fully occupied in trying to revive them.

That evening we had a rest, but the following morning we found that the deal had spun out of control. Canadian counsel in Ottawa reported that the anticipated tax relief from the Canadian authorities didn't seem to be forthcoming. Counsel had asked for a promised ruling on the sale of the Canadian Utility stock that would save IU approximately $20 million, but after the announcement of the negotiations with the two Canadian buyers, Canadian tax officials had had second thoughts.

We met with Jack to discuss the Canadian tax situation and held a telephone conference call with all the Canadian counsel, including the tax counsel.

"The Canadian tax collectors know we have a deal going," Jack said, "and they've decided that it would be hard or impossible for us to back out." His face twisted in anger. "So they decided they want to collect the revenue." He paused. "Is that a fair summary?"

Canadian counsel told us politely that the tax authorities were no longer receptive to their arguments. They didn't want to attribute reasons to the tax officials' actions.

"What does the Canadian government want more than the tax on this transaction?" I asked Jack.

"The sale of Canadian Utility to Canadians," Jack said.

"Then pull the deal," I said. "And let them know definitively that you won't do the deal."

"They may not care," Bob Calman said. "We'll still have to go back to selling control by degrees."

"Not so," Jack said. "That also was premised on tax relief."

"You still have the benefit of the U.S. tax situation. You save $70 million," I said.

"The U.S. tax position is risky," Jack said. "The Canadian tax position was supposed to be certain. If I have to pay the Canadian tax and have a risk on the U.S. tax, the deal isn't attractive." He was firm.

"Pulling back on the deal," Bob Calman said, "and terminating it is a risky strategy." He didn't like playing brinkmanship with the Canadian tax authorities.

"It's a negotiation," Jack said. "We have to let them know that we have alternatives. Otherwise, they have no reason to give us anything. And the political implications have to be given a chance to percolate."

"We've been at this a year," Bob Calman said. "What happens if we announce that we've withdrawn from the deal and the Canadian tax authorities come back and grant us the tax relief we wanted? Will we be able to put the deal back together?" He saw the IU stock depressed after the failure of the deal and trading again at $12, with the company risking a hostile takeover.

"Both Calgary Power and Atco want this deal," I said. "They too will put pressure on the Canadian tax authorities. If the tax authorities relent, I'm sure one or both of them will be willing to go forward again."

"There are always intervening events that change things," Jack said, affected by Bob Calman's remarks. "What do you think?" he asked, turning to Calman. No one likes to terminate a deal that's about to be made.

"You've convinced me. The risks are worth taking," Bob Calman said. "Let's withdraw from the deal." His decisiveness made up Jack's mind.

Jack issued a press release to the effect that IU had withdrawn from negotiations over the sale of Canadian Utility because of failure to get expected Canadian tax concessions. Concurrently, he called Calgary Power and Atco and told them each that the company wasn't for sale. Canadian tax counsel in Ottawa was instructed to deliver the press release to the taxing authorities and then leave, without discussing the matter.

The next day the tax lawyers in Ottawa got a call from the taxing authorities. Reconsideration was being given to the tax concessions. None of us had anticipated such prompt action. The following day the tax lawyers were handed letters from the revenue authority granting concessions on the disposition of the Canadian Utility stock.

With the Canadian tax ruling settled, we were in a position to have Atco, the high bidder, begin a tender offer, but Jack delayed calling Atco. He'd been brooding about the tax issues for about two days and was concerned about the risks of a $70 million tax bill from the Internal Revenue Service.

We all came together again in my offices for the express purpose of deciding whether we should go forward with the sale of Canadian Utility. No one had any doubt that the IRS would assert a claim for the $70 million and IU would oppose it. Despite resistance, a claim of such magnitude would affect IU's financial statements. IU's auditors would have to determine the chances of success on the part of the IRS. If they thought the IRS would likely succeed, they would want a full reserve for the tax, which was tantamount to having IU pay it. Even if they didn't seek a reserve, they would note the contingent liability of $70 million plus interest on the financial statements. How would such contingency affect the ability of the company to do business and to finance itself? A claim like that could dissuade people from doing business with the company.

Second thoughts about the transaction had blossomed into doubts about the advantages of the deal. "Businessmen are doomed to have their most interesting exploits reported and measured by accountants," Jack said. Today he wore a black suit with a white shirt and a black-and-white tie, stark colors for sobriety.

"Bill Goldstein is prepared to give a strong opinion that the company will prevail on the tax point," Bob Calman said, starting to cut away at the obstacles that seemed to be hindering the deal. "That should go a long way with the auditors." The auditors always relied on outside counsel with respect to matters subject to litigation. They wouldn't require a reserve, but would note the contingent liability.

"I don't think the company will be hurt by the contingency," Bob Calman said, "and it won't affect our stock price." His basic optimism gave everyone assurance.

"You'll have to accept uncertainty for five or ten years," Bill Goldstein said. "It will take that long to resolve the case with the IRS."

"That's a long time," Jack said.

"There's no way to do it any sooner," Bill said. "To win with the Service, it will have to go to trial."

"That's not so bad," Bob Calman said. "Who knows what will happen in five to ten years."

It was then that one of the Canadians told us the story that we all came to refer to as the "camel story." He began in an offhand way, triggered by the thought of the changes that five to ten years could bring. It seems that an important sultan had a camel that had been with him for at least thirty-five years, and over time the sultan had gotten very fond of the camel. The camel not only carried the aging sultan and his supplies wherever he traveled but also was a constant companion. The sultan concluded one day that he would enjoy it very much if the camel could talk. The sultan knew, of course, that this was a difficult, if not an impossible, undertaking, one for which he wasn't equipped. But it was an idea that fascinated him. Talking would enhance the camel's companionship, and of course give the sultan a very different view of the world, one to which few were privileged. He called his counsel of many years, who acted for him on all important matters, and asked him if he knew if there was anyone in the kingdom who could teach the camel to talk.

"Sire," said the counsel, "no one can teach a camel to talk."

"Then you should do it," said the sultan.

"Sire, I said, no one."

"No one has tried," said the sultan. "It's very important to me, and I'm prepared to pay extremely well."

"You are serious, sire."

"Very," said the sultan.

"It will be very expensive," said the counsel, "and since we are not all that experienced, it may take very long, five to ten years," said the counsel.

"I can understand that," said the sultan, "but if the camel could talk, it will be worth the wait."

"Then it will be done, Your Highness, and I will do it," said the counsel.

At home that evening, the counsel told his wife that he'd agreed to teach the sultan's camel to talk.

"Fool," she said. "No one can teach a camel to talk."

"You don't understand."

"There's nothing to understand," she replied.

"Yes, there is," he said. "I'm going to be paid extremely well to do this, and it will take long. And as I see it, the sultan is seventy-five, the camel is at least thirty-five, and I am seventy-three. A lot can happen in ten years. By the time ten years has passed, one of us is sure to be dead."

We all laughed. Over time every problem goes away—or becomes someone else's. What gripped one about the tale was its offered temptations.

"Unfortunately, what we know," Jack said, testing the moral, "is that the IRS won't die."

"Nor will the company," I added. The story was a cynical way of looking at business matters, but a common one, and of questionable morality, telling you to take the immediate benefits and leave the mess for someone else. In business, at every level, there is always a way out of the consequences of failing to teach the camel to talk; there is always an opportunity to move on to another job, another town, a new frontier, taking the bonus in the paycheck before the bitter harvest.

"But the camel may talk," Bob Calman said, getting back to the real issue. He could see that, when considered, the story was sobering and having the opposite effect from its teller's intent.

"That's Bill's opinion," Jack Seabrook said, smiling. "You have to believe in the camel's talking. In our case, no matter what happens to us there won't be any dead camels or dead sultans."

"The camel will talk," Bill Goldstein said.

And with that, Jack decided to do the deal.

DESPITE OUR EXPOSING the story as meretricious, it persisted in our minds. Something about it caught our fancy as credible and intriguing, for it dealt with the effects of time on expectations. Once we acted, we were a first cause, but the events that followed were outside our control. That alone made you think, but waiting five to ten years to know the result was a further and substantial part of its engrossing attraction. All our lives were in transition. We could all look back at the past ten years and see what had happened to us. In the next five to ten years, as we all got older, significant change would be more likely than ever before and probably not always as anticipated. At a certain point in your life, you have to recognize that the future isn't life-enhancing. We could see how we would all age, and we could envision desired changes in our lives, but we knew that our individual and collective speculations could only explore likely outcomes. We were thrust into a mystery with its own spell and time limit. Would the consequences of our actions be someone else's problem? Among us there were bound to be survivors who cared and who would be affected. Someday in the next ten years the survivors would meet and reflect and bear witness. At no time in all my practice had I ever been so bonded to a group or so curious about the outcome.

Almost immediately events took an unexpected turn. The deal didn't go unnoticed by other companies. The structure (especially the tax advantages) appealed to the many conglomerate companies looking to sell their subsidiaries. Within a month, Esmark, formerly the holding company for the Swift meat-packing businesses, while trying to sell its subsidiary Vickers Energy Company to Mobil, decided to restructure the cash purchase arrangement into a transaction like IU's. But when Esmark did the deal, all the subtlety and artifice that Jack had brought to the transaction were ignored. Jack and Bill Goldstein had been careful to make sure that Canadian Utility had never been for sale for cash. At all times only a swap transaction was contemplated. Esmark and Mobil ignored the first principle because their transaction had begun as a cash deal.

But more than first principles were different in the two transactions. In its deal with Mobil, Esmark had started out expecting to pay the tax and then learned of a method, not previously contemplated, that might be used to avoid the tax. These distinctions meant that not only was Esmark's factual situation different from IU's, its economic and psychological positions were also different. For Jack and IU, payment of the tax crippled the transaction, and for Esmark, avoidance of the tax would be nice, but not essential. Esmark could settle or fight, probably creating a bad precedent either way. None of us had anticipated a companion case with a cruder set of facts and less risk to the taxpayer.

Easy emulation of the transaction didn't escape the notice of other companies or the Internal Revenue Service or Congress, and Congress changed the tax law almost immediately to eliminate such tax-free swaps. The Internal Revenue Service, however, wasn't satisfied only to eliminate this method of tax avoidance in the future and brought suit to recover taxes from both IU and Esmark.

Tax litigation is a protracted matter. It doesn't start as a case. First, ordinary year-end tax returns are filed, and then subsequently claims are disallowed. A deficiency assessment by the government results, and then there are the inevitable attempts at settlement. Finally there is a case, with other attempts at settlement. Few matters go to trial. Improbable as it seemed at the outset, no one settled, and both Esmark's and IU's cases went through their full careers, taking eight years before being ready for trial. Given a choice of two cases, the government chose to take to trial first the Esmark case, the more egregious and easier to win of the two. After the government won that case, the IRS would be prepared to deal with IU. Having no control, IU saw that it could be levered into some objectionable settlement or wind up at trial faced with an unfavorable precedent that the government had earned against Esmark.

What had happened in the eight years? Jack had stepped down as chairman and chief executive officer of IU, but remained on the board of directors until 1987, when he became an honorary director. He continued to serve as the chairman of Gotaas Larsen, the company he'd spun off from IU. John Christie, Jack's heir apparent and chosen successor, had taken over as chairman and chief executive officer of IU, and Bob Calman, the chief financial officer, had left his position at IU to become the chairman of Echo Bay Mines, a major North American gold producer, also a spin-off of IU. Bob Calman continued to serve on the board of IU. Over the eight years, Jack had provided corporate vehicles for the talented executives around him and for himself, making about as graceful a transition as one could imagine.

Bill Goldstein had changed law firms to become the senior tax lawyer at the Philadelphia firm of Drinker, Biddle & Reath, but still acted as a tax adviser to IU, and Peter Canellos and I were still on call to do deals for IU.

For all of us it was striking that the group was largely intact, and shifts in circumstances hadn't materially mattered. The tax situation had become so familiar after eight years that it was largely ignored, although occasionally we'd all recognize that the government was still pursuing the matter, working out its rights against Esmark. Experiencing a gradual, largely foreseeable evolution, we assumed that there wouldn't be any sharp changes.

In January 1988, however, we were all forced to review the tax situation in an unexpected context. A company called Neoax made a cash tender offer, totally unsolicited, to acquire IU. I was called on by John Christie to defend IU against the hostile attack. In that connection an evaluation of IU had to be made as to its worth against the bid. As is usual in those situations, a bidding package was prepared, first to bank lenders and then for third parties. For both the lenders and prospective buyers, the $70 million tax claim, plus interest (which by then had practically doubled the government's claim), had to be evaluated. Unfortunately, the evaluation wasn't based so much on the subtlety of Jack Seabrook's maneuvers as on the likely result of the Esmark case, which by then had been tried in the tax court and was awaiting decision. The tender offer couldn't have happened at a worse time. Everyone had a negative view of the outcome of the case, and the tender offer didn't allow for waiting until the tax court decided, although the decision could come down from the court at any time.

It didn't matter from whose point of view you looked at the tax case; the impact of the case was harmful. Take John Christie, who was a believer that the $70 million tax wouldn't ultimately have to be paid. Defending against the tender offer, he first tried a recapitalization of the company and then proposed a leveraged buyout. In both cases the banks weren't sympathetic to any assumption that didn't provide for payment to the government of at least $70 million. Every evaluation was forced to assume liquidation of the company, the corporate equivalent of the company dying. That was a situation we hadn't considered, showing the limits of our vision.

The benign view was that the cost of the tax case would be in the range of $70 million, or about $2 a share. IU, as reconstituted at the time of the bid, had doubled its shares from the time of the Canadian Utility transaction and was traded at about $14 or $15 a share. Stretched to the limit, the company might be worth about $21 if you didn't give it credit for winning the tax case. In other words, the tax case was worth about 10 percent of the value of the whole company.

In 1988 the average time to completion of a tender offer was about forty-five to sixty calendar days, although the initial expiration time was always set for twenty business days (about twenty-six calendar days). In defending, we delayed the contest as long as we could with every dilatory move I could manage, hoping for a decision by the tax court. Given all the negative assessments of the outcome of the tax case, only the tax court offered any hope.

Delay worked. The decision came down before the last round of bidding for IU. The tax court found for Esmark against the government. The decision immediately increased the value of IU by $2 a share. If Esmark won with its crude case, then IU would win hands down.

When we all met after the tax court decision, we felt like survivors, privileged to see the result of our efforts. We were at an IU board meeting, and Jack was attending as an honorary director. "Well," Jack said, "I was getting worried, but the camel learned to talk." He paused and smiled broadly. "And at the right time." And then he added, looking thoughtfully at all of us, "What will the next ten years bring?"

A FOOTHOLD
IN THE BRONX

▼

*"The fallout from corporate warfare
has its civilian benefits."*

"That's the deal breaker."

"What's that?" asked Dr. Mitchell S. Rosenthal, president of Phoenix House, a drug-free residential treatment program for drug addicts.

I'd slipped into business argot that hadn't crossed into the not-for-profit sector. We were in Phoenix House's conference room in an old West Seventy-fourth Street building that had been purchased in 1972 when the neighborhood looked unsalvageable and the building sorely needed repair. The residents had renovated the building and, with Phoenix House's guidance, renewed themselves.

"It means the point over which the deal fails unless resolved," I explained.

"Got it," the doctor said.

It was intriguing that I was introducing the language of deals to him, because the doctor was on a parallel course with many of my business clients. In this meeting in 1978 he faced his first strategic acquisition, a failing treatment program in the Bronx, and we'd come together to do a deal. In this context, he was in step with his time, expanding by acquiring others.

Dr. Mitchell S. Rosenthal was a builder. After training in psychiatry, he served as a Navy physician at the U.S. Naval Hospital in Oakland, California, and came in contact with Synanon, a residential drug-treatment program. Impressed with their methods and results, he came home to New York after his Navy stint committed to fight drug addiction, and joined the city's Addiction Service Agency in 1967 as one of the two commissioners. Immediately, he bumped against the city's limits and its bureaucracy. Effective treatment required changing the addicts' environment and restructuring their lives in residential facilities. But there were none that the city owned, and the city, for political reasons, couldn't easily buy tenements, even for drug treatment. To buy the run-down buildings, a private foundation, known as the Phoenix House Foundation, was formed. The patients helped repair the buildings as part of their work therapy.

The doctor then enlisted the help of the Department of Human Resources to classify the addicts as totally disabled, which entitled them to federal aid to the disabled that could be contributed to Phoenix House for their care. With the Foundation holding the real estate and federal welfare support providing necessities for the resident addicts, Commissioner Rosenthal could use his agency's budget to pay for staff to deliver health care and treatment to the addicts. It worked, and the Phoenix program was a model program, an exciting initiative of Mayor John Lindsay's administration.

It's impossible to end-run the bureaucracy in the city for long or avoid its politics. Abe Beame, city comptroller and an aspiring candidate for mayor, challenged the conflict of interest he saw in the doctor's acting as a commissioner for the city and as a director of a private foundation holding real estate improved by addicts. Beame started an investigation and wrote a report about claimed abuses arising from the conflict of interest: the principal one was the improvement of Foundation-owned real estate with city and state funds. The "Beame Report" spawned two other investigations: one by the Department of Welfare and another by the New York State attorney general.

Exposed to intense examination by politicians hoping to make names for themselves, the doctor needed a lawyer, preferably a corporate lawyer, to restructure the Phoenix program's arrangements with the city. Nancy Hoving, an early enlistee in the fight against drug abuse and chairman of the board of the Foundation, introduced the doctor to Roswell Gilpatric, then head of the Cravath firm. The case got turned over to Cravath associates, and Carol Bellamy worked on it for a short time. On leaving Cravath to work for the city, she turned it over to me in 1968, thus providing me with a balance to my representation of United Fruit. This was one of the few opportunities at the time for a corporate lawyer to do work in the public interest. Most of such work required court appearances and litigation skills. Work in the public interest required artful juggling of the matters for which you were responsible, because the corporate clients always came first. To take on a client in the public interest also meant that you lengthened your day, since time spent that couldn't be billed didn't seem to count as much as billable hours.

I met the doctor and the Foundation's board in the conference room on West Seventy-fourth Street. The doctor was my age, filled with his mission and at ease with his position as the leader of the Phoenix program. The board members were mature, well-connected New Yorkers looking for an able advocate. The purpose of the meeting was to take my measure to see if I could do the job. I'd been at Cravath eight months and was inexperienced, relying solely on my own native shrewdness and the patina of professional competence that goes with holding down a job at a law firm. Inexperienced or not, I was judging them, while being judged, for a lawyer must know his clients. It was probably my brassy stance of not accepting their version of the story and of evaluating them by asking demanding questions that got me through the meeting without them calling Cravath for another lawyer. Phoenix House became one of my earliest clients, the first that I represented without direct supervision of a partner.

The city's investigation was distasteful to the board. They'd set out to fight drug abuse and were in a political cross fire. Cravath litigators were defending them to show that there was no self-dealing, but that effort was only a holding action and wouldn't solve the problem. Beame's inquisition was a platform from which to ask nasty questions with the assurance of press coverage. Not finding anything wrong wouldn't keep him from continuing to posture or probe, which impeded the program's ability to treat addicts. Beame's interest was in extracting any concession that gave him a political victory over John Lindsay.

The solution was already known when I stepped in to represent Phoenix House. Beame would require that the doctor resign from his city post to join the Foundation, and thereafter the Foundation would negotiate contractual arrangements with the city and state to deliver drug-treatment services. The Foundation would then be an independent vendor of services, and its performance would be monitored.

Simple as it sounded, it was totally unreasonable when examined. The board assessed Beame's proposal and were noisy about it. At their meetings, everybody spoke, without the usual show of restraint found in business boardrooms. Nancy Hoving was a spirited advocate and often led freewheeling and heated discussions. All the members had contributed time and money to the Foundation and were committed to fight the drug problem, and even the city, if it interfered with their efforts. They saw that the doctor would lose his job and then have to negotiate for the funding of the program, including his salary. Drug treatment would stop. Compromise lay in the doctor's resigning but with the city continuing to fund Phoenix House's drug treatment program until the contractual terms could be worked out. It meant that the doctor would have to fund his salary through charitable contributions, which was a lot to demand. The self-interest of politicians is more than most good-minded people should suffer. There was little reward in victory for him other than the opportunity to deal with the drug problem in the city for a marginal salary that he raised by pleading for contributions. At any time he could have opened a Park Avenue office and become a psychiatric physician for the rich, with success assured. But the doctor was willing to leave his job to free the board from the cloud of investigation. I liked him for that and told him that I thought the compromise would work. Assuming Beame accepted, I was prepared to work out the contractual arrangements with the city.

He resigned from the city job, and it took another eighteen months to spin off the program, have the city withdraw all charges, and get a clean bill from the Welfare Department and the state attorney general. During that time, the doctor and I got to know one another well. Our professions were a bond. As a lawyer, I was in his view called on to serve Phoenix House, as if I too had taken the Hippocratic oath: in my case, to facilitate medical treatment through law. That obligation to serve knew no time constraints. One night he called me after midnight, waking me to ask me what to do about a boy who had been arrested during the day in New Jersey while trying to solicit charitable contributions for Phoenix House.

"How am I supposed to know?" I said irritably. "I don't do that kind of work."

"You're a lawyer. If he were sick, I'd treat him. But I don't know what to do here."

"Wait till morning," I said with enough authority to put him at ease. "We'll get him before a magistrate and get him released on bail." That satisfied the doctor, and it worked: so he was encouraged for the next time. I bought two copies of *The Bust Book*, a primer on dealing with the police, one for the office and one for home, all for the next time.

The next time was having me work on the tag end of a hopeless criminal appeal for two residents who said that they hadn't committed the robbery of a drugstore for which they were convicted. They had an alibi defense, claiming to be at a Phoenix House facility at the time the crime was committed. The witnesses in their favor were Phoenix House residents, former addicts. The jury didn't believe them and found the defendants guilty. The conviction had been devastating to morale at the facility.

"No one has any faith in this case," he told me. "You have to do it. You clerked for the Chief Justice of California. We need leave to appeal to the Court of Appeals from the Chief Judge. This is right up your alley. The residents need their faith in the criminal justice system restored."

I worked on a brief (trying to overturn a jury verdict based on claimed errors of courtroom procedure and the charge of the judge to the jury) and made an appearance in Chief Judge Charles D.

Breitel's chambers in lower Manhattan. A chubby young man from the Queens district attorney's office was there to oppose my application. As we waited together in the anteroom for the Chief Judge to see us, I inspected my adversary. Nothing he wore seemed to fit. He saw me examining him, knew what I was seeing, but was unconcerned. He was a tough little man.

"You write that brief?" he asked.

"Yes."

"Pretty good," he said, acknowledging my pride.

Of course it was good, damn good. I'd given it a lot of effort and felt that the sentences sang out for justice.

"For an amateur," he added.

I clenched my teeth, and didn't respond, waiting for him to eat his words before the judge. But it wasn't to be. The judge gave me less than five minutes for argument and denied the request. I left the chambers, pausing only long enough to let my adversary shake my hand in his pincer grip, forcefully pressing home his victory. There was a reason why no one had believed in the appeal: it was hopeless. And residents of Phoenix House would have to find faith in the criminal justice system through another example. If I'd known more, I'd have been less sure, but I learned about the benefits of legal specialization.

Our professional relationship permitted me, in turn, to make demands on the doctor. For example, the city, a short time after the Phoenix program was spun off, sent a team of auditors to the West Seventy-fourth Street office on a surprise visit to screen confidential patient records. The doctor made an emergency call to me for advice on how to deal with this intrusion. I told him to throw the auditors out. They didn't need those records for an audit and weren't entitled to access to confidential patient information. In working out the spin-off arrangements with the city, I'd specifically negotiated confidentiality arrangements that precluded the auditors from looking at portions of the patients' records where the patients gave confidential information about their past history, which could include information about prior criminal activity. My sense of privacy had led to my seeking and obtaining the provision from the city's counsel, who apparently hadn't discussed the arrangements with the city's auditors.

The doctor said, "They told me that if we don't allow access, they'll cut off the money."

"Throw them out," I said. "They have no right to look at the information. Tell them we'll see them in court." I was adamant and my voice was harsh. No compromise was possible.

It was a tense moment. No one likes to oppose their main source of funding. The doctor was being put in that position, with the future of Phoenix House at stake. The city's ability to cut off the money and starve the program was a highly potent weapon. I recognized the high stakes and then realized that the position I'd taken was more than that of a legal adviser. I'd left him no room for decision. The effort I'd put into representing the program had me speaking as a partner in the enterprise, which was stepping over the line. No matter my emotional feelings, I had to step back into my role as lawyer and only advise, leaving him free to make the decision.

I said, "I don't mean to preclude your decision. Let's discuss this situation." I didn't have to say anything more.

He had already made up his own mind. "If we can't keep the patients' confidences, we won't be able to treat them. We have to take the risk."

He threw the auditors out, and we waited. We got nasty calls from city officials, but the city backed down. They reluctantly acknowledged that they didn't need confidential patient information to make audits.

For him, I was a general practice lawyer. He called me when there was trouble or when he needed advice, no matter the type of problem. For me, participating in a common enterprise offered a sense of continuity that balanced the brief encounters that mainly made up doing deals. I watched him over time become an able administrator and build a staff that could deliver low-cost and effective treatment, which made Phoenix House the premier national drug-treatment program. Working closely with him enabled me to understand my business clients better, for I could appreciate their sense of achievement in building their organizations. Some of my investment banking clients were interested in fighting drug abuse and I encouraged them to go on the board. The clients, astute businessmen, were able to make more direct contributions to the running of Phoenix House than I could, because the business part of the doctor's operations was similar to many of the businesses they advised. But then came an instance where my main legal experience could be put at the service of Phoenix House.

"Do you know anything about acquisitions?" the doctor asked me one day in 1978.

"Yes," I said.

"This is a difficult one. We don't know how to do it and we're competing with other programs to acquire it."

At last, a matter for which I was trained.

In the conference room on West Seventy-fourth Street, he told me about Logos, a treatment program in the Bronx. I got myself a cup of coffee from the pot that was always available and sat back and listened. The conference room's proportions made it an intimate working room, and here we'd worked through many of Phoenix House's problems.

Ron Coster, the chief financial officer of Phoenix House, sat with us to explain the costs. The doctor stated the facts. Logos treated about forty residents in a facility in the lower Bronx. A state audit had turned up questionable expenses that, on further examination, exposed fiscal problems and mismanagement. The state, having uncovered a waste of funds and other fiscal problems, would cancel Logos's contracts to deliver services unless a reputable, well-managed program took it over.

The Logos program had run up debts in a number of quarters for well over $50,000, including a $30,000 loan from Chemical Bank that had been personally guaranteed by the chairman, a local Catholic parish priest. The problem, as the doctor saw it, was: "If we take over the program, we take over the debts, which isn't worth it to us. For that much debt, we'd set up our own program in the Bronx."

The doctor had it fully analyzed: "If we deal directly with the state, the program will go under and the priest will be responsible for the $30,000 to Chemical Bank. No one wants that. The priest didn't know about the poor management, and neither did the outside directors. The board wants someone who will come in and assume the loan and get the priest released."

"Even the state wants the priest released," he continued. "They are reluctant to write new contracts if it means the priest will be liable. But no one who has looked at it is willing to take on the debt."

"Did anyone ask the bank to forgive the debt?" I asked.

Ron Coster smiled. "Everyone. The answer is no. That's why the bank took the guarantee."

"Who did you speak to?" I asked.

"The loan officer," Ron said.

"Nasty?" I asked.

"Firm," Ron said. "Very firm."

"Did the state try?"

"The state won't do that," Ron said.

"You guys want all the assets without paying for them," I said. "And you won't assume any liabilities. That's better than I've ever been able to do for my clients."

"I told you, it wasn't easy," the doctor said.

"Let me back up. Why do you need this program?"

"It's an old program that has community acceptance and involvement. We have only one treatment program in the Bronx. This acquisition gives us a firm foothold in the Bronx. We have to be well represented there. Otherwise, we haven't done our job for the city. And it's not so easy to start up programs now. Communities are afraid of us. They believe we bring crime, which is totally untrue, but prejudice is hard to dispel."

"Let's deal with the logic of the situation."

"Go ahead," the doctor said.

"If no one is prepared to assume the debt, then the state will have to choose someone to take over the program. It's only a matter of time," I said. "You're the best qualified to run it, and if you wait, you'll get it on your own terms."

"This is not a situation where you can wait," the doctor said. "There are too many variables. The state may do nothing. Some other program may plunge in and assume the debt. Or a number of other possibilities could occur that we can't see right now. Besides, the kids need treatment."

"The priest is the key," I said. "That's the deal breaker."

"Is there anything that can be done?" he asked.

"Well, the bank should release the priest. That was a goodwill loan."

"Everybody's tried the bank," Ron Coster said, his frustration showing.

"I'll call Dick Simmons at Cravath," I said. "He represents Chemical Bank and is a sensible man. Let's see what he can do."

The last time I'd spoken to Dick Simmons was about three years before, when I told him that Wachtell Lipton was prepared to do Cravath a favor, but didn't need any favors from Cravath. Now it looked like I needed a favor, or politely put: a concession for a mutual client, Phoenix House.

I called Simmons and told him about the situation. He listened and didn't ask any questions until he had all the facts.

"What do you want me to do?" he asked.

"Have the bank release the priest," I said.

"Who is the loan officer?"

I gave him the man's name.

"It'll take me about an hour," he said matter-of-factly. "Call the loan officer in about an hour and he'll make arrangements to get you the release."

"Thank you," I said.

"It's small," he said.

"Big for Phoenix," I said appreciatively.

I called the loan officer and was met with: "You delivered the bank." I could hear the anger in his voice. I didn't say anything: he hadn't said anything to which I could respond.

"Who do you know?" he asked.

"I need the release," I said. "We're on Park Avenue." I gave him our address.

"I'll send it over to you this afternoon," he said. And then: "Who do you know?" he asked again.

"It's the right thing to do," I said, this time choosing not to respond.

"It's somebody very important, because until an hour ago we had all made up our minds," he said, retaining in his voice the resistance Ron Coster and everyone else had met.

The doctor was delighted. "The legal old-boy network really works," he said.

"It wasn't that at all."

"It wasn't?" He looked puzzled. We were in the West Seventy-fourth Street conference room and Ron Coster was with us. He too looked perplexed by my response. They were used to seeking and taking favors for Phoenix House. This looked like another one.

"There weren't any favors delivered here," I said. "The bank is not in the business of giving away money. That's why the loan officer was upset about giving the release."

"Then what was it?" the doctor asked. He liked to know how things worked. I could see his interest.

"I asked for the release and Simmons evaluated his client's position. That is the way lawyers always deal with each other. We didn't have to push the pieces of this game to the end of the board. He could see that to collect on the loan, the bank would have to try to enforce the guarantee by suing the priest in the Bronx Supreme Court. There would have to be a jury trial. From that it followed that in a charitable loan, where the priest never got any money, the bank couldn't win, and the matter would probably be picked up by the newspapers. Why should the bank generate ill will trying to collect on a loan meant for community goodwill? Without my saying anything, he knew that it was best to be gracious. That's the way all cases are settled."

"Simmons is a powerful guy," the doctor said.

"Of course," I said. "That's why I called him. But his power comes from his good sense," I said, "and not from being able to give arbitrary directives."

"The fallout from corporate warfare has its civilian benefits," the doctor said, enjoying his insight into the way lawyers work.

STANDING ON
THE LINE

▼

*"There's one overriding rule in the merger
wars that must be observed: take no notes
and avoid leaving a paper trail."*

Stanley Sporkin, the man in
charge of the Enforcement Division of the SEC, spent his days
pursuing swindlers, cheats, frauds, and other miscreants. Blessed
with more than ordinary cynicism, he was better able than most
to recognize con artists, even those clothed in conservative business
dress. In his world, liars had agreeable manners and avoided gold
chains and other ready signs of irremedial sharpness. This deepened his distrust of everybody. Like all prosecutors, he knew that
there was no end to scoundrels, but that awareness, enervating to
many, hadn't sapped his energy or efforts.

This endless villainy, however, affected Stanley physically. The
weight of it seemed to have lodged on his shoulders. They sagged
as if he'd never be able to unburden himself. His waist had spread
from fast-food meals taken at his desk and his eyes, always ringed
by dark circles, looked like he'd spent too many nights in sleepless
vigilance. He often growled when he talked. And when he was
angry, he was like an Old Testament prophet railing against de-

clining values. Looking at Stanley, you saw a forbidding moral
force, which made him seem twice his rather average height.

Despite his air of constant irritation, he had a sense of humor.
There was even an illustrative anecdote, told as gospel. The story
begins in Stanley's office, where it was his usual practice to collect
suspects and lecture them about their transgressions. There were
always plenty of misdeeds. The SEC monitored the sale of securities
(common stock and debt instruments) to the public and the purchase of securities from the public, and required fair and accurate
disclosure of financial information so that public investors (and
not just insiders) could make informed decisions. In takeover offers
the SEC required raiders to disclose information not only about
themselves but also about the target companies. Considering the
high stakes, many raiders were tempted to misstate damaging facts,
omit them altogether, or trade on information before it became
publicly known. Accordingly, Stanley was always busy and his office
full. Others, next in line, waited in the anteroom to his office in
full hearing of his booming voice. Snared in his room, there was
little opportunity to deflect his anger. Even good defense lawyers
couldn't get a word in in opposition. In the course of one of Stanley's
harangues, the object of his anger had a heart attack, probably
while trying to sputter a protest. An ambulance was called, a
stretcher was brought in, and the prostrate victim was wheeled
from Stanley's office as the crowd, businessmen and their lawyers,
beheld the effects of his vehemence. Immediately after the stretcher
passed, Stanley entered the waiting room to face the assemblage.
As if unaware of their concern, he smiled, put his hands on his
hips, and impatiently inquired, "Okay. Who's next?"

That kind of reputation created and concentrated power, and
Stanley used it. Lawyers weren't immune. Indeed, we all came
under his special scrutiny. Many a lawyer was lectured by him to
stop trying to stand on the line. In matters of judgment, it's easy
to go astray, and if you're standing on the line, it's hard to see it.
Stanley wanted lawyers to be in the forefront of enforcement, part
of his task force. In his view, if the leading lawyers pushed their
clients to make early disclosure of important pending matters, others would follow and the securities markets would function more
efficiently. But a lawyer's stock-in-trade is his judgment of the

applicability of rules. No lawyer was willing to cede that judgment to Stanley or the government. As a result, there was growing tension between Stanley and certain practitioners who refused to heed his exhortations.

In 1979 Stanley brought an action against William Carter and Charles Johnson, senior partners of Brown & Wood, a prominent Wall Street law firm, for failing to make early disclosure in press releases and in quarterly financial reports with respect to the failing financial position of a company to which they were legal counsel. The stock market, in Stanley's view, was trading in the company's securities without fully appreciating the declining value of the company. As punishment, he sought to have Carter and Johnson suspended from practice before the SEC for as long as one year. It was the first case of its kind challenging the judgment of lawyers. After a hearing, an SEC examiner found against the lawyers, and suspended Carter for one year and Johnson for seven months. They appealed, insisting that they had both acted properly. In 1981, the case was awaiting review by the full commission.

The case against Carter and Johnson was a warning from Stanley, letting all lawyers know that he'd monitor their behavior. His next major case, we all suspected, would be against a leading law firm over a merger matter. Stanley was more than a tough traffic cop, making sure that rules were followed. He wanted to impose strict constraints on a rough-and-ready marketplace which was largely ordered by lawyers for participating parties. Sure enough, at the end of 1981, before the case involving Carter's and Johnson's suspension from practice was decided, Stanley started an investigation of the lawyers involved in the acquisition of a company named Belden, in which I was actively engaged.

Everything went wrong from the start in the Belden merger with Crouse Hinds. The business combination made sense, which was a rarity and reason enough to believe the deal would follow a straight path. Crouse Hinds made circuit breakers and electric safety devices, and Belden fabricated electric wire and cable. They served similar markets and their products generally complemented one another. The rationality of the joining of the two companies encouraged a conventional and workable agreement. Crouse Hinds would acquire Belden solely for its common stock. So structured,

Belden shareholders would swap their stock for Crouse stock, tax-free. Skadden Arps represented Crouse, and Wachtell Lipton represented Belden. There was little that was adversarial, and nobody remotely contemplated anything like all-out warfare or Stanley's investigative ire.

The agreement was signed on September 8, 1981, and announced immediately thereafter. When a stock deal is announced, the stock price of the acquirer invariably drops. Declines of as much as 10 percent and even 15 percent aren't unusual, because the acquirer is issuing a quantity of stock which sharply increases supply over demand in the marketplace. Also, arbitrageurs and other speculators will sell the acquirer's stock short (that is, selling stock they don't yet own) in anticipation of covering the short sale with the surplus of stock that will be available when the transaction closes. Such sales also put downward pressure on the acquirer's stock.

Contrary to conventional expectations, Crouse's stock price rose sharply. At first the feeling was that the market had applauded the transaction and saw the synergies inherent in putting the two companies together. My image of the average market maker was a plump man (formerly a cigar smoker) who now ate too much, spent his days watching the computer screen, and was skeptical that any deal made sense and reluctant to buy when others were logically selling. Pleasing these market skeptics was highly satisfactory: it showed true insight in conception. Everyone likes to participate in a deal that is well received. In those moments it's as if you've produced a play that gets rave reviews. The glow of the favorable reception carried us forward for a number of days and addled our minds. But the stock price continued to rise beyond the fundamentals of the deal. Finally everyone realized that no one could be applauding for that long, and we tried to account for the aberration.

Once we probed, we found that Internorth, a midwestern natural gas distributor, had been buying the Crouse stock from all sellers. Crouse had been trading in the mid-20s immediately before the announcement of the Belden merger; by September 11, it closed at $36⅞. On September 12, 1981, Internorth announced a cash tender offer for Crouse at $40 a share. How had Internorth gotten ready in only four days? Such decisiveness was notably unusual—and why was it interested in Crouse? Not until much later did we find out that Internorth had been preparing for an acquisition of Crouse Hinds for about four months. It wanted Crouse without Belden, which it had never previously considered acquiring and knew relatively little about.

Facing what it viewed as a lost opportunity if the merger between the two companies went through, Internorth accelerated all its plans. The novel aspect of its tender offer was its announcement to the Crouse shareholders that it wouldn't buy the Crouse shares unless Crouse dropped the deal with Belden—or the Crouse shareholders rejected the Belden merger by voting against it. Internorth had a winning hand. It was axiomatic that the Crouse shareholders would prefer the cash offered by Internorth to the merger proposed by Crouse.

A two-pronged defense against Internorth was worked out. On behalf of Belden, Wachtell Lipton brought a lawsuit in state court in Chicago, where Belden was based, claiming that Internorth's tender offer for Crouse was wrongfully interfering with an advantageous contract for Belden, which wanted to merge with Crouse. On behalf of Crouse, Skadden Arps sued in federal court in Syracuse, where Crouse was headquartered, arguing that Internorth's coercive tender offer had violated certain disclosure requirements of the federal securities laws. Wachtell Lipton and Skadden Arps were now acting together against Internorth. It was a satisfying moment to work with the most polished of your adversaries. Wachtell Lipton had consistently attempted to be on the opposite side of Skadden Arps, which meant representing target companies, as Skadden Arps was noted for its offensive strategies. Wachtell Lipton's position was meant to assure the business community that in every hostile takeover there would be access to first-rate legal help, since there were only a handful of firms as experienced in takeovers as Skadden Arps. As a marketing tactic, it was brilliant, for it defined Wachtell Lipton as the antidote to Skadden Arps, setting Wachtell Lipton above its competitors. The marketing ploy was Marty Lipton's idea, and helped generate substantial defense business.

With litigation on two fronts, well situated in hometown courts for the local advantage, we hoped to win a skirmish against Internorth. The better of the cases was the Wachtell Lipton challenge in the state court. Takeovers had already gotten to the point in the marketplace where no deal was honored until closed. This was definitely against us. And there were decided cases from which inferences could be drawn that deals, subject to a shareholder vote (like ours) to approve the issuance of shares to effect the acquisition, could be interrupted by competing bidders before the shareholders voted. But there were no cases directly bearing on this point. Our argument was that something more than the morals of the marketplace should govern. It was an appeal to the high-minded. The case was promptly heard, and the state court judge found, to our delight, that Internorth was improperly interfering with the merger and enjoined it from continuing its hostile tender offer. As expected, Internorth promptly appealed to get the order reversed.

We assumed that Internorth had an excellent chance of winning on appeal, but the appeal would take about forty-five days to be heard. Having gained the advantage of that time, we regrouped to fashion a new set of defensive actions. Defeat was certain if we stayed with our original plan of seeking approval from Crouse's shareholders to issue shares to be swapped for Belden's shares, because it would take about sixty days to clear soliciting material with the SEC and to call and hold a meeting. By that time, Internorth would be free to continue its tender and the Crouse shareholders would favor Internorth and disapprove the merger with Belden. Completely ignoring Crouse's stockholders, however, wasn't possible. But Crouse could, under New York Stock Exchange rules, exchange up to 20 percent of its shares for Belden's shares without first getting stockholder approval. Belden's shareholders would gladly exchange their shares for the premium offered by Crouse. Since Crouse was more than twice the size of Belden, 20 percent of Crouse's shares represented, based on the exchange ratio, a majority of Belden shares. Such an approach had been rejected initially because approval of Crouse's stockholders would have to be sought anyway to finish the purchase of the minority interest in Belden. A two-step approach was an inefficient way to proceed under ordinary circumstances.

But reexamined in light of Internorth's tender, an exchange offer would be powerfully effective. If Crouse were able to effect the swap and acquire a majority of Belden's shares, sensible economics required that the entire deal be completed. Crouse's stockholders would have to approve the remainder of the transaction; otherwise Crouse would suffer accounting charges to its earnings that would devalue the Crouse stock. Even Internorth wouldn't then interfere with the completion of the deal, for it would make no financial sense to do so. And if Internorth couldn't sensibly interfere, it would have to acquire both companies or quit and acknowledge defeat. Acquiring both was more than it was prepared to do. A transaction contemplated at about $500 million would escalate to approximately $750 million. Internorth would have to drop its tender offer. We'd found a winning gambit to use in the forty-five days pending the appeal of the state court case.

Internorth reacted immediately to the announced exchange offer. George Kern, of Sullivan & Cromwell, a knowledgeable and seasoned advocate, counterclaimed for Internorth against Crouse in the federal court in Syracuse, asking that the swap be enjoined. His argument was that Crouse was taking away from its stockholders the opportunity to decide whether they wanted to do the Belden deal. The exchange offer was an underhanded move: coercive of the Crouse stockholders, depriving them of the Internorth tender offer. George bellowed when he talked in ordinary conversation. Filled with indignation, he shouted. Skadden Arps's response was that Internorth had no standing to object, which translated to: Don't listen to him. Good litigators always try to impose procedural obstacles to keep their adversary from getting to the merits. Skadden Arps's argument was that Internorth had only become a substantial stockholder after the deal was announced. As such, Internorth wasn't representative of the other Crouse stockholders and was acting only to advance its own acquisition interests. Skadden Arps argued that Internorth's high-and-mighty claims about coercion ignored the finding of the state court in Chicago that Internorth was wrongfully interfering with the deal. And so on. The substantive argument that Skadden Arps made in favor of the exchange offer was that the Crouse directors could reasonably use their business judgment to pursue the acquisition of Belden as part of its business plan, even though it would defeat the Internorth offer. After hearing everyone out, the district court ruled in favor of Internorth, enjoining the closing of the exchange offer. The decision was immediately appealed.

The outcome of the two cases in the trial courts was that we'd effectively blocked each other, since neither Crouse nor Internorth could finish its actions. The matter would be decided on appeal. And after hearing argument, both appellate courts reversed the trial courts. When the dust cleared from all the litigation, it looked like we were back to where we'd started (we each had won one case and were free to fight), but it wasn't all a waste. Internorth was a step behind. Crouse could close the Belden exchange offer the next day, which thwarted Internorth, leaving it to buy both companies or none.

It wasn't a waste in another sense: both cases decided fundamental propositions. The Illinois state appellate court sanctioned behavior that thereafter became quite common, raiders insinuating themselves into an announced deal by offering a better price. And the federal appellate court in New York found that boards of directors had the power to follow their business plans, even if it amounted to an end run around shareholder approval and defeated a favorable offer. These cases were the precedent for Paramount's attempt in 1989 to acquire Time Inc. and for Time's defense: acquiring Warner. Time and Warner had entered into a merger agreement, like Crouse and Belden, providing for Time to acquire Warner for its stock. Paramount tried to break up the deal and relied on Internorth's victory against Crouse in Illinois to make a cash tender offer for Time alone. Time Inc. followed Crouse's strategy by making a cash tender offer for Warner. By acquiring Warner, Time defeated the Paramount bid.

The Crouse contest with Internorth, however, took an additional turn. Since Crouse could close the Belden exchange, Internorth was faced with a very difficult decision. Did it withdraw or did it now offer to buy both Crouse and Belden? Contrary to all our expectations, Internorth announced that it would now go forward and acquire both. Sometimes, I wonder how those decisions are made: from anger and frustration or good business judgment. I could see the frustration and had experienced George Kern's anger. The argument for sensible reevaluation by Internorth was that the merger of Belden and Crouse made sense. Internorth, stretched by the additional cost of the acquisition (purchasing all the new Crouse shares issued to acquire Belden's shares, representing about a 50 percent increase in the consideration required for the purchase), saw an opportunity to take advantage of the situation. Its new offer was $37 per share cash for Crouse, including Belden. Except for a similar gambit by Tom Evans when the target company made a small, frivolous acquisition in an attempt to defeat the Evans bid, none of us could remember a time when the raider lowered its price. If the two companies fit well together, then Crouse should be worth more per share—at least $40—not less. Internorth was seeking, and on the verge of getting, a bargain.

The management at Crouse was despondent. All the defensive actions had worked, but they were fighting a predator more voracious than ever imagined. Crouse, at this stage owning 50 percent of Belden and still in the process of acquiring the other half, now sought a buyer that would be willing to acquire both it and Belden. Crouse's board had to take such action to prevent Crouse's shares from being acquired for an inadequate price. Its defense had turned out to be a burden. How many buyers would do what Internorth was willing to do and acquire both companies? But Crouse's investment bankers, Lazard, were cautiously optimistic. In this heated merger market, if you put out a distress signal, recent experience showed, there was usually another buyer, at a higher price. The ebullience of the eighties had started.

For the Belden shareholders, the decision of Crouse to sell itself (and Belden) offered them a double dip: a premium in addition to the one they had just received from Crouse and a ringside seat at an auction as they waited for the Crouse stock certificates to be delivered to them, ready for sale to the highest bidder. What an introduction to corporate acquisitions! None of us could remember something like this ever happening before.

Finding a buyer for both, however, didn't prove easy. A number of companies considered bidding but then had second thoughts. Cooper Industries, a well-managed Houston conglomerate, finally emerged as interested in acquiring both companies. Cooper had a history of making acquisitions as a White Knight, and all had been successful. In this case, however, Cooper was cautious. It would only offer its stock against Internorth's cash and was concerned about its chances of winning against a cash bid. Also, it faced a determined adversary that had shown resilience.

Cooper's stock was trading at about $60 to $61 a share, and the ratio it offered was a .725 share of Cooper stock for each Crouse share. At the contemplated ratio, Cooper's offer was worth about $44 a share. Cooper's bid would take two or three months to close because it had to be pre-cleared by the SEC. The bid price had to be discounted by the cost of money for the period and for the uncertainty of completing the transaction. These were all serious negatives. Cooper anticipated that on the public announcement of its offer its stock price would decline, that the downward pressure could be severe, and that if its stock fell below $50 its offer would fail. The ratio it proposed was its best price and it wouldn't change it. While Internorth was now offering $37 a share for both companies, it was possible for Internorth to raise to $40 for both (the price it was prepared to pay for Crouse alone), which would probably put it on high ground with a winning bid. Based on a $40 offer by Internorth, Cooper's stock couldn't fall below $55 to be competitive. Such a decline was very likely. Moreover, arbitrageurs prefer cash deals. For them, stock deals are risky transactions requiring them to speculate in two securities, those of the target and those of the acquirer. At comparable prices, the market professionals would choose cash and Internorth.

Realizing the risks, Cooper wanted a leg up, some advantage that would show that it was a wily competitor and had figured out a clear route to the goal line. Corporate prestige was at stake, which Cooper didn't want tarnished, and the perceived risks were bothersome enough to Cooper to raise doubts about the common sense of making the offer. Poised to commit, Cooper drew back.

Cooper asked Skadden Arps and Wachtell Lipton to attend a meeting, seeking our tactical advice. The request immediately made me wary. Cooper and Lehman Brothers, its investment banker, and all their lawyers didn't need us as tacticians or critics. At the meeting, we learned that Lehman Brothers, responsive to Cooper's concerns, had come up with an approach that they thought would drive the deal forward. What they had in mind called for Crouse and Belden to attempt to induce key holders of Crouse and Belden stock to agree to tender to Cooper and not to Internorth. Crouse was a New York corporation, and a two-thirds affirmative vote of the outstanding shares was required to approve any merger transaction. If one-third of Crouse's shares could be tied up in some fashion in favor of Cooper, then Cooper would be willing to be a White Knight. Looking at blocks of stock held by various trusts close to Crouse management, Lehman could only account for about 20 percent of the stock, a significant shortfall. If the plan was to work, arbitrageurs would have to be asked to commit. What Lehman Brothers had in mind required that the lawyers for Belden (Wachtell Lipton) and the lawyers for Crouse (Skadden Arps) call arbitrageurs holding large stock positions in both companies and get them to commit in writing not to tender their shares to Internorth but to tender them to Cooper. The arbitrageurs could be induced to play because their commitment would produce a higher bid than Internorth's offer.

This plan made me supremely uncomfortable. Getting the arbitrageurs to agree to a certain action in advance of making a tender offer had never been done before. Novel ideas aren't always bad, but this one would attract the SEC and get the direct attention of Stanley Sporkin. When carefully thought through, the plan didn't work because a majority of the shares couldn't be found in the hands of a small enough group to be definitively tied up, and therefore it wasn't worth the pain of confronting Stanley. This deal had already inspired cartoons of a series of mindlessly open-mouthed fish of increasing sizes lined up to swallow each other. It didn't need any more attention. If we weren't careful, it would be hard for Stanley to resist an opportunity to lay down restrictive rules for the eighties.

Talking to Cooper, I was unabashedly critical of the plan. So what if one-third of the shares agreed to tender to Cooper; a majority was needed to win. Commitments from one-third of the shares was no more than a push in the right direction. If Cooper's stock price dropped sharply, Internorth would get a majority of the shares. The majority could always force the minority to sell, even if the minority held one-third of the shares. Nothing that we could do would change the rules of corporate warfare. Cooper felt, however, that commitments from arbitrageurs could have a calming

effect on the market and ease some of the downward pressure on
Cooper's stock. There was merit to those claims that my arguments
couldn't fully dismiss. But the benefit was marginal and wasn't
worth the detrimental effect of litigation and government
investigations.

We all agreed to meet on the weekend in Houston, the second
Saturday in November, to discuss the strategy. Waiting for the
weekend, a delay of three days, would allow us all to calm down
and decide which concerns were most important. The meeting was
supposed to begin promptly at 9 a.m. on Saturday at Cooper's
offices. I took an early-morning flight and arrived to find a three-
ring circus already in progress. Cooper intended to make a go or
no-go decision by Sunday, and all related issues were being debated
in concurrent meetings in three different conference rooms. In one
room, investment bankers, financial executives, and accountants
were sifting financial information, recasting projections of earnings
and cash flows. In another, operating executives and engineers were
sorting business data to understand the health of the business and
the benefits of the combination. And in the third, investment bankers and lawyers were analyzing strategic considerations in making
the offer. Senior executives of Cooper participated in each of the
conferences, walking from room to room to assess progress and
problems in each of the sessions. Financial and operating executives
also moved through all the conference rooms being briefed on all
aspects of the deal. In their usual thorough fashion, all the senior
Cooper officers would meet at the end of the day, share their
assessments, express their doubts, and decide. In the third conference room, I was asked to discuss the background of the transaction and evaluate the chances of success against Internorth.
Others also presented their evaluations.

I was told that the presentation would have to be repeated for
the benefit of the other groups and the senior executives. People
walked in and out of the room, however, as if it were a continuous
showing, and no one seemed to have much time to fully focus on
what was said. As new people came in, I would have to give a short
summary and begin anew to bring them current. Often the attentive
people began to lose interest. And so I was never sure that anyone
heard fully all that was said. To be effective, I determined that the

best way to make a presentation that everyone could follow was to use the blackboard and outline all the information there. I was used to this kind of instruction from my regular evening teaching at NYU Law School. From the top left-hand corner down, I detailed all the considerations, making neat rows of information, and juxtaposed critical assessments. Dan Neff, the associate working on the deal with me, reviewed the display to make sure it was complete.

Seeing as well as hearing the message, I believed, would reinforce it: price would determine the outcome. As a corollary, and for emphasis, I firmly said that there was no way to lock up the transaction, the market would decide the winner. At every turn I tried to discourage suggestions that dealing with the arbitrageurs would be an artful way of proceeding. I didn't mention Stanley Sporkin, but my voice carried all the negative overtones of my discomfort.

The other message I gave was the overriding rule for the merger wars: take no notes and avoid leaving a paper trail. Many deals had failed because company executives had written to one another about the competitive advantages of an acquisition, naïvely making the government's antitrust case. The government was not the only one to be feared. A clever adversary can turn unguarded statements to his advantage. In litigation all notes and memos would be discoverable, exposing our doubts and weaknesses. Boldly on the board I wrote: "TAKE NO NOTES," and then added parenthetically for a bit of humor: "(including of this board)."

It was a long day. The meetings went well into the evening. When I left, senior management was just getting together to pool their impressions and make a decision. I returned to New York on the last flight into JFK, arriving well after midnight. My car was at La Guardia Airport, and I took a cab from one airport to the other. At about 1 a.m., I found my car in the La Guardia garage, but it wouldn't start. Someone had stolen my radio and battery. At that hour the airport was closed and deserted, bereft even of cruising cabs. I found a phone, called a taxi service, and finally got home at about 2:30 a.m., tired and debilitated, feeling a cold coming on. More than one meal per day on an airplane is a health hazard, proven innumerable times to me and always ignored.

I was awakened at 7 a.m. on Sunday by a partner at Lehman Brothers who had stayed over in Houston. The energy in his voice was more startling than the ringing phone. Beginning without apology for the early hour (probably he'd showed about fifteen minutes' restraint while waiting for the clock to strike the hour), he had the moral momentum of being in an hour-earlier time zone. Cooper, I was brusquely told, was prepared to go forward but only if it received positive assurances in writing from at least one-third of the shares that they would tender to Cooper. Hardly awake, I may have hesitated too long before protesting. My momentary silence was taken as consent and he began to issue instructions. I sputtered an objection which halted him long enough for me to recount the difficulty of getting agreements and what little effect they would have. My pitiful outcry was peremptorily dismissed. He'd prepared himself.

"This is the only way Cooper will go forward. It's your job to sign up the arbitrageurs."

"Give me a reason, just one, that makes sense," I said, trying to leaven my consternation with a reasonable tone of voice, realizing that I sounded shrill.

"If they agree to tender to us, it expresses a belief in the value of our stock," he said. Cooper and its advisers had come back to the cosmetic benefits of the action rather than the tactical aspects.

"All that the arbs will agree to is that at equal prices they'll prefer the Cooper stock." From their point of view that would induce an auction with little or no risk to them.

"That's enough for Cooper."

One more time, I tried to protest. He would have none of it.

I called Don Drapkin, my counterpart at Skadden Arps, who represented Crouse. I knew him quite well, since he'd been at Cravath during the time I'd worked there. He was knowledgeable, careful, and astute. Years later he went on to become vice chairman of Revlon. I found him at his mother-in-law's house in Bayonne (he'd married his Cravath secretary), and we attempted to devise a form of agreement to be signed by the arbitrageurs. Our solicitation of the arbitrageurs had to be completed in one day, Monday, otherwise there would be leaks. We concluded that we couldn't approach more than nine arbitrageurs, a magic number indicating that the solicitation was select and private. A letter agreement was needed to assure prompt approval. Keeping the letter simple, he and I finally settled on one sentence which said that the arbitrageurs weren't free to tender to Internorth unless the price of the Cooper stock dropped below $50. If Internorth raised its price, the agreement terminated. Drapkin then undertook to get covenants from three trusts holding 20 percent of the Crouse shares and left me to deal with the arbitrageurs.

How to approach the market professionals was the next question. All their names were known, but not their stock positions, and we needed promises from the maximum number of shares held by the fewest number of people. I called Marty Lipton at home on Sunday and explained the situation to him. He called his friend Richard Rosenthal, then the head arbitrageur at Salomon Brothers. Rosenthal had a sizable stock position in Crouse, agreed to participate, subject to his lawyer's approval, and told us which other arbitrageurs to call. Following his lead, I called everyone on Monday morning. All agreed to participate. But first they all wanted approval of the arrangements by their respective legal counsel.

What ensued thereafter was painful. Each arbitrageur had his own lawyer, and each lawyer knew that the arrangements would be painstakingly inspected and vigorously challenged by Internorth (and perhaps by the SEC) as market manipulation. No one liked the letter agreement. Fearful, each had his own approach. My inclination was to agree to whatever each would commit to as a practical solution, but I soon discovered that such a technique wasn't possible. Everyone wanted his own version but also wanted to know what everyone else would do before fully committing. So after I finished with one and went to another, I had to go back to the first, who then wanted to make changes, which meant going back to the second. It was almost impossible to get to the third, let alone to all the others. The more time they spent on trying to reach airtight arrangements in contemplation of a challenge, the more uncomfortable they became with the validity of what we were doing. All this was exhausting and time-consuming. Most of the working morning was over before I concluded that I'd have to go back to the original sentence and insist on no changes.

Starting negotiations with a degree of flexibility and switching to total rigidity is a strategy that defies common sense. What I had going for me was the gamesmanship of the arbitrageurs. They believed that Cooper wouldn't go forward unless it got the affirmation of these agreements, and their lawyers were told to do everything possible to promote the transaction. How could a one-sentence letter prove so difficult to produce?

More was at work, however, than I first realized. All the lawyers wanted to know what Charlie Johnson, representing the arbitrage department of Merrill Lynch, would do. They expected that he would be gun-shy, since he was still appealing his proposed suspension from practice. I'd avoided approaching Charlie early, wanting to get a number of lawyers representing substantial arbitrageurs to agree before talking to Charlie. I also expected that he'd be difficult to deal with, knowing Stanley Sporkin would be watching. Taking any undue risk could affect the commission's attitude toward him and hurt his pending appeal. In his shoes, I'd tread lightly and not too close to the line. If Charlie advised his client not to sign, the others might bolt and run. Indeed, they may have been expecting Charlie to object and were looking for a way out. Without Charlie agreeing, nothing would get done. Reluctantly, I called him.

"What do you think, Charlie?" I asked as he pondered the sentence.

"Stanley's going to bark."

"Do barking dogs bite?" I asked.

"Sometimes." His tone offered slight assurance. As we talked, however, I sensed that he wasn't rejecting the letter agreement. The problems covered by the agreement interested him. "What are the others going to do?" he asked.

"I've told them that there can be no changes in the sentence. They're waiting for you," I said frankly.

"It's one of those days," he said. He was a senior partner and used to people waiting for his opinion.

"Yes," I said.

"Am I wrong to think that the nine arbs can sell their stock to Cooper anytime they want?"

"You're not wrong," I said, responding although it was a rhetorical question.

"Can't they then agree on the terms under which they sell?" He meant pricing and timing terms, if the sales were not immediately made.

"I believe they can. But it can be said their agreement with Cooper influences others to sell to Cooper."

"So does the sale," he said. "Am I missing anything?"

"Not that I know of."

"I'll recommend it to my client," he said.

"Do you want to make any changes?" I asked, impressed with his professionalism.

"I thought there could be no changes."

"I'd like to keep it simple, but if you have any I'll take them."

"It's fine the way it is," he said.

Nine arbitrage firms signed, but we fell short with 30 percent of the shares rather than the 33 percent that Cooper had insisted upon. Close was good enough, and Cooper committed by issuing a press release announcing the exchange offer. Special mention in the press release was given to its arrangements with the 30 percent of the shares held by arbitrageurs and trusts, all with the hope that the agreements would keep its stock price from precipitously dropping.

The predictable reactions followed. Internorth challenged the validity of the contracts in the federal court in Syracuse, and the SEC started an investigation. Ordinarily the Internorth lawsuit would be prosecuted vigorously, and the SEC wouldn't seriously investigate until after the contest was over, leaving the matter for the court and the marketplace. In this case, the SEC immediately began a campaign to invalidate all the agreements, and Internorth waited while the SEC acted.

Characteristically, Stanley said, "This smells. Everything about it smells. Those guys can't do that." Stanley had spoken. We knew that his concern was that the contracts interfered with the free market and he considered that manipulative. Stanley never gave his reasons, but prophets don't need or use justification, argument, or other forms of ratiocination. Their moral force obviates reason. Nevertheless, for the moment, we were satisfied that his fury was empty, for he didn't (and couldn't) point to any broken rules. Even Stanley needed fractures, if only hairline breaks, to claim transgressions; otherwise his exquisite moral sense was merely personal, without the force of his office.

We underestimated him. Ever hardheaded and uncompromising, Stanley worked his will. He called Cooper's lawyers in Texas, told them to come down to his office in Washington. Confronting them, he asked Cooper to release the arbitrageurs from the letters. But he was met with stone-faced silence. So ridiculous a request didn't deserve an answer. Stanley then demanded that they be released and was met with headshaking. Lecturing the lawyers came next: Stanley reminded them that approval of the SEC was required before Cooper could begin its exchange offer. Slowly they understood.

If Cooper couldn't commence its offer with reasonable promptness, it would lose its credibility and Internorth would win. Stanley told them that he'd teach them about bureaucratic murder. The neatly printed exchange offer on fine white paper would yellow from age while they waited for his approval. No court could or would order the SEC to hurry. He didn't have to lecture for very long. Without Stanley's cooperation, Cooper's game was over. The lawyers told Cooper that Stanley had them blocked. Cooper wanted to make the acquisition and had no choice but to agree to drop the agreements. All our work was for nothing.

And Cooper, it turned out, didn't need the contracts. Once it began the exchange offer, its stock price dropped as expected, but the price remained higher than Internorth's bid and Cooper successfully completed the acquisition of Crouse, including Belden. That victory should have been the end of the matter, but Stanley wasn't satisfied. Nasty deals like this with the arbitrageurs could happen again. Continuing his investigation, he called in all the lawyers to take their testimony.

I was served with a subpoena by the SEC and directed to appear at the commission's New York office with all my, and the firm's, records pertaining to the matter. I wasn't prepared for this turn in the investigation. The context was wrong. In every action that I'd taken I thought I'd be fighting to uphold the validity of the agreements, but Cooper had conceded. Stanley had outmaneuvered us all, and there were no principles at stake. What was even more humbling, he was investigating why we'd gone astray, making us targets. The investigative process was now part of our punishment. Bringing or defending a case for a client is the lawyer's role, but being the target in the case is different, not part of our training or emotional expectations. Sitting beside the client doesn't prepare you for being in the client's hide.

At least I hadn't taken any notes. Stanley would have to formulate his own questions, work out his own theories. When the subpoena came I assumed that our files would contain only public documents. I was wrong. Dan Neff, the Wachtell Lipton associate participating with me at every meeting, had made an extensive file. Every question I'd asked him had been recorded. All the legal uncertainties had been followed up with careful research, indicating all the doubts and none of the resolutions. And he had issues of his own, ones more remote than mine, something a cautious and inexperienced person might want to review. All the concentric circles encompassing the problem were documented, showing every aspect of our thinking. Ordinarily, much of the firm's work product would have been protected from the investigator's eye, but Stanley was one step ahead of us. Our client, Belden, had been absorbed by Crouse, which in turn was merged with Cooper, which waived all rights to confidentiality, knowing that it had settled with the SEC and that there would be no claims against it. Whatever we'd thought or had done was fair game. Seeing the file, I knew that my deposition was going to be a long and worrisome one. Looking back over the decision process, all the second thoughts were obvious.

My examiner was Gary Lynch, who subsequently became the head of the Enforcement Division and prosecuted such people as Dennis Levine and Ivan Boesky and Michael Milken. Stanley had brought in the first team. The New York examining room was a small, windowless conference room with a battered table, whose gritty undersurface held the remains of more than one mouthful of gum. The room smelled of other cases, acrid and sour reminders of distress. Gary Lynch sat facing the door, his papers arranged on his side of the table. As soon as I arrived, he locked the door so that we wouldn't be interrupted, retaining, like a valuable fixture, the stuffiness of the room. The stark, straight-back chairs were the final assurance of discomfort. A stenographer sat at the end of the table, equipped with both a stenographic machine and a tape recorder. I'd come with two litigators, who were there to object to questions and to allow only crisp answers. The less said, the better.

Taped to the wall behind Gary Lynch was a large chart, practically blackboard size, which reproduced in full the blackboard that I'd drawn in Houston.

"Where did you get that?" I asked, unguardedly showing my surprise. On the chart, carefully reproduced, was my bold admonition: "TAKE NO NOTES (including of this board)." Lynch smiled evasively, letting me know that he'd be the one asking the questions, gratified by my reaction and satisfied that the subpoena had been effective. Someone from Cooper had taken careful notes, making sure that no word or number was lost. Even without testimonial evidence, Stanley had complete documentation of all that had gone on at the Houston meeting.

Of course, Gary Lynch began his questioning by asking me to explain the blackboard. He had all the time in the world to explore every nuance, more so than anyone attending the meeting. Under such scrutiny, there is no perfection, and even a smooth surface has its burrs. For eight hours he asked piercing questions. Answering carefully, I relived each decision in slow motion. Lynch even had the various drafts of all our false starts in formulating the letter agreement with the arbitrageurs. The care taken by us weighed against us. Each version was a probe, like burglar's tools, looking to make a passage. You could frame a case from our implements and what we'd tried to avoid. My distress added to the corrosive character of the room.

Where was this investigation going to lead? Would we too wind up in disciplinary proceedings just like Charlie Johnson? Would it depend on our answers to the questions? When the deposition was over, Gary Lynch and I shook hands. Interestingly, we'd gotten to appreciate each other. He'd gotten to see what we do. The shared experience, strained as it was, made a bond. I asked, as I felt I could: What did Stanley want? He was direct: Stanley didn't want us to do it again, ever.

Stanley was very effective. It took me almost four years before I tried anything like that again.

▼

CHARLIE JOHNSON'S CASE was decided a month or two later, in February 1982. The commission found in his favor and the case was dismissed. Stanley Sporkin left the SEC when William Casey, the chairman, was appointed to head the Central Intelligence Agency. Stanley became Casey's general counsel and then was appointed to be a federal district court judge in Washington, D.C.

FAMILY BUSINESS

▼

"The alchemy was in leverage."

William Stokely III controlled about 20 percent of Stokely–Van Camp. His great-grandmother and her sons founded the business in 1898. Subsequently his father and then his cousin headed it. The business was started in eastern Tennessee, to grow and can local produce for sale, mainly in the Southeast. In 1933 the company moved its headquarters to Indianapolis after the acquisition of Van Camp's and added the Van Camp name to reflect the business combination. The company, however, remained the Stokely family business. In 1981, at the age of forty-one, Bill Stokely III became the chairman and chief executive officer. The company's products represented three generational innovations: canned foods, frozen foods, and Gatorade. And there was a young William Stokely IV, which told volumes about the family pride and character and its hope for further business development.

I always thought of the company in terms of shades of green, which suggested renewal. From the drab olive of the boiled beans to the electric, almost Day-Glo virescence of Gatorade, the character of the green intensified in each new product. And like the depth of the green, the family commitment to the business also seemed to have strengthened as the stewardship was handed down. Few families in America pass anything along to third and fourth generations and have it respected enough to be preserved and treated like a trust.

Bill Stokely III was short and compact, built to last. Without pretense, he maintained the company's headquarters in an old Indianapolis warehouse building, close to operations, watching costs. Running the company wasn't all duty or bean counting. There was a twinkle in Bill, who had found life-enhancing opportunities in the business. Gatorade required resourceful marketing, which one year justified the company's supporting a car in the Indianapolis 500, the most important sporting event in the city. Thereafter Stokely sponsored a car on the Nascar circuit to increase Gatorade's exposure. Making the company marketing-oriented, Bill also became knowledgeable about dieting and exercise trends, necessary information for him to capture market share for Gatorade. Being sensitive to youthful aspirations, he shared them, which dispelled the stodginess that often seems to come with middle age and running a large business.

In starting the company, the great-grandmother and her sons had controlled it. Over time the company sold stock to finance its growth. In 1935 the company began to trade publicly, and thereafter public ownership became broad enough to list and trade the company's stock on the New York Stock Exchange, evidencing the firm's success. That attainment bore with it a disturbing vulnerability. Bill Stokely's ownership, while substantial, wasn't enough to preclude anybody from buying a controlling stock interest in the open market or making a bid to acquire the whole company.

The company was the last independent, publicly traded canning and food-processing company in the United States. All the others had been folded into larger companies, objects of the conglomeration and consolidation of American industry. Inevitably, Stokely would be acquired. The signs were already there: City Investing, a huge conglomerate, had acquired over 5 percent of the common stock and had publicly filed documents indicating that it might be interested in acquiring control. The company had fought off those advances, paying greenmail, by repurchasing City Investing interest in its stock at a premium price. Another company, called Minas Basin, a private company located in Nova Scotia, had crossed the 5 percent stock-ownership threshold and continued to buy stock with the hope of forcing the company to swap canning assets held in Canada for the recently purchased common stock.

The holders of large blocks of stock were outside agitators for sale of the company. Whether Minas Basin or another would move to acquire the company was unknown, but each incursion put up a "For Sale" sign for the company without its permission. Every time the trading volume in the company's stock rose, new questions stirred as to its fate. It was an uncomfortable position for the management and more so for Bill Stokely. Running the business was part of his birthright, and the thought of losing it was devastating. As a reflective man, there was no limit to the amount of time that he could spend contemplating the possible loss of the company. As a practical man, he sought a sensible answer.

It was the public ownership of about 80 percent of the company stock that took away his ability to control his destiny. The solution to his difficulties had to lie in repurchasing the public stock, but the amount required was well beyond his individual capacity. The money would have to come from the company itself, which meant a leveraged buyout. Once he fixed on the idea, and worked it through, it was captivating. The more he talked about buying the company, the more real it became.

In November 1982, Bill Stokely engaged Goldman Sachs and Wachtell Lipton to consider the possible buyout. We flew out to Indianapolis on a Sunday morning to meet with him in a hotel room so that our activities wouldn't alarm the employees or cause a leak. Most of the morning was productive and we worked through lunch, eating sandwiches in the room. In the afternoon, he turned on the football games to get the scores, and as the camera panned to the benches, he proudly pointed out the Gatorade containers prominently available to all the players.

"The boys have been doing their job," he said, referring to his marketing staff. "We supply it free. Seeing the players drink it is the best advertising." Once the games were on, it was impossible to resume the meeting.

What emerged from the meeting was the idea that in a leveraged buyout Bill Stokely could wind up controlling 50 percent of the company and still realize in cash more than the full current market value of his stock interest. To recite the conclusion was not fully to appreciate it. The result sounded specious, like having your cake and eating it too. To think about it in concrete terms and prove the result, you had to do some simple arithmetic. Bill controlled about 565,000 shares out of the 2.7 million outstanding. The current market price of the stock was $40. If he sold all the shares, he'd realize $22.6 million. That was a lot of money, but selling everything was contrary to his dynastic intentions. He sought to end up in the same position as his great-grandmother and then his grandfather, controlling the company. How, then, could he get more than $22.6 million and own 50 percent when he'd started out by owning only 20 percent?

The alchemy was in leverage. In a leveraged buyout, about 90 percent of the money used to buy the company is borrowed money, and the remaining 10 percent is equity. If Bill Stokely already controlled 20 percent of the company, then he held a sufficient number of shares to supply twice the equity needed. One-quarter of his shares, representing 5 percent of the current ownership of the outstanding shares, would supply half of the equity needed in a leveraged buyout. Accordingly, the other three-quarters, or the 15 percent interest, would be available to be cashed out along with the public shares.

These percentages translated into dollars in the following way: In his contemplated transaction he assumed that he would initially offer $50 a share and be prepared to pay up to $55 a share, for an aggregate cost of about $155 million for all shares, including expenses and the repayment of certain indebtedness of the company. About $15 million would be needed for the equity. At $55, Bill Stokely's 565,000 shares were worth over $31 million, and if he deposited $7.5 million in shares (for half the $15 million equity), he would have more than $23 million in cash remaining. If the banks were prepared to lend $125 million and the insurance companies provided $15 million as subordinated lenders, the deal would work without a hitch, and he would have cash amounting to more than the current market value of his holdings and still own half the company.

Indeed, the arithmetic showed that no matter how much Bill paid for the company, he was always in a position where one-quarter of his stock would purchase 50 percent of the equity and the other three-quarters would be cashed out. The limit on him and the management was in their ability to pay back the debt from the earnings of the business measured against the risk of bankruptcy. The banks and the insurance companies would carefully review the assessment, of course, and set limits on what could be borrowed.

At the end of our meeting that Sunday, we asked if the company plane was available, hoping to avoid the inconvenient commercial flight schedule, and Bill Stokely offered us the use of the aircraft. It was a propeller plane, which made it economical, he told us, and it was very airworthy. Then, as he adjusted his glasses, he informed us that a month earlier the pilot had forgotten to put the wheels down at the point of landing and had ripped off a piece from the bottom of the plane before he realized the error, but the pilot was still able to pull the plane up and get the landing gear down. This incident was supposed to illustrate the plane's safety. Rather than inconvenience the pilots on a Sunday, we chose to go home commercially. On the ride back, we all acknowledged that Bill was gracious and the story about the pilot's blunder well timed.

Single-mindedly, Bill pursued the buyout. The purchase price for the company had to be high enough to discourage others but not so high that it left the company unable to grow. Estimates of debt costs at varying interest rates were made and then matched against projections of income over five- and ten-year periods. From those calculations, all the judgments would be made. The question that had to be addressed in estimating future income was how much could you reduce overhead, if you were a private company rather than a public company. Although Bill Stokely was careful about costs, there was always more that could be done. Was he prepared to run the operations on a leaner basis and cut down on capital costs for a few years? Was he prepared to close down some marginally performing businesses and dispense with all the perquisites that usually come with managing (rather than owning) a public company? In that regard, was he prepared, for example, to eliminate the corporate aircraft? To answer those questions required a hard look at the way the company was being operated.

The analysis sounds dryly mathematical, a variant of cost accounting, but it isn't. A new psychology is required, free from the hindrances of emotional predilections. If competition developed for the purchase of the company, the buyers would be prepared to make radical cuts in direct and indirect overhead. It's difficult to assume the point of view of outsiders, for they are relentless and indifferent to the pain inflicted. Even so, it was possible intellectually for Bill to make the assessment, although he may not have been prepared emotionally to implement all conceivable cuts in expenses. On the emotional side, there's always the desire to leave some cushion so that the stresses of leverage can be absorbed.

Before undertaking the buyout, Bill Stokely had to be reasonably sure that he could win. Looking at various models for purchasing the company, it was fair to conclude that he had an edge over anyone trying to buy the company on the basis of the company's own earnings and assets. His advantage was that he owned a significant amount of stock and could afford to pay more than a full price because he didn't need a high return on his investment. Financial buyers like KKR and others aggressively doing leveraged buyouts in the last few years would recognize his advantage. Reasonably, then, he needn't expect competition from them.

What about corporate conglomerates interested in a new business opportunity? Could he compete against them? The simple answer was that no one had approached him or any of his board members about buying the company. That said a lot, but not everything. If Bill Stokely offered to buy the company, and the price he offered was deemed to be fair, then the company was for sale at any higher price. There were probably some companies that would like to buy the company but weren't prepared to make an offer unless invited. If the company was for sale, those buyers might step forward. There was no way of knowing the extent of the interest, and the risk was significant. Could a corporate buyer pay more? Of course. The corporate buyer could borrow against its own assets as well as those of the company to support a higher price. But the answer wasn't conclusive. Another question had to be asked. If the buyer significantly leveraged to effect the sale, what would it earn? The $55 price would require all the cash flow of the company, more than the current earnings, to service the debt and would be detrimental to the earnings of the corporate buyer, unless the buyer was very large. Most corporations, committed to reporting consistently higher earnings each quarter, would find the acquisition cost unattractive.

That analysis was comforting, but again it wasn't the final answer for Bill. There was a class of corporate buyer that might be interested anyway, despite the lack of earnings necessary to support the high price that the company would command—namely, strategic buyers, companies that needed or wanted the assets of Stokely–Van Camp because they would extend their product base, or companies currently not in the business but who regarded it as related or as a good business into which to expand. Were there any? Probably, but not many. Would any come forward? That was the most difficult question and everything hinged on it. The answer was that it was possible, but not likely, because there was a potent deterrent on Bill Stokely's side: his name was on the door. It wasn't as if he were buying it as a stranger, some Johnny-come-lately who could see that there was a profit to be made here. There had to be enough honor left in the business community to respect the legitimacy of family business interests, to treat the business as if it weren't for sale to the highest bidder. I believed that sentiment in favor of family businesses existed—especially in the Midwest, where the most likely bidders would be based. The Stokely family name and continuing management should dissuade people from raiding the company. That was a warm feeling. Those kinds of impressions, however, never fully dissipate the chill of risk.

Fifty dollars a share was chosen as the starting price, leaving the ability to raise by $5.00. The trading room was to put Bill Stokely in a position to satisfy any demands of the independent directors for more money. It was inevitable that they would seek a price higher than the one first offered in order to fulfill their role of representing the interests of the public shareholders. That kind of accommodation had to be taken into account in the initial pricing, and there was room to go to $55. To initiate the process, Bill

Stokely announced the buyout at the end of November 1982. The work of the committee of independent directors assessing the fairness of the offer would span about three weeks, and it was anticipated that after three or four weeks the committee would report to the board that the price wasn't satisfactory and the negotiation would begin. The committee hired its own independent investment banker, Dillon, Read & Co., and regular company counsel, Lord, Day & Lord, acted as the counsel for the independent directors.

To our surprise, before the committee rendered its report, Central Soya (a midwestern food-processing company) called Bill Stokely and told him that they were interested in acquiring the company at $55 a share. That was the first indication that outside third parties would step into the process. From the way Central Soya's proposal was voiced, however, it aimed to do a friendly transaction: it wouldn't publicly state its interest if the bid was opposed by the management. Since Bill Stokely was prepared to offer $55, Central Soya's bid would be matched, and it wasn't considered a contender. After the initial surprise, Central Soya's approach was a comfort. It confirmed that the pricing was reasonable and that there was a reluctance on the part of third parties to try to break up the family-sponsored buyout.

Bill Stokely raised the offering price to $55, and at the end of January 1983 the committee of independent directors, acting on the advice of its adviser, endorsed it as fair. Then Goldman Sachs began its work of putting together the financing for the transaction, which would take between thirty and sixty days. Thereafter, the buyout would be presented to the stockholders for their approval, which required an additional thirty days. During that period, the company was in its most vulnerable position. Any new proposal from any source at a higher price couldn't be ignored. The only way to counter a higher price was to find more money to top it. While Bill Stokely could possibly stretch to $60, anything more put the company at great financial risk in the event of a downturn in the economy.

The first indication that Central Soya wasn't the only interested party came from increased activity in the Stokely stock at the end of February and the beginning of March 1983, while financing was being arranged. The rising trading volume meant that somebody was accumulating stock, buying on rising prices to induce more sellers into the marketplace. It was like hearing the pounding of hooves without being able to see the horse or rider. Finally, Esmark, a Chicago-based conglomerate, filed a schedule with the SEC publicly stating that it owned over 6 percent of the shares of Stokely (168,000 shares purchased at prices ranging from $53 to $55) and that it was considering acquiring Stokely. Goldman Sachs then got a call from Esmark Corporation—from the chairman himself, Don Kelly.

Kelly wanted to talk, and we met with him and his chief financial officer in Chicago, knowing that it wasn't going to be a pleasant session. It was an afternoon meeting, but Bill Stokely looked like it was well past midnight. He'd had a sleepless night and was tense. Kelly tried to treat the meeting as a routine event, but he didn't relax any more than Stokely. Kelly was a rotund, fastidious man who had alert eyes and looked like he spent most of his time searching for deals. Bill Stokely's tenseness made Kelly guarded, and he seemed to choose his words carefully. He took some time to put on a show about having the economic muscle to buy the company, which meant that something else was on his mind. Fairly soon, however, he got to the point. Nothing about Stokely fit into the immediate thrust of Esmark's businesses, but Kelly saw that there was growth potential in the marketing of Gatorade. He liked the company, he said, and he didn't want to lose his investment to the management when they bought the company. With those words he introduced the idea of his becoming a partner.

Kelly was an able businessman who saw an opportunity that he felt entitled to explore. After a tense start, his performance had been adept and efficient, although as the meeting wore on, he again appeared to become unsettled. Insinuating oneself into the middle of a transaction wasn't novel, but it was something tried only in the last few years. Kelly's midwestern sensibility hadn't deterred him, but it may have contributed to his discomfort. His proposal was met with a frigid stare from Bill Stokely. In response, Kelly drummed his fingers on the conference-room table and said, "We can play hardball or softball. It's up to you." His face flushed with anger as his fingers continued to beat on the table, filling the silence.

"We've heard the hardball," Bill finally said. "What's the softball?"

"No, no," Kelly responded. "That's the softball. The hardball is I buy the company or I sell my position to somebody else who will buy it." His fingers relaxed now that he'd fully articulated his position. "We'd like to be friends," he said. "We want to be co-investors. That's the softball."

None of the choices was pleasant. No one had thought of Kelly as a partner, particularly in this case where all the partners had been hand-selected. The limited few that were to participate were Bill Stokely himself, the operating management, and certain financial institutions. But Bill Stokely was defenseless, and there was no choice except to negotiate. At that moment Bill was put in the position of trading an interest in his heritage, something few of us have experienced. To remain in the room took a strong stomach and a sure sense of what's important.

"What percentage are you looking for?" Bill asked.

Kelly didn't hesitate: "Twenty-five percent."

That was a large interest: it would force a significant reallocation, even cause some participants to be dropped, since Bill Stokely wanted to hold control, more so now, if Kelly's company, Esmark, would be participating.

"Something less would be easier to deal with," Bill said. Now that he was fully involved, the strain seemed to have eased.

"I'm firm," Kelly responded.

"I can see that," Bill said without humor. He paused, and before committing himself, said, "I'd like you to invest $15 million in subordinated debt of the company." It was a bold move on Bill's part. Subordinated debt, the financing junior to the bank loans (later known as junk bonds), usually came from insurance companies at that time. If Kelly furnished the money, Stokely could get it on better terms than customary since Kelly wasn't a pure lender and would take into account his equity return in determining the rate on the debt.

"You're increasing my commitment," Kelly said.

"That helps get the deal done," Bill said. Kelly nodded, indicating he would furnish the additional funds. They then talked about the terms of the subordinated debt and reached an agreement satisfactory to Bill. Before everything was settled, Bill said, "I assume you'll agree not to buy any more shares. And not sell your shares to anyone else."

Kelly said, "I can't agree to all of that. I won't buy, but I have to be free to sell my shares if someone makes a tender offer."

"Then you have an option," Bill said, disturbed. Kelly was positioned to take the benefit of the deal if he wanted it or sell out at a higher price to someone else if a hostile bid was made.

"That's what I want," Kelly said flatly. He knew the power of his position, and exercised it. "There probably won't be another bid," Kelly added.

"What do we get?" Bill asked, more for the sake of embarrassing Kelly than as an inquiry.

"You get . . ." Kelly began, and then stopped, his eyes hardening. He pursed his lips, choosing his words carefully. "You probably get us as a partner."

Kelly wouldn't budge, and Bill agreed to the terms. When the meeting was over, Bill shook hands with his new partner, giving no hint of distress. Like all good businessmen, he curbed his personal feelings.

Once the deal was cut with Don Kelly, we all thought we saw the finish line. We prepared definitive financing arrangements, including those required with Kelly. Just about the time we cleared our disclosure material with the SEC and were about to sign with the banks, Don Kelly balked at requirements set by the banks that Esmark not sell its shares in Stokely until the bank debt was more than half paid down. Kelly wanted Esmark to have complete control over its investment. Neither the banks nor Kelly would change their position. Kelly had Esmark withdraw as an investor in the buyout. The withdrawal occurred at the beginning of May, two months after the original handshake with Bill Stokely. While Kelly stated publicly that he would support the buyout, he qualified his support by adding: as long as it continued to be the highest-priced alternative. The failure to bring Kelly along cost a month, the time it took to find substitute financing with an insurance company. Finally, at the beginning of June, a shareholder meeting was set for July: the buyout would get done about nine months after it had first started.

Again the finish line was in sight. But in the third week of June, Pillsbury contacted Stokely about making an offer to acquire the company. Bill met with William Spoor, Pillsbury's chief executive officer. Spoor indicated that Pillsbury was prepared to pay $62 a share. Nothing Bill Stokely said could dissuade him. That meeting wasn't the last word. Bill Stokely's arguments were taken up at the Pillsbury board meeting by John Whitehead, then co-chief executive officer (along with John Weinberg) of Goldman Sachs. He was on the board of directors of Pillsbury and came to a regular meeting to find on the agenda the proposed takeover of Stokely–Van Camp. Before that meeting they had never hinted to him of the contemplated takeover.

Because of his firm's involvement in the buyout of Stokely, Whitehead was told that he wouldn't be permitted to participate in the Pillsbury board's consideration of the proposed tender offer. He objected, and the board gave him an opportunity to be heard at the outset of the meeting. An articulate and polished speaker, Whitehead told the board that even if his firm wasn't representing Stokely, he'd have objected to this takeover. As a matter of principle, he was opposed to hostile takeovers. In this case, the Stokely family involvement in the business counseled against any hostile interference with a reasonable transaction. The Pillsbury board, largely Midwesterners, listened politely, asked no questions, and dismissed him when he was finished. Then they met without him.

In the Pillsbury board's view, Stokely had been put up for sale and was underpriced. Gatorade was the attraction for Pillsbury, a high-profit-margin product that could benefit from its marketing expertise and access to shelf space in the supermarkets. Why shouldn't Pillsbury bid and give the Stokely shareholders a reasonable alternative? Considered from a market perspective, it would be wrong for them not to bid and take the opportunity for Pillsbury's shareholders. In their view the offer wasn't hostile or even uninvited, since the company was for sale. And so, if there had ever been an exception for family transactions, it was overridden. A free market admits to no impediments.

Immediately after the board meeting the tender offer was announced, assuring speed and surprise. The swift action freed John Whitehead from the totally uncomfortable position of knowing about an imminent takeover affecting a client that, as a matter of law, he couldn't talk about. In the disclosure of the tender, Pillsbury was careful to state that Esmark, formerly part of the Stokely buyout group, had sold out to Pillsbury for $62.

No one on Bill Stokely's team had ever contemplated paying $62 per share. The question for Bill Stokely was whether he could compete with Pillsbury's price. What number would best Pillsbury? Obviously, Pillsbury had more in its pocket. Pillsbury probably could bid as much as $65 or even $68. The next plateau was $70. Could the company pay $70 for itself? The decision wasn't Bill Stokely's alone. The banks would have to go along with him and so would the insurance companies. He'd have to show unequivocally that the company could service the additional debt, which, for a $15 per share increase, amounted to a raise of approximately $45 million, of which $40 million would be additional debt. The management recomputed the financial information assuming various purchase-price levels. Everyone was eager to find a clear path to competing. What they found was that the company couldn't bear as much as $60 from its own resources. The lenders wouldn't lend more and the management didn't feel comfortable taking on the risks. Bill Stokely had to acknowledge that he'd been outbid.

We had a short meeting at our offices to consider alternatives. There was no basis for attempting to remain independent, because the Stokely board of directors had already concluded that the company should be sold and that $55 was a fair price. All the board could do was seek a higher price. Bill Stokely understood the position of the board. No one said anything to him about having to sell, however, leaving him to utter the words. He was entitled to speak first. His compact shoulders heaved as he bore the weight of the decision and its consequences. "Okay, let's sell it," he said. "That's the only alternative." With that, he turned to Goldman Sachs and told them to see if they could find a higher bid. The best buyer was now someone that, like Pillsbury, was looking for a chance to extend its product base. Such a company would have its own management and wouldn't retain Bill Stokely.

Goldman Sachs and Bill Stokely held an auction, and Quaker Oats was the high bidder at $77. Ira Harris, the Chicago-based deal maker for Salomon Brothers, had done most of the preparatory work of convincing Quaker to step in after the announcement of the Pillsbury tender. When Goldman Sachs called, Quaker was ready to discuss price, prepared by Ira Harris to make a preemptive bid that would discourage all other players. Once Pillsbury made a hostile tender, Harris knew that Stokely would seek the highest price. On Quaker's announcement of $77, Pillsbury withdrew its bid, acknowledging defeat.

The $77 price, startling when compared with the $55 price originally found fair, engendered public criticism of the Stokely insiders. They were charged in national business and legal publications with trying to take the company from the public shareholders at a low price. The charge was made without understanding that the company wasn't being purchased by Bill Stokely and the management to be resold for a profit and without appreciating that bootstrap acquisition prices are limited. Nevertheless, the sale of Stokely came to be accepted into common wisdom as showing that management buyouts take advantage of inside information and that enormous profits are made by the groups that buy out companies. At the same time Stokely proved the contrary: that it isn't possible to buy a company at a bargain price, since someone will always take it away from the bargain hunter. It took another three years to find a structure that resolved the contradictions. But after Stokely, no one could have any illusions about the values of the marketplace.

KEEPING PEACE

▼

*Experts have the assurance of ready
answers and closed minds.*

Stokely had tested the limits of leveraged buyouts by management, and its lesson didn't need renewal. So in 1985 when representatives of Multimedia, headquartered in Greenville, South Carolina, told me that they wanted to do a buyout, I recited all the difficulties to them in exhaustive detail. Countless times before I'd listed the obstacles. Rote telling had apparently made my rendition pale, and nothing I said discouraged them. I decided that more graphic details were needed, loss of job and station, the corporate equivalent of blood. Vigorously and with passion, I used my best material. Still, they stood their ground. What were they seeing?

The only situation that justified attempting a buyout, I told them, was the one in which management faced a hostile tender offer for control, and the company had to be sold. Buying the company in that situation was trying to save it. If the attempted purchase failed, management was no worse off. Trying the buyout at any other time was foolhardy. I avoided using stronger words, although I was tempted.

Wilson Wearn, chairman of the board, headed the management team, and he was accompanied by David Freeman, counsel to the company. They were a study in contrasts. Wilson, the older man, was thin and quick and decisive, while David Freeman was a large bearish man, slow-moving, as if every step and turn were thought through. Freeman, once his mind turned the matter over, was equally decisive. They were of one mind on these matters, having worked out all aspects before coming North to deal with strangers. Wilson Wearn was a thoughtful and proud man who had a vision for Multimedia: he wanted it to grow independently and remain in Greenville. Multimedia was a diversified communications company, operating largely in the Sun Belt. It published ten daily and twenty-nine nondaily newspapers, owned and operated television and radio stations, ran more than a hundred cable television franchises, and syndicated television programming, including the Phil Donahue show.

There was depth of management in the company and its prospects were excellent. Wilson Wearn and David Freeman feared that it would become, like many fine companies, a victim of the takeover frenzy. They didn't like my attitude because it was unexpected. I'd become an obstacle for them. Multimedia's circumstances were different from Stokely's, they told me. And the time was ripe for a buyout.

I explored the differences. Four families (the Peace, Jolley, Furman, and Sisk families from Greenville, South Carolina) owned about 42 percent of Multimedia's stock, a powerful block that excluded others from control. That was the principal point of departure from Stokely that made a strategic difference.

Would the families, I asked, be prepared to buy an additional 9 percent of the shares to get to 51 percent? The answer was that the families were sellers of stock and couldn't be expected to buy additional shares. What's more, the families didn't participate in the management of the business. They were a loose confederation at best, willing only to get together in a transaction like a buyout that would make their holdings liquid, expecting for all the families about $300 to $350 million from the deal. From that information,

I concluded that the 42 percent block of stock was insufficient to exclude someone else from getting control. Nothing less than owning a majority assured control.

What about, they asked, using the corporation's money to buy back shares from the public if someone else attacked Multimedia before the buyout was completed?

That was a thoughtful question. If Multimedia repurchased about 16 percent of its outstanding shares, thereby reducing the outstanding number of shares, the families' ownership would increase to a majority. But the quick answer was that the approach wouldn't work. In a leveraged buyout transaction, the family members would be relegated, along with management, to the status of bidders. The corporation would be in the hands of independent directors appointed to evaluate all offers. If a competing bidder made a more favorable proposal, the independent directors would have to favor the better bid, irrespective of any sentiment toward the various founding families and the management. Corporate money wouldn't be permitted to purchase shares and defeat the competing bid.

There was, however, they told me, another element that favored a buyout. They were impatient with me now. Multimedia was a South Carolina corporation, and a merger required a two-thirds vote. The four families acting together held more than one-third of the shares and had a veto over any merger, putting them in a position that certainly barred others.

Again, I examined the assertion. The veto, while imposing-looking, worked only if the families were prepared to continue to hold their shares. If a raider bought a majority of the shares, then the families would lose their representation on the board. With no voice in corporate affairs, they'd find that the majority stockholder had cut the dividend, shutting off economic benefits, much like an embargo. Inevitably, the families would capitulate and sell. There was no effective veto.

Looked at realistically, I told them, announcing a leveraged buyout was attempting to bluff everyone into thinking that the families would buy additional shares up to 51 percent of Multimedia stock and would stick together. While 42 percent looked formidable, it wasn't much different from Bill Stokely's 20 percent interest. Knowledgeable advisers to a raider would see all the vulnerabilities.

For those advisers the only question would be whether the families were prepared to spend their own cash for additional shares, and they would test that proposition. If the raider worked at gathering intelligence, it would be able to pull enough information together to know that the families would collapse under pressure. Someone on the raider's side would know one or more members of the various families and there are no secrets. Even if the families were tight-lipped, after the first two probing moves in the game, all the other turns would be known. After the probing moves, family advisers would have to tell the family members not to wait for the embargo, subjecting their shares to substantial price discounts, and all defenses would collapse.

Was there any way to arrange the pieces in the game so that the positions would be better? The answer was no. The state of the art hadn't advanced since Stokely.

"What about the so-called poison pill?"

Martin Lipton had recently conceived and developed the "poison pill," which was a major and innovative advance in takeover defense. The pill worked by giving shareholders a right to buy shares at half price in the event of hostile purchases of the target's stock, a right that the raider couldn't acquire. It was novel at the time, and controversial. Only at the end of 1985 did the Delaware Supreme Court validate the defense technique in a case involving Household International. But Multimedia's objectives, a buyout of the public, rendered the device unavailable to it and the management.

Just when I thought I'd discouraged them, they turned the question around on me. Was there anything to be gained by announcing a buyout?

It depended, as always, on what you wanted. For the family members who weren't involved in the management, the buyout offered enticing opportunities. If the buyout was successful the families would wind up owning approximately one-third of the outstanding shares (while pulling out of the company approximately $350 million). That result would be achieved by setting up a new company in which they would take their desired ownership position, while selling their Multimedia shares, along with the public, to that company. If a higher offer was made by a third party, they could cash out their entire stock position at a price in excess of the buyout price, perhaps $400 million or more. Announcing a buyout was an invitation to an auction, with the families prospering in all events. But for the management, it was a significant risk. Winning, management would acquire a hefty stock position of 15 to 20 percent with job security equivalent to tenure. Losing, they would be replaced. Losing was more likely than winning.

What management currently faced, however, was immediate erosion of control, they told me. Various family members were looking to sell their stock. As their aggregate interests fell below 40 percent, the illusion of control would disappear. And it wouldn't be long before the sales of stock reduced ownership to less than one-third. Selling shares couldn't be contained, because everyone needed some cash. Once anyone got a good price, others would be induced to sell, and there would be no stopping the flow. Control would be lost in a year or two at the most. This situation was the direct opposite of Stokely's. From that perspective, the risks associated with a buyout weren't great. Indeed, they knew what they were doing and brought me around.

Shortly after our meeting and before everyone was fully prepared, the volume of stock buying in Multimedia increased sharply on rising prices, which indicated a possible leak of the proposed buyout. I counseled prompt action, and on the first morning of active speculation, I tried to get the company to close down stock trading. But the company wouldn't act without talking to Dot Ramsaur, a member of the Peace family, who spoke for all the founding families. Southern sensibility was at work. Good manners, I was told, required prior notification to Dot before any action, regardless of the exigencies. And then, to my dismay, no one would call Dot before 3 p.m. My arguments for an earlier call were ignored in favor of the human dimension, the scope of which I couldn't fathom. My Southern gothic musings were ended when I was told that Dot suffered from back problems, which gave her sleepless nights and made her a late riser. Only late in the day, after the market closed, did they speak to Dot and get her approval. For the first time I had an intimation that Wilson Wearn and David Freeman were only a part of the leadership team.

Three years after Stokely, in mid-1985, Multimedia announced its leveraged buyout, with the price eerily like Stokely's, about $55 a share, part cash and part subordinated debt, now widely known as junk bonds. But I didn't bother myself about reminders of failed deals. If there was to be a confrontation with a competing bidder, it would happen soon enough. The antagonist would wait until the buyout price had been found to be fair by the independent directors. Knowing that an ambush was likely didn't make the preparatory work easy, but I lived with my misgivings.

After the announcement, I was invited to Greenville to meet with Dot Ramsaur and members of the founding families at Dot Ramsaur's home. The meeting, of course, would be late in the afternoon. I didn't know what to expect. A few years before, a lawyer in Columbia, South Carolina, had driven me into the countryside surrounding Columbia to show me the foundation of an old mansion belonging to his family that had been burned by General Sherman on his march to the sea in 1865.

"That's what you Yankees did to us," he said. "My family's never been the same." I had to explain to him that although I might seem to him to be a representative New Yorker, I couldn't take even remote responsibility for his family's woes since I was a first-generation American. But for him, I was still a Yankee.

What I found in Greenville was that the considerable wealth of the families was largely locked up in Multimedia. Dot's house was a modest brick colonial, much like you would find in suburban New Jersey. The living room was barely large enough to accommodate representatives of the Peace family (by far the largest stockholders), which produced about thirty people. Dining-room chairs had been brought into the living room and set up in rows to give everyone a seat, and I at first had a sense of being present at an old-fashioned Tupperware party, and then at a makeshift adult education class. Dot Ramsaur was the instructor and I was a guest speaker. She ran a disciplined meeting. People raised their hands when they had questions and wanted to be recognized, and the young people deferred to their elders. They asked me to go over the timing of the transaction and the risks. There was no doubt that they wanted to unlock the treasure from the company, especially to alleviate pressure from the young people. Dot Ramsaur was gentle and kind and shrewd, wanting to take care of everyone's

needs, which the money would do. After the meeting we went into
the library for tea and pimento cheese sandwiches on thin, crust-
free white bread. I felt a long way from home, but was treated like
family. Dot, I found out later, had community concerns and interests. Contemplating a successful deal, she would make arrangements with Betty Stall (another Peace family leader), all with David
Freeman's help, to assess the Peace family members for a substantial contribution toward a performing arts center in downtown
Greenville across the street from Multimedia's offices.

Soon after the family meeting, the committee of independent
Multimedia directors approved the $55 bid. Within days, William
Simon, timing his actions perfectly, thereafter made a bid for Multimedia on behalf of his company, Wesray, at $60 a share. Wesray,
formed to do leveraged deals, had experienced great success in the
buyout of Gibson Greeting Cards in 1982. Gibson had been purchased by Wesray from RCA in a leveraged buyout for about $80
million. Only eighteen months later, Wesray sold Gibson in a public
offering of its stock for about $290 million. That quick turnover
and remarkable gain got Wesray a lot of backers. Drexel Burnham
would be acting as Wesray's banker and would finance the Multimedia takeover. As Simon intended, Wesray's bid halted all progress on management's buyout. But even before management could
put pen to paper to see if they could raise their price, Lorimar
Pictures made a copycat proposal, duplicating Wesray's offer in
all respects except the per share price: Lorimar upped it to $62.
Both bids were invitations to the independent Multimedia directors
to negotiate. Lorimar said that it too would be backed by Drexel
Burnham.

None of us had ever seen competing bidders backed by the same
investment banker. Why were they stepping all over each other?
Bill Simon belatedly met with us and attempted to explain. Drexel
would act for anyone making a deal with Multimedia. Wesray was
prepared to acquire Multimedia only on a friendly, negotiated basis. Drexel had its doubts about whether Wesray would be able to
convince management to do such a transaction. Lorimar, on the
other hand, had told Drexel that, if necessary, it would make a
hostile tender offer. Simon smiled broadly and said that with management's cooperation he could negotiate a better deal than Lori-

mar could offer. He made Lorimar the common enemy, and before our eyes repositioned himself as a White Knight. He seemed to have forgotten that he'd initiated the hostile takeover bidding.

What we'd seen exposed, as if the lights in the theater had been turned on too soon, was the raw machinery of Michael Milken's business. As head of Drexel Burnham's junk-bond operation, he was the force behind the firm. Not until 1984 had Milken sought to finance mergers with his junk bonds. Subordinated debt had been used in the early leveraged buyouts, the source for such financing being insurance companies. Once Milken turned to financing mergers, he displaced the insurance companies as direct suppliers of the debt and they ultimately began buying the bonds from Milken, leaving him to originate the loans. This bid for Multimedia was early for Milken in the merger field, and while he was very formidable, all his deftness hadn't yet been developed. Before mergers, he'd furnish capital to ventures that couldn't raise money from banks or in the public debt markets where the bonds most readily bought were usually investment grade, rated as such by rating agencies like Moody's or Standard & Poor's. Working with small companies, Milken had developed a loyal following and a network of savings and loan and insurance companies and managers of pension funds and investment companies as well as other institutions investing money. Their attraction was to the high yields on the bonds and the conviction that the yields more than compensated for the risk of default.

Calling the debt instruments that Milken dealt in "junk" was no accident. He preferred calling them "high yield" securities, but junk (if not garbage) they were because most of the securities industry disdained dealing in weak securities from third-rate companies. Drexel Burnham was a third-tier investment banking firm, without clout. The firm entered the marketplace by functioning where it could, shouldered out of better opportunities by stronger competitors like Goldman Sachs, Morgan Stanley, First Boston, and Salomon Brothers. The debt instruments of once strong companies that had fallen on hard times were known as "fallen angels" and then just "junk." In that marketplace for junk bonds, largely without competition, Milken made Drexel Burnham the major player and then lifted it into the first rank of investment banks.

Milken was a man in the service of an idea: that junk was gold because a balanced portfolio of junk bonds yielded better returns over time than any other debt. He had a book which stated that conclusion, *Corporate Bond Quality and Investor Experience* by the economist W. Braddak Hickman, an analysis of all U.S. bonds issued from 1900 to 1943. Junk in Milken's hands became special, accumulating new meaning from his commitment, as he extended the boundaries of the term "junk" to include subordinated debt of good companies.

Milken was able to cultivate interest in the junk debt because savings and loan companies were competing with banks and money market mutual funds to capture deposits based on the interest rates they offered. The savings industry and the insurance industry had become highly competitive, and high-yield junk bonds helped aggressive savings institutions offer attractive yields to their customers and enabled insurance companies to offer favorably priced insurance products to theirs. Once these savings institutions and insurance companies found junk debt as a way to get a competitive edge, they became "junkies," needing high-yield securities to stay in business. The need Milken created gave him substantial power. But despite a large network of institutions committed to these high-yield securities, Milken and Drexel Burnham were outsiders, without the clients necessary to participate in the merger market. Their corporate clients didn't fit the profile of target companies and were not capable of acquiring large companies. Milken sought, and found, entrepreneurs who had some success in making acquisitions, such as T. Boone Pickens, who in 1984 made a bid to acquire Gulf Corp.; Nelson Pelz, who acquired National Can; Ronald Perelman, who took over Revlon; and William Farley, who outbid Don Kelly for Northwest Industries. For target companies, Milken often looked to those that were in the process of doing a transaction, such as Multimedia. What Milken was doing was selling companies he'd never seen because he could arrange financing from institutions. By placing junk bonds he could get as fees for his firm as much as 6 percent of the principal amount of the bonds plus a portion of the equity of the company being acquired. Also, he could demand and get the merger advisory fees paid to investment banking firms. The upstart Milken had positioned himself so that he didn't need large corporate clients, and the merger market had become his playground, like the various oceans for freebooters of an earlier time. After 1984, few takeover transactions did not involve Milken in some direct or indirect way.

His presence was so potent, and the fear he engendered in the corporate community so real, that Martin Lipton chose not to represent him (leaving that to Joe Flom of Skadden Arps and a host of other takeover firms). Opposing Milken positioned Wachtell Lipton as primarily a defense firm. The choice was not a necessary one. Skadden Arps flourished representing both sides. But limiting representation to target companies was a choice that Goldman Sachs had made years earlier, and it had proved very profitable for them, expanding their defense business. The early decision of Lipton to say that the firm would not join with Skadden Arps in raids (remaining available for the corporate target) had also proved very successful and encouraged Lipton to reject Milken and his firm as clients. When the poison pill defense was developed by Lipton and validated by the courts at the end of 1985, just about the time Milken had become a factor in the marketplace, Wachtell Lipton's place as the premier defense firm was assured.

We now had our Multimedia board game set up with all the players positioned and the anticipated problems ready for confrontation. If the families and management didn't come forward with a better price than Lorimar, the independent directors would be obligated to negotiate with the high bidder. Even if the families stated that they weren't prepared to sell their shares and refused to negotiate with either bidder, that stated position would induce a hostile tender offer. If Lorimar announced a tender, in my view all family resistance would collapse. The only thing that hadn't been foreseen was the names of the contestants.

We called a meeting at our firm to work out a counterstrategy. Wilson Wearn, David Freeman, and members of management came to our offices for the session. For them the higher bids were storm warnings, signs of impending disaster. They were looking to navigate through this dirty weather. To me the situation was one in which there was no chance of winning. The course they should follow was to sell the company. Attempting to defeat higher bids through litigation or other tactics would only waste precious time.

The Greenville contingent complained about the structure of the transaction and not our imminent failure. On their minds was criticism of friends in Greenville shut out from participating in the leveraged buyout. Multimedia had started in Greenville, and there was a significant shareholder population locally. What management and the families had heard at home was that there was no reason for the four families to get a different deal, and a better one besides. Everyone should be treated equally. Why did they have to sell out to the families and a group of New York investors? Various family members had pooled their information and found that the local stockholders had been uniformly harsh and insistent in their condemnation.

For me this criticism was totally irrelevant. It was elementary to me that the leveraged buyout structure couldn't accommodate friends and friends of friends. The purpose of the transaction was to cash out all the public stockholders. Then the risks of high leverage would be borne by a small group of sophisticated investors. But somehow the Greenville group seemed to think that the buyout could go forward despite the bids from Wesray and Lorimar. That was where the failure of communication lay. Although I didn't want to explain the limits of the buyout structure, I would have to do just that. We were so far apart in our thinking that it would take a full day to explain the difficulties we faced. Had I gone wrong at the first meeting? Hadn't I described precisely this impasse when I told them about all the risks? Higher bids always win. Why did they want to tinker with the structure when it couldn't work?

Everyone took coffee and Danish from the sideboard, and fueled with refreshments, they ignored my consternation. They wanted me to listen to them. The outcry of their friends had been enough of a reproach to deeply affect them and the families. They all had to have a chance to express themselves. Only when they had fully vented their concerns would we be able to get back to the real issue: a $55 bid wouldn't be able to defeat a $62 tender offer. The committee of independent directors would take the sale of Multimedia away from the families and sell it to the highest bidder.

I listened—nodding politely, annoyed at our cross-purposes. Wilson Wearn and David Freeman thought that they were addressing my problem—that $55 was not as good as $62. People in

Greenville don't care, they told me. They would take $55 if they could also reinvest in Multimedia like the families. I knew that the simple and irrefutable answer was: "They can't." The leveraged buyout structure was as tight and as demanding as a sonnet. There was a strict limit to the number of investors in the same way that there was a set number of lines in a sonnet. If you changed it, you had something else. I was short with them, filled with the ardor of my own expertise. Experts have the assurance of ready answers and closed minds.

They didn't care if they changed the form. "Leveraged buyout" was a Wall Street term. I could hear Dot Ramsaur saying that. My off-the-rack answer was that everybody in Greenville couldn't be satisfied. Otherwise, there wouldn't be a buyout. The essence of the transaction was the people would be bought out. The incontrovertible truth of the proposition was right in the name— "leveraged buyout."

Taking a new tack in a further effort to be convincing, I reassessed the shareholder base for them. What percentage of the Multimedia stock do you think is held in Greenville by people other than the founding families? About 15 percent, I was told, in the hands of about a hundred or more people. With the founders' 42 percent, another 15 percent was a very hefty percentage—enough to block a tender offer, but not sufficient to buy out the rest of the company. For that, a two-thirds vote was required, and the directors would never approve a $55 price against a $62 bid, whether or not offered by a majority of the shares. At best, even with an additional hundred or more friends recruited in Greenville to join the families, we'd be stymied without a chance for a payout. The families wanted liquidity, and for them, $350 million in cash was part of the buyout package. Without the possibility of getting the cash, the families (and their friends) would sell to Bill Simon at $62.

I'd restated the problem and had come up with the same answer, like footing a column of figures from the bottom up rather than the top down. At least I'd proved the point to myself.

They asked: Why couldn't the public be offered the same thing as the family, $55 per share and a chance to invest, say, $10 of that amount for a share in the leveraged buyout company. They were back to the same question. They wanted me to go through the complexities and legal impediments to prove that it couldn't be done.

Fred Eckert of Goldman Sachs joined us then. He had been orchestrating the deal and was an experienced banker. They asked him the same question. He turned to me and asked: "Why not?" He was never put off by complexity and saw that we had a losing position. Against taking a loss, he wanted another approach. "Suppose we offered the public the same deal as the family," he said, reframing it as a statement.

I shook my head. "If I took you through all the steps, you'd see that it isn't worth trying." And then I had another idea, which arose out of the pressure of the situation. "You could give shareholders a dividend of $45 and let them keep their shares," I said.

"Can we do that?" everyone asked. I had a very attentive and interested group. What would the shares be worth, they wanted to know, after all the shareholders were given $45? Fred Eckert understood and articulated the answer immediately: "Whatever the company was worth after it had incurred the debt to make the payment." If shareholders were given $45 as a dividend on each share and the company was worth $55 per share, then each share was worth $10. Logic didn't require that the analysis stop at that point, and Fred spelled it out further. "If someone was prepared to pay $62 a share, and if the shareholders were given $45 in cash, then the share should be worth $17. And if someone wanted to pay $65, then the share should be worth $20."

The question was whether the shareholders would prefer to take $45 a share from Multimedia and keep their shares, maintaining their relative ownership interest in a highly leveraged company, or take an all-cash deal from a third party. We would be leveraging Multimedia, but the company would continue to trade publicly. We were, in effect, turning the leveraged buyout vehicle inside out. In that meeting, prepared to resign, we'd found a winning strategy. It was only then that we realized that we were on to a new structure. It had to be called something other than a "public leveraged buyout." We chose to call it a "recapitalization" to get away from any hint of a buyout. Naming what we'd done made it different from a mere idea; it gave it substance. Finally, the newness of the form didn't bother me, if it would defeat Wesray and Lorimar.

In the recapitalization structure the company wasn't being sold. On the contrary, it was being mortgaged. We could tell the independent directors that all shareholders would participate on the same terms, including the families. The shares (which we referred to as the stubs because their value had been significantly reduced by the dividend) would continue to be publicly traded. Highly leveraged, the Multimedia stock would find its own trading value. There was no limit to what it would trade at. It could sell at $10 a share or $17 a share or $20 a share or more. What was strongly in our favor was Bill Simon and Lorimar tripping over each other to buy Multimedia. Who knew what Multimedia could be worth? Most telling was Bill Simon's desire to buy Multimedia, for he was known for uncovering hidden treasure. The stories of the successes of leveraged buyout entrepreneurs had probably made the public ready for leveraged equity.

Fred Eckert endorsed the approach as financeable with the banks. His assessment was that the public would favor the deal over Simon's or Lorimar's offer. No one thought of the new form as a radical innovation, only as a necessary tactic. Everyone liked the idea that the company was no longer for sale. That turn of events would check, if not cripple, all buyout proposals for Multimedia.

And as anticipated, the new approach frustrated Lorimar and Wesray. For them, there was no attractive or foreseeable route to victory. Cohesive holders of shares now blocked their approach. So confronted, Bill Simon and Lorimar withdrew.

Before victory could be toasted, yet another bid was made, this time by Jack Kent Cooke, owner of the Washington Redskins. First, in the wake of Simon's and Lorimar's withdrawal, he'd bought about 10 percent of Multimedia's stock in the market, showing seriousness of purpose and committed capital. Then he offered the directors and the shareholders $65 a share for the company. Where had he come from? What was the source of his interest? All the questions were answered when we learned that his banker was Drexel Burnham. Milken was a banker in search of a client. Each time one lost heart, he found another more intent than the last on acquiring the company. For Milken, money was no object. With him behind the bidders, the price could be raised again.

While Milken attacked on the basis of price, Jack Kent Cooke, advised by Milton Gould, the senior partner of the law firm of Shea & Gould, determined to attack the underpinnings of our defense. Their assessment was that the only way that a $45 dividend could be sustained against a $65 bid was the coercive decision of the founders not to put their shares up for sale. Cooke, advised by Milton Gould, brought an action in the state court in Greenville, South Carolina, charging the families with breach of fiduciary duty and improperly using their dominant stock position to thwart more favorable bids.

Milton Gould's legal theory, which had merit, was that once the families offered to buy the company and set a fair price, they couldn't back off when someone offered a higher price. There are numerous situations in the law where there is no duty at the outset, but if a task is undertaken it must be completed. Here was one of those cases, Milton argued. No one could have asked the families to sell initially, but now they had to sell their shares to the highest bidder.

There was also an appealing public relations aspect to the attack. Milton Gould contended that the families had wanted Multimedia solely for themselves at an absurdly low price. Now suddenly it wasn't for sale and they were blocking a stellar price. Either it was their game or no game. The families looked entrenched and infinitely greedy. Milton Gould could call up the spirit of American fair play, exposing the families as selfish and domineering. If anybody could dramatize that theme it was Milton Gould. He was a great trial lawyer, one whose talent had matured and flowered over the years. At seventy-five he was still fully active. His most recent notable trial victory was the winning of a major libel case on behalf of Ariel Sharon against Time Inc. Passionate and vital, he could make any courtroom come alive, and arguing a case in a South Carolina country courtroom was to his advantage, although he was a big-city lawyer. Milton had striking ivory-white hair and the ragged cragginess of men who have spent their lives seeking justice,

reminiscent of Clarence Darrow. He commanded unbounded respect, which absolved him of his urbanity.

Milton's adversary was my partner, Bernie Nussbaum. Also a
trial lawyer of great experience, Bernie knew that he had the
tougher side of the case, especially with Milton as his opponent.
And without doubt he'd be taken for the New York lawyer in the
courtroom. Bernie had a cherubic face and a balding head with
tufts of curly gray hair, much like a friar's, which he kept closely
cropped. He exuded warmth and was charming, but his speech and
suits and clipped, precise style would all say "big city." Bernie had
on his side that he was representing the local establishment. But
often that is resented, looked on as an aspersion on indigenous
talent, and is expressed as: Why did Multimedia go to New York
to get a lawyer? What also made his case hard was its complexity.
It had changed from a leveraged buyout to a new form, only recently
labeled by us as a recapitalization. In New York the judges would
probably understand it, but this case was going to be argued in a
small-town courthouse where such matters were never heard. He
had to distill out all the perplexing elements and reduce them to a
simple theme that a country judge could understand. The more he
explained, the greater the likelihood of offending all the locals,
including the judge.

The process of arguing involves taking the opportunity to educate
the court. And there is never much time. There would be an hour
for opening argument, then the presentation of one or two witnesses
by both sides, and finally short closing arguments. The case would
be fully presented for decision in one day. Unfortunately, in mid-
1985, financial technology had advanced beyond common
understanding.

And if all that wasn't hard enough on Bernie, I'd made arrangements with arbitrageurs to enhance the chances of approval of the
new recapitalization plan. Only once before had such arrangements
been attempted, on behalf of Cooper Industries, and Stanley Sporkin had managed to strike them down. But Stanley had left the
SEC, and the SEC under Ronald Reagan, despite memory of past
matters, was no longer actively interfering with ongoing transactions (except for insider trading), leaving the challenges to the

parties and the courts. I'd overcome my reluctance to make arrangements with arbitrageurs because no one on our side was certain that we'd be able to withstand a tender offer at $65 or more. We wanted to have at least another 8 to 10 percent of the outstanding shares tied up and committed to the recapitalization transaction. The means we used was to contract to sell shares in Multimedia at $10 a share after the recapitalization to about seven arbitrageurs. The agreements bound the arbitrageurs to buy the shares and to vote for the transaction so long as there was no bid by Jack Kent Cooke over $70 a share. We picked $70 because we thought that he wouldn't bid above that amount. The arrangements were then publicly disclosed.

Bernie, of course, wasn't happy with the agreements, for they gave Milton further evidence to show how the deal had been wired together against the interests of the public stockholders. Bernie had been served with Milton Gould's trial brief just as he got on the plane to Greenville, South Carolina, the evening before the trial. He intended to read it on the plane and make responsive revisions to his argument during the flight and in the hotel room. There would be no time in the morning for preparation. On the plane Milton Gould and his assistant, also in transit to the courtroom, were sitting across the aisle from Bernie. Milton was reading a novel and enjoying himself. Nothing in his demeanor indicated that there was a demanding trial about to take place. His apparent absorption in the book was complete, and he had the kind of carefree attitude of a man on the way to watch his college football team, as if he were going to be a spectator judging the performances.

Milton and Bernie acknowledged each other and exchanged warm pleasantries across the aisle. Bernie, a compulsive man, wanted more than anything to be able to open up Milton's papers and go through them with care. But with Milton sitting there relaxed, reading his novel, Bernie reached into the pocket of the seat in front of him and took out the airline magazine. He wasn't going to show Milton that he was still in the process of preparation or let an unguarded moment on the plane indicate to Milton how difficult the issues were for him. All through the flight he thumbed and rethumbed the magazine, left finally to reading the advertisements for the distraction they offered. Only after the flight, in the privacy of his hotel room, did Bernie begin his final preparation and fully develop his theme at an hour much later than he would have liked.

The courtroom was packed and many of the family members came to hear the argument, seeking some vindication. Milton Gould had the benefit of being the first to speak at opening argument and the last to speak at closing argument. Bernie was sandwiched in between. Milton masterfully wrung out the spirit of unfairness that he saw as inherent in the families' actions. Like a surgeon, he used his words incisively to peel away what he considered cant, and he pointed out what he regarded as the meanspiritedness of what the family was trying to accomplish.

On Bernie's turn, you could see all the effort that he'd put into trying to make complex ideas simple. "Your honor," he said. "A man has a house, which he discovers is worth a lot more than he paid for it." Bernie paused to let everyone know that this was going to be homespun, radiating a warm smile that rarely failed to charm. The judge nodded for him to proceed, not acknowledging the blandishment. "The man goes to the bank and asks them how much they would let him borrow on the house, and they tell him that even though he paid, let's say, $25,000 and has a mortgage on the house for $15,000, they'd lend him another $85,000, your honor. The bank thinks that the house is worth $125,000 in this market. And so, your honor, the man borrows against the house and puts an additional mortgage on it. Now that's not a sale, your honor. He's still going to live in the house. He's still going to take care of it. All he did was borrow money against it. He can use the money any way he likes. The bank is not telling him what to do with the money."

Bernie paused and walked to the side of the room, letting everyone digest his story and apply it. "Brokers may come around and say, 'Gosh, we could get you more for the house. Let us put it on the market and let's see what we could get.' Probably $125,000 is a low figure. But if he sells the house, your honor, he can't live in it. And more importantly, if that house is going to become more valuable over time, he can't get the growth in the value the property may experience if he sells it. That's our case, your honor. This is a mortgage case, not a sale case. What's all the fuss about? The fact that we thought about selling the house doesn't matter. We didn't sell it, your honor. We went back to the banks and said, 'We're not selling. We want to mortgage it.' "

Bernie went over his theme, waiting for the court to nod and nod again. The court nodded for his benefit, giving him every assurance of understanding. And then Bernie switched themes. "What kind of offer is Mr. Cooke making, your honor? He's asking us to interrupt our stockholders' meeting and consider his offer. He's not making a tender offer to the shareholders. He's not taking his case to the marketplace. He's playing a public relations game, your honor. There's always time to consider his offer after the shareholders have had a chance to decide whether they want to mortgage Multimedia. If they want to mortgage it, that's what we'll do. If they reject our mortgage proposal, then there's time enough to consider Mr. Cooke's offer. If Mr. Cooke wants immediate attention, he should make a tender offer. He knows that at $65 the shareholders are not interested in selling and that's why he's in court, your honor. But how can the shareholders be ordered to sell to him? All the court can do is make sure everybody has a fair hearing. If Mr. Cooke wants a hearing in the marketplace, let him make a tender offer."

Milton, of course, had a chance to deal with Bernie's obfuscation, and he pressed his points, getting the nods from the judge. He too was assured that he was fully understood. After closing argument the judge reserved the right to decide and indicated that he would have an opinion in a day or two on this matter. The parties would be called into court when the opinion was ready for the court to read it to them.

True to his word, the judge decided the case promptly. To our good fortune, he decided in favor of the founding families. Reading the opinion afterward, I felt that the court chided us, the lawyers, on too simplistic a presentation. The opinion begins with two critical words, "Simply stated," and the court, in two sentences, neatly lays out the issues in all their complexity with more precision than we did in our briefs.

The court found bedrock law in the proposition that no shareholder need be required to sell his shares. Even if they had put the company up for sale, the founding families couldn't be forced to sell their shares if they didn't want to do so. They could change their minds even if the implication of their actions was to put their shares up for sale. That was a proposition without exception in the law, and the court adhered to it. The court, however, said that Jack Kent Cooke was free to address all the other shareholders by making a tender offer. The court indicated that it was up to Jack Kent Cooke to find the price at which everyone would sell, and it wasn't the court's role to require sales or influence the market.

The joy of victory was relatively brief. With the kind of energy and intensity that only the fully committed can command, Jack Kent Cooke made a tender offer at $70.01 per share. Having exceeded $70, he freed up all the arbitrageurs bound by contracts to favor the recapitalization and picked a price that was higher than any price thought achievable. With Mike Milken in his corner, he was formidable. We were in a situation reminiscent of the Stokely–Van Camp buyout. This time, however, there was no Quaker Oats or its equivalent to act as a White Knight.

It was an interesting situation: on the one hand, Jack Kent Cooke was offering $70.01 a share, and on the other, Multimedia was offering $45 and a chance to retain your stock certificates. Was each stock certificate now worth $25? The stock had stretched from $10, but was it infinitely stretchable or did all the elasticity snap by $25. What we knew was that the families were still committed with their 42 percent, but they weren't truly economic players. The $45 a share would give them as much liquidity as they wanted (an aggregate of $350 million) and they would continue to control Multimedia. The swing vote was the arbitrageurs and the coterie of people in Greenville who had earlier indicated that they wanted to be in the same position as the families. No one knew what they would now do.

A tender offer takes twenty business days to close, and opinions can change and so can the marketplace during the course of the period. The outcome wouldn't be known until it was all over. We called all the arbitrageurs, but no assurance from them would be final. They would all act in their own economic interest as they saw it in the last minute. At the outset, some arbitrageurs said that they favored the family recapitalization, which put pressure on Jack Kent Cooke to raise again. With Mike Milken behind him, they thought that they could extract more money. Cooke wisely indicated that he'd gone as far as he could go, or would go. Then the pressure turned back on Multimedia. Was there more money that could be distributed to the shareholders? Why limit the payment to $45? In this kind of give-and-take it was very difficult to determine where everything would come to rest. A fulcrum point had been reached, and the outcome could swing either way.

The legal case between Jack Kent Cooke and Multimedia continued on other grounds. Each side took the other's depositions, like boxers sparring, as if they would mix it up again in court. At one of those depositions it was suggested by a lawyer for the Cooke team that perhaps the parties should talk. That was the kind of signal that couldn't be ignored, and we all met to see how to proceed.

Looking at the situation from the perspective of Cooke's signal, it looked as though he was worried and would be prepared to be bought out. Buying him out would end the tender offer. With Cooke out of the way, the family recapitalization could go forward without mishap and the shareholders, offered no alternative, would vote for it. Although buying out Cooke was desirable, we didn't have access to the corporate treasury. It seemed unlikely that the committee of independent directors or its counsel would approve a buyout that looked like a raw form of greenmail and eliminated the shareholders' option of choosing the $70 cash tender offer. Whether it was unlikely or not, we had to ask the question, and I called Morris Kramer at Skadden Arps, who was representing the committee. I called him while everybody in the room waited. Morris listened and expressed his sympathy and told me that he would have to recommend against a buyout of the shares. No cash was available.

"What if we offered Cooke $60 to $70 cash per share, payable on closing of the recapitalization?" I asked the group. In that deal, Cooke would withdraw his tender offer and wait for the recapitalization to be approved. It would take about sixty days for him to get paid.

"That's not cash," everyone said. "It won't work."

"We don't know that it won't work," I said.

"In the same way you knew that the committee wouldn't give us the money, you can know that this won't work."

"It depends on Jack Kent Cooke's assessment of the situation,"
I said.

"He's not getting anything out of waiting."

"He has a chance of losing if he continues his tender," I said.

"Losing is not so bad. He gets $45 and a share of stock."

"That's not what he wants," I said. "That's why he put out the
signal to talk. He probably wants $70 a share."

"Are we prepared to give him $70 a share?" someone asked.

"Let's start at $65," someone else said.

"There's no point in negotiating if he wants cash," someone else
said.

"We could agree to indemnify Cooke if he waits for shareholder
approval," I said. "There's bound to be legal actions by some
Multimedia shareholders to force him to disgorge his profits. Greenmail is not favored by the courts. An indemnity could be attractive
to him."

Everyone felt that an indemnity would be appealing to him and
it was agreed that we ought to find out what he had on his mind.
It was thought best that I call Milton Gould, since the inquiry had
come from Gould's firm.

Milton Gould was waiting for my call, and he promptly told me,
without hesitancy, that his client was a seller at the right price. I
started at $62 a share, and there was an offended grunt at the
other end of the line.

"Sixty-five," I said, and added, "The Multimedia stock is trading
at $62 despite your tender at $70."

"There's a premium there," he acknowledged, "but it's not
enough. Look," he said, "we're buyers at $70 and a penny, and
we're sellers at $70. You can forget the penny."

"I may be able to go that far," I said, "but the terms have to
be right."

"Cash," he said.

"Cash at the closing of the recapitalization," I said.

"That's not cash," he answered. His response was prompt. He'd
anticipated the exchange.

"You want cash immediately?" I asked, expressing my disbelief,
as if that would change his position.

"That's what cash is," he said firmly, his voice sharp enough to dispel further pretense.

"I'd have to check with my client," I said. "I'm not sure we would do that. In any event, we wouldn't give any indemnity."

"We need that," he said.

"Only if the shareholders approve the transaction, including the purchase of your shares. Then it's clean. Otherwise, it's your risk."

"I have to talk to my client," he said. He knew he'd heard all I had to say.

"I understand," I said. "Get back to me when you can."

"I'll call you after lunch," he said.

After the conversation, I felt exposed, for there was no doubt that he understood everything, including the tenuousness of our position. He knew that we didn't have the money, and he understood full well that we were afraid that he'd win if he persisted in the tender offer. The settlement discussions had shown us in our underwear. When he hung up, he could take all the time he wanted, analyze the positions and options, reassessing his interest in doing the deal. Interestingly, he'd given relatively little away in the conversation. He was prepared to buy or sell. In our conversation, he was a seller, but he could very well change his mind.

Settlement discussions offer the opportunity to talk to the other side and canvass their strengths, and the result may not favor settlement. Starting out, I felt that there was nothing to lose, but now I saw that we could have eroded our position. I reported my conversation to the group, and everybody began to speculate on what Jack Kent Cooke would do. How solid was our position? Speculation about our weaknesses occupied us until we were depressed.

In midafternoon Milton called back, his voice gruff and curt. "We'll do it," he said. "We'll take $70 cash per share at the closing of the recap and we get indemnified."

"Agreed," I said. From his voice I couldn't tell whether he was satisfied or dissatisfied with the result, and I couldn't ask.

What made him do it? Again it's speculative. But I always assumed that Jack Kent Cooke wanted Multimedia; otherwise he wouldn't have fought as hard as he did. Selling out under those terms meant that he saw the family and the arbitrageurs holding firm and thought he couldn't win.

And with that we created and completed the first recapitalization. In all these corporate machinations, were the shareholders overlooked? How well did they fare? To our amazement, within a short time the stub stock went over $25 a share and continued its upward rise. Within a year the stub was trading at over $45 a share. The technique of recapitalization, created out of necessity to achieve Multimedia's objectives, was immediately duplicated in other major transactions. That kind of success bred more deals—more leveraged deals.

Multimedia, having successfully recapitalized, emerged with its management and shareholders unified, committed to pursue an independent course. Aware of the difficulties of fending off a raider, management adopted carefully thought-out long-range plans fortifying the course of independence. Given Multimedia's unique situation, its defenses continue to be state of the art. In addition, the South Carolina legislature, shortly after the recapitalization, adopted strong anti-takeover legislation, designed to protect native businesses from takeovers.

INSIDE TRADER

▼

The human heart has multiple chambers.

On July 8, 1986, the Securities and Exchange Commission served Ilan Reich, a young partner at Wachtell Lipton, with a subpoena demanding all his and the firm's files relating to certain transactions that Ilan or the firm had acted on over a six-year period. These were transactions in which Dennis Levine, an investment banker at Drexel Burnham Lambert, Incorporated, had traded on inside information. Levine had been arrested on May 12, 1986, the first in a series of arrests that would expose the largest insider-trading ring in Wall Street history. Here was the grimy underside of the past decade's merger activity. Before Levine's arrest there had been little reason for those professionals involved daily in the merger markets to question each other's ethics. Until then, misuse of inside information had rarely involved professionals. Most often, exposure of abuse unmasked peripheral parties like typists and proofreaders. But by July 1986, Levine had implicated a number of young investment bankers from other major firms as part of his ring, while leaving no doubt that other professionals directly involved in merger transactions would also be named. We had all been affected by the fraud, without being aware of it, and that summer we intently followed the course of the investigation, waiting for further revelations.

The SEC's subpoena, in addition to requesting specified files, called for all of Ilan's office and personal records, including bank accounts, travel and expense vouchers, and telephone logs over the last six years. These constituted cartons of information about his daily affairs that, when artfully pieced together, would provide a topographical map of his activities. In response to this inquiry, Ilan shrugged in his typical relaxed and acceptingly benign fashion, telling everyone that he was resigned to the indignity of the SEC getting into all aspects of his life. On that afternoon, Ilan came into my office to talk to me about the scope of the SEC's request, which he had been trying to satisfy most of the day, and to seek advice.

"What will the records show?" I asked.

"Nothing," he said, finding a seat by the window, the sun to his back.

"Do you have anything to worry about?" I asked, raising a broader question. Any investigation by the SEC is a warning signal, and almost involuntarily I judged him, wary of deceit.

In the strong afternoon light his prematurely gray hair looked almost white and his skin glowed the way it would with a lamp behind it, pink and luminous, nearly baring his finely wrought bone structure. Everything about him was at rest: even his long, lean fingers, usually curled around a pencil, were relaxed. Sitting comfortably in a slouched position, one leg slung over the arm of his chair, he seemed at total peace with himself. Is a troubled conscience reflected on the surface? If so, I thought, it would show now. Composed with the stillness necessary for an X ray, he faced me without a hint of any inner tensions. As I observed him, he leaned forward and drank slowly from the can of soda he held, his eyes finding mine.

Waiting for an answer, I lowered my eyes, as if ending my scrutiny, but my mind insisted on posing questions. If the surface wasn't revealing, shouldn't the judgment be made from known actions in the past six years? There were dozens of moments of stress we'd

shared, disarming enough to show character in all its aspects. Are
moments of depression a basis for a damning judgment? What about
arrogance? Annoying questions, sufficient to make me feel a stitch
of self-reproach in raising them, more so because the mind can
always work up doubts. If anything, there was a bewildering confusion of detail in these experiences, with his life and mine and the
firm's history entwined.

Ilan was twenty-five when he'd joined Wachtell Lipton six and
a half years before, his hair already gray. The gray was touching,
as if he'd been singed by an internal fire. He was slight and lithe,
with the physique of a dancer, almost elegant. Never quick to make
friends, he was an outsider whose business suits were all an acceptable dull gray and whose shirts were always white—an un-
changing uniform, without flair or self-expression. You found the
man in his expressive face and hands and in the language of his
body. His smile was shy and sweet and made him look vulnerable.

He was one of the four or five lawyers that Wachtell Lipton hired
annually in the late 1970s. The firm's founders had decided that
young lawyers should be hired with the intention of making them
partners, contrary to the Wall Street system of admitting relatively
few of the associates into the partnership. Growth of the firm would
be controlled by being selective in hiring. Wachtell Lipton told the
young people that they could trust their elders to promote them to
partnership status, and that promise affected the partners' attitude
toward the associates: there was no need to keep aloof from the
associates, for they would almost certainly become partners. Cravath discouraged social contacts by partners because the associates
were not part of the firm; here I could be close to the people with
whom I worked. Accordingly, I regularly had lunch with them,
occasionally dined with them, and even met their families. There
were substantial benefits in eliminating the traditional barriers, for
I got to understand the world from another generation's perspective, which made life fresher.

Ilan began working exclusively with me after graduation from
Columbia Law School in 1979 and an initial three-month period at
the firm. He worked with me for about a year. Although he was
headstrong and needed guidance, within a short time I knew that
he was a truly gifted and imaginative lawyer who had an intuitive

feeling for the work. His interest and aptitude increased my desire to teach. And while the working relationship was tutorial, it centered on the day's events, which weren't organized for learning, leaving room for personal expression and an exchange of points of view that affected the outcome of the work. Through Ilan, I understood the role I'd served for my mentors in acting as an intellectual foil and companion, though I carried the mentor relationship further than I'd experienced it and made Ilan a friend.

We ate lunch together regularly, mostly discussing the work at hand. Sometimes we talked about personal problems, and Ilan gradually told me about his life. Ilan was driven to be more successful than his brother, Yaron. I enjoyed that competitive spirit in him, familiar as I was with family rivalries, which were common to many of my partners and myself. Yaron, a year and a half older, always excelled, and Ilan had followed in his brother's shadow for over twenty years, in all their schooling, including Columbia College and Law School. Yaron's achievements had continued and were even accelerating: he was a well-regarded lawyer at Cleary, Gottlieb, Steen & Hamilton, a prestigious Wall Street law firm. The brother was close to the family and had embraced its Orthodox Judaism. As if in response, Ilan rejected Judaism completely: he worked on all the holidays and observed no dietary restrictions. Like most at Wachtell Lipton, he was totally secular and made the firm an outlet for his ambition.

While Ilan's brilliance showed itself early, it was accompanied by impatience when his point of view wasn't immediately accepted. He became easily irritated and then angered at others when they disagreed with him, referring to those lawyers outside the firm as "empty helmets." While working exclusively with me, he was sheltered from the rest of the firm, but when he worked for other partners, there were sometimes needless confrontations. Ilan did better with the younger people: he understood their limitations, and his brilliance engendered awe and adulation in them. Inverting the usual formula for success, he was liked by the people below him and disliked by the people above.

The partners reviewed the associates annually and graded their performances. At such meetings, all the partners pooled their information and exchanged views. With the associates not present, there was always a frank exchange, often an emotional one. Most of the partners found Ilan exceptionally talented, but many were distressed by his arrogance, which was interpreted as lack of judgment. I was the apologist for his behavior. He was young, I said, and the rough edges would wear smooth. Despite that, he was given bad reviews for three years running and was then told that he might not become a partner. In his fourth year, Ilan talked to me seriously about leaving Wachtell Lipton. His rejection of the firm came from an anticipation of failure and also from contemplating expected adjustments to the partners that strained his personal flexibility. On a late-afternoon flight back from Chicago, he spent the entire trip discussing the situation with me. I felt that it was a moment of decision and told him that I wanted him to stay, that as the practice grew he would share it. He asked me then, as he had from time to time, what he had to do to develop his career. The best advice I could give him was to avoid confronting the partners.

He tucked in his chin and became less assertive in the firm. For the next year his relations with the partners were untroubled. Freed from his confrontations, they could enjoy tilting with their adversaries, and recognize his brilliance. The final challenge was Martin Lipton, who wasn't easy for any young person to work with. Ilan, however, developed a good relationship with Lipton, first by allowing the older man to take the lead and then by respectfully acting as a foil, much as Ilan did with me. Lipton ordinarily needed a mature mind with which to exchange ideas, but in Ilan he found a fine and eager one. First Lipton appreciated him, then he became proud of him, and the relationship became almost that of father and son.

Ilan became a candidate for partnership after five years at the firm, a year earlier than the usual six-year track. Just as his early partnership looked assured, I opposed it, the only one who did. I was concerned that Ilan was immature and, just turning thirty, was still not seasoned. I felt that he could benefit from another year's apprenticeship. In his favor was that everyone in the firm knew him and, by then, trusted him. With his trouble in getting along behind him, he was integrated into the firm.

Debate about early partnership was academic, however, because there was a need for new corporate partners. At the end of 1981,

Carlo Florentino, a young partner, had been forced to resign as a result of trading on inside information. That loss, and two other young corporate partners leaving to go to other law firms, had created a gap that needed to be filled, and no one took my objections seriously. Ilan was my friend, and they knew that if everybody who had previously opposed him recognized his talent, I wouldn't vote against him. The partnership met in November 1984 and made him a member of the firm as of January 1, 1985. The early elevation to partnership was especially poignant for him, he told me, after the trials he'd experienced at the firm—and for once he had gotten to the goal line before his brother.

Judging Ilan in my office that summer afternoon, nothing countered my feeling that he was entitled to my loyalty. As I examined him, I asked myself one further question: What about his friendship with Dennis Levine? Less than a week before the subpoena, Ilan had told me that he'd just gotten a telephone call from Dennis Levine, who sounded as if he were speaking from a pay phone. Ilan had heard the unmistakable ring of coins at the beginning of the call, giving the illusion that the call was safely being made from some remote place where it couldn't be overheard or recorded. Levine, free on bail, said to him, "The prosecutors are asking me a lot of questions and I wanted to hear from you what I should tell them about us." Ilan told him he didn't know what he was talking about, and abruptly hung up.

That call came to mind now, with a picture of Dennis Levine, in his aviator glasses, hunched over the phone in a posture of guarded intimacy. I felt that the subpoena was part of a concerted action on the part of Levine and the government to entwine Ilan: the next step after Levine's obviously recorded and deceptive call. Telling me and others about Levine's actions validated Ilan's status as victim.

Sitting opposite me, Ilan now appeared to be judging me, evaluating our friendship, which was his right. Nonetheless, it was disconcerting, and I stood up to adjust the blinds, deflecting the stark light away from me. This was the moment to give him assurance of my loyalty. Friendships are fragile, and I didn't want to offend him. Ilan was working on some of my matters again, after a year as a partner, sharing an important part of my life. Knowing him as well as I did, how could I doubt him? When he told me that he was innocent, I was ready to accept his assurance and embrace it.

Sipping his soda, he became contemplative and asked me then whether he should get his own lawyer to handle the subpoena. I told him we were all in this together and the firm should represent him. There was no reason that the investigation should cause a division in the firm, leaving him outside. He looked gratified by the support, rewarding me with his sweet smile, and I acknowledged his appreciation by smiling back at him, satisfied that representing him was the right thing to do. How could he hide anything from me?

Within a week, he confessed.

ILAN MET DENNIS LEVINE at the end of 1979 in the offices of Wachtell Lipton while working on one of his first deals. Ilan had been out of school only a couple of months and hadn't yet begun to work with me. Levine had been employed a little longer as an investment banker at Smith, Barney & Co. Both Levine and Ilan were part of a large team of professionals involved in the merger of Gifford Hill and Amcord, two cement companies. Ilan admired Levine's affability and easygoing manner. Though Levine was more knowledgeable than Ilan when they met, the balance would soon shift, and Ilan would remark that Levine was not a rocket scientist. He still felt, however, that he could never achieve Levine's level of grace and charm. Levine told him that he wanted to be his friend, and Ilan was flattered.

Was there something in Ilan that Levine could see that we could have or should have seen? I don't think so. What Levine did, which no one else could do, was test Ilan—and others. For example, at the time Levine met Ilan, he also met Dan Neff, who had been out of law school and with the firm about two years. Neff was the senior associate working on the Gifford Hill merger. Levine approached Neff in an offhand way and told him that they were fools for working so hard for so little when others were able to benefit from all the merger information. Everybody does it. Neff bristled and told Levine that it doesn't matter: there's no amount of money that justifies the action. Levine, of course, backed off, and Neff, now a partner in the firm, would only think of the incident again after Ilan was caught.

That was the way Ilan was approached. He didn't strongly object, and Levine then knew that Ilan was vulnerable. After that he cultivated Ilan because he wanted a source of inside information at Wachtell Lipton, which was a center for merger activity. Ilan and Levine would have lunch together, and Levine would talk about his aspirations, and Ilan about his frustrations. Ilan wanted to be a partner in the firm, and Levine wanted to be an independent principal, with enough money to do his own deals. In that kind of revelation there is always a sense of intimacy. With intimacy, the groundwork of conspiracy is laid. When the parties conspire, it is as if the relationship has moved to a new plane: the secrets shared look like building blocks for friendship.

Ilan furnished inside information to Levine within six months of joining Wachtell Lipton. They met at the Plaza Hotel on Fifth Avenue, walked into Central Park, and sat on a bench. Ilan had set the place of meeting, on the street where there was no one to hear them or suspect the nature of their conversation. Levine told Ilan that he was familiar with foreign banking systems and arrangements and that he could set up secret or nominee numbered accounts through which stock trades could be made that were untraceable. If the information about proposed mergers was obtained early enough, Levine's trades would never be noticed. Ilan would share in the profits made from trades in which he furnished information.

The information Ilan had obtained Levine already knew from another source, making the event merely a dry run, though impressing Ilan with his knowledge. Subsequently, while walking on the street after lunch together, Ilan told Levine about the pending sale of the Jefferson National Life Insurance Company of Indianapolis. This was a deal that I was working on and had discussed with Ilan in order to keep him informed about all my work, although another associate was working on this particular matter with me. Ilan knew that it would be difficult to trace any leak to him because he wasn't working on the acquisition. From me he'd learned that there would soon be an announcement of the sale of Jefferson to the Zurich Insurance Company, as well as of the price the Swiss company was prepared to pay, and he thus could calculate the rise that would occur in the stock price on the announcement. After again getting Levine's assurances that there was no risk of their being discovered, Ilan told Levine what he knew, and Levine purchased stock in Jefferson National.

Since Ilan was not working on the matter, he couldn't keep current with changes in the transaction, and didn't learn that the deal was about to fall apart. When I realized that the negotiations had definitely failed, I had the client promptly announce that Zurich had withdrawn. The Jefferson National stock price plummeted. Dennis Levine sold at a loss, and learned a lesson. He should only take information on deals that Ilan was certain of or those on which he was actually working. Ilan, however, resisted tipping Levine on deals in which he was personally involved. His reasoning was that he didn't want the tipping of information to cloud his judgment or color the professional advice he was giving to the client. When Ilan finally began tipping Levine on deals on which he was working, he gave Levine the information very early in the transaction, and would subsequently avoid any discussion about what Levine did with the information. Ilan thus would never know whether he stood to benefit from his action. In Ilan's mind, this distancing himself from his actions left him free to give appropriate professional advice. But by tipping on his own deals, Ilan increased his risk and was moved closer to exposure.

Dennis Levine told Ilan that he would set up a separate account for Ilan's share of the amounts Levine made on trades from information furnished or verified by Ilan. But Ilan rejected all offers to document the arrangement for fear that it would increase his chance of being caught. The basis of the sharing was never specified by Levine, although Levine gave Ilan supposed "accountings" as to amounts held for Ilan. Ilan, ambivalent about his activities, doubted whether there would ever be a payout.

IN SEPTEMBER 1981, when Ilan had been at the firm about two years, we discovered that Carlo Florentino, a partner in the firm, had been trading on inside information. The firm had hired Carlo in the spring of 1979, about six months before Ilan joined the firm. He had worked at Davis, Polk & Wardwell for eight years, and as a fully trained journeyman lawyer, became a partner at Wachtell Lipton in January 1981. He was a shadowy figure for Ilan, less so for me, until Carlo confessed and left the firm.

Carlo precipitated his own exposure. He had a trading account at E. F. Hutton, in his own name and with Wachtell Lipton's address. Before joining Wachtell Lipton he'd used the address of his former employer, Davis, Polk & Wardwell, and had traded on inside information while an associate there. All of Carlo's trades were made through that account, which was ultimately his undoing. While his early trades hadn't been for amounts large enough to arouse suspicion, in 1981 he told his broker at Hutton to purchase over $1 million worth of stock in a particular company, committing almost all the money accumulated in the account. A $1 million trade was unusual for the broker. The one thing in Carlo's favor was that he was a partner in Wachtell Lipton. Everything else was against him.

Examining the account, the broker saw that Carlo never lost money and never sought advice from Hutton or discussed stocks. The broker called Hutton's general counsel, the firm's chief legal officer, who saw the problem immediately and called Martin Lipton. Lipton told him that someone from Wachtell Lipton would have to examine the account, and it was opened to the firm. The pattern in the account was obvious; each trade related to a deal Carlo was working on. When he learned about a bid to acquire a company at a premium price over the current market price, he'd buy the stock of the target company before the public was told. An initial few thousand dollars had been run up to over $1 million. Carlo never took any money out of the account; he always reinvested it. The trades went back to the time when he was employed at Davis Polk.

Members of the firm confronted Carlo in his office. The door to the office was closed as Carlo met with the partners, and when Carlo realized that the firm knew about his account, he collapsed into a ball and started to cry. The shame was too much for him. In seeing his destruction, we all felt that we'd lost our innocence and would no longer freely trust anyone. We were rendered more innocent, however, by our attempts at understanding. Rational analysis showed that Carlo was irrational. He was earning about $350,000 a year as a first-year partner and could look forward to much more over the years. It didn't make sense to destroy this opportunity. On reflection, we noted a few unusual things about his behavior in the office. He had often complained about insider trading and was particularly secretive about his transactions. Sometimes even the associates working for him didn't know the names of the target companies, which was unusual.

After Carlo confessed, Ilan was very curious about him. Ilan came to my office and I cleared away some papers from my table, inviting him to sit down and share a moment with me while we talked about more than the day's events. Often we would discuss this deal or that, but it was rare to take a moment to reflect. Looking at the moment now, it appears very different from what it seemed then. Ilan knew about his own tipping activities, and I only knew about Carlo's insider trading. While we both had curiosity about Carlo, our questions were different, but then his questions seemed like extensions of mine. I asked: Why did Carlo do it? All I got from Ilan was a shrug, which meant that it was unknowable and anybody could speculate. He asked: What had happened to Carlo? I saw his question as merely different in emphasis. He wasn't asking about why Carlo had started, but what had happened to him once he'd started. I am transfixed by the exchange between us. It was a moment closer to revelation than any others because we were exploring motives. He didn't answer, but wanted answers from me. I had hired Carlo, shared his anguish over his not being made a partner at Davis Polk, and therefore knew more about him than most. In a speculative mood, I told Ilan what I knew.

I'd met Carlo for the first time when he was interviewing for a job at the firm. He'd been warned that he wouldn't become a partner at Davis Polk, but he didn't quite believe it. He was thin and intense, had dark, glistening black hair and bright, black intelligent eyes that were lively and took in everything around him. His résumé showed that he grew up in a working-class Italian family in Queens, had gone to Queens College, where he showed intellectual promise, graduating Phi Beta Kappa, and had gone on to NYU Law School, where he was at the top of his class. His background was a comfort to me. It packed in a nutshell a lifetime of effort to excel and tested his discipline and intellect against others also disciplined and intellectually gifted. I respected his achievements and told him that we were interested. He'd never failed at anything and told me that he thought that there was still a chance for him at Davis Polk. He had given everything he had to Davis Polk and he wanted to stay there to see if they would keep him. I told him that we would wait for him to be ready. Within four months he called, devastated that he'd been dismissed. He wanted me to tell him that they were wrong, and he sought my comfort and confirmation of his worth. I told him that Wachtell Lipton had taken rejects from a number of large firms, including myself, and understood such dismissals. That appeared to be the assurance he needed, although we both knew that the social aspects of the rebuff couldn't be healed by Wachtell Lipton.

"His actions were self-destructive," Ilan said.

"It looks that way," I said.

Ilan ticked off the failures to conceal. "Keeping an account in his own name," he said, "was stupid." For Ilan that was the term of greatest condemnation, an ignominious and demeaning defect. The speculative moment didn't quite satisfy. I'd been able to muse, but couldn't see why Carlo would trade on inside information.

"Ilan," I asked, "why would he do it?"

"For the money." And then Ilan shrugged again, and I have his sweet smile in my mind.

"He never took the money," I said, satisfied with the last word.

What I didn't know then was that Carlo had once told Ilan that he wanted to be very rich. And Ilan believed that Carlo "took" the money because the account was directly under his control and accessible to him, in a manner never available to Ilan in his arrangement with Levine. Given the openness of the account, Ilan was sure that Carlo paid taxes on the trading profits, a tangible step very close to taking the money. Ilan didn't explain these distinctions to me, which would have given him away, leaving me to feel that I'd made a telling point. Ilan's silence in response to my comment was meaningful only later. But by then the moment was gone.

Despite the damage to the firm, including adverse publicity,

Wachtell Lipton rallied to Carlo's defense, convinced that his actions proceeded from forces beyond his control. In that view, Carlo was a victim and shouldn't be punished. As a firm, the partnership pleaded with the court not to put him in jail. The firm sent a letter, on behalf of the partners and associates, asking for clemency. The court also saw Carlo as sick and pitiable, and was lenient. His trading account was taken by the government, and he was suspended from law practice for five years, but he wasn't disbarred from practicing law or sent to prison, nor did he sustain fines or any other penalties.

The firm concluded that others—not us—had ruined Carlo. He had been cheating before he came to the firm and that relieved everyone in the firm of guilt. If his sole working experience had been at Wachtell Lipton, we might have thought of the firm as the root cause, as if the pressure of the practice generated his behavior. Wachtell Lipton concluded that the solution to the problem was to stop hiring people who had worked at other firms and only hire directly out of law school. Our innocence comforted us. With changes in hiring policy, no one expected to see a repeat of his behavior. We also concluded that Carlo was unique. Whatever my doubts, I accepted the collective conclusion. It took five years to discover Ilan's breaches of trust.

NOTHING IN THE way Carlo was caught could lead Ilan to believe that the same thing would happen to him. Nonetheless, Ilan gradually tried to extricate himself from Levine, and for over a year, beginning in 1983 and until the spring of 1984, Ilan refused to give Levine any information. To counter Ilan's resistance, Levine asked him, at various times, if he wanted money from his account. Ilan always refused the money. But Levine kept telling Ilan about his share. In the spring of 1984, Ilan resumed giving Levine information, and Levine insisted on regularly mentioning the amount Levine allocated to Ilan. In the last such description, Levine told Ilan that there was $300,000 for him.

Ilan would say: Dennis Levine is my friend. But on this new plane of shared secrets there were new rules. Ilan had to have a basis for extrication. There is rarely a reason for thinking about how to extricate yourself from your friends. Here, however, there had to be a way out. For Ilan, the way out was deniability. He'd signed no papers, opened no accounts, had access to none, and had taken no money. Several months before he became a partner he stopped giving Levine information. He could say: I was never a party to this. I never exchanged any information. Levine, however, wanted him entwined. Ilan would tell him: "You are to tell no one about us." And Levine would assure him that he had told no one. But Levine was uncontrollable. He told Robert Wilkis, part of his ring at the investment banking firm of Lazard Frères & Co., that he had a source at Wachtell Lipton, whom he described as being "a young associate close to Lipton" to give credibility to his statement. Levine wanted to hold a dinner party for all his informants so they all could meet each other. Ilan thought Levine was crazy and told him so in vehement terms. Frightened of exposure, Ilan told Levine that he wouldn't go to the dinner.

It wasn't exposure that Levine sought. He wanted to tie everyone to him. He was the hub, and the others were the spokes. There was power in having a hold on others, and Levine wasn't about to relinquish that power over Ilan. Noting that power, Ilan saw his vulnerability. Also contributing to Levine's power was Ilan's well-known friendship with Levine. If Levine was caught, questions would be raised about what they did together. If enough questions were asked, there could be damaging answers. At various times, Ilan told me that he was trying to get Levine to use the firm on his deals. Levine was moving up the investment banking ladder: he had gone from Smith Barney to Lehman Brothers at a more senior level. But I had worked on a deal with Levine and was not impressed. Ilan told me that I underestimated Levine and should have lunch with him sometime. He was offering me a reason other than friendship for their meetings. I never had lunch with Levine.

Levine always gave Ilan the impression that he was making a lot of money at his jobs. After he moved to Drexel Burnham from Lehman Brothers in the fall of 1984, he told Ilan, who had just ceased giving Levine any information, that he was being paid so well it was "almost enough to make me an honest man." Ilan took that to mean that Levine was nearing his financial goal, but given the glee with which it was said, Ilan was certain that the goal would soon increase.

On May 12, 1986, Ilan was with his wife, Diane, at a black-tie fund-raising dinner for Mount Sinai Hospital, held at the Waldorf-Astoria, when she heard that Dennis Levine had been arrested. Ilan had heard the news earlier in the day. The room was filled with lawyers and investment bankers who knew Levine. Levine was supposed to be at the dinner but had been arrested in the afternoon and spent the night in jail. The room buzzed with speculation. Ilan's face showed a certain confusion. Diane, aware that Dennis Levine was Ilan's friend, told me that when she saw Ilan's face she first suspected that he might be involved with Dennis's illegal trading.

It was inevitable that Levine would get caught. His assumption was that early purchase activity, long before there were any merger rumors, wouldn't be picked up on any enforcement radar screens. As convincing as that may have been to him, he was looking at only one source of exposure. In that environment there are always numerous sources for discovery. In Levine's case, certain brokerage employees in a Merrill Lynch office in Venezuela noticed the successful trading of a certain Bank Leu account in the Bahamas, which confirmed for them that there was smart money at work. They didn't know the owner of the account and didn't care. Their interest was in making money by doing the same thing. Nothing prevented the Merrill Lynch brokers from making trades paralleling the smart money Bank Leu account. That is what they did until a disgruntled Merrill employee, not included in the trades, sent the New York office an anonymous letter reporting the activity. The New York office sent the information about the Bank Leu account to Gary Lynch, then head of the enforcement division of the SEC. It didn't take the SEC long to pierce the veil of secrecy surrounding the numbered Bank Leu account and uncover Levine and his trading activities.

Once Levine was arrested, Ilan was forced to consider what Levine might reveal. Thinking about it was painful and enervating. Shortly after the arrest, while on a business trip in Southern California, Ilan contemplated suicide. He drove his rented car to a cliff and stared down, thinking of killing himself. What stopped him was his ability to deny everything. Who would believe Levine? That had been his plan all along, and he would adhere to it.

On the red-eye flight from Los Angeles to New York, he listed, on a yellow legal pad, the facts as he saw them: he never took any money; there were no records; and no one involved knew his name except Levine. On the pad he filled several pages with his analysis to confirm the common sense of his plan, but he had nagging doubts about his ability to disclaim everything. Levine had lied to him about the amount in the account. When caught, Levine had $12.5 million in his account, much more than Ilan had ever imagined. Suppose Levine had told someone about him. While possible, it wasn't likely. It was wrong to speculate, and he would only deal with known facts, which limited what he could put on his yellow pad. The known information showed that he had been careful. Who would believe Levine? Didn't that make him safe? He had no one to talk to or confide in, and the only exterior expression of his situation was on that pad. The pad, with the list of known facts, told him that he had to adhere to his plan.

Once Ilan concluded his analysis, he acted as if he was unaffected by Levine's arrest. There were moments when the stress may have showed, such as the transaction in which Drexel Burnham was leading a bid to acquire a Wachtell Lipton client and Ilan found out that Drexel Burnham had represented the target company a number of years before. Here was a possible conflict of interest. Ilan decided, with the client's permission, to take out a full-page advertisement in *The Wall Street Journal* questioning Drexel Burnham's integrity for being on both sides of the transaction. Specifically, he wanted to embarrass Drexel Burnham by mentioning Dennis Levine and questioning whether Drexel Burnham should play so fast and loose with client relationships. Since he was challenging Drexel Burnham's integrity, he showed the text he'd prepared for the ad to the litigating partner working on the transaction to see if there were any accusations that might be considered libelous. The partner was disturbed by the text and brought it to Lipton. Lipton told Ilan not to do it: it went too far and wouldn't work to benefit the firm's client. It was a strange moment, perhaps the final assertion of integrity. Or was it an involuntary scream of pain?

When the SEC issued a subpoena for the firm's and Ilan's records on Tuesday, July 8, 1986, the firm assigned four partners to respond. They confronted the SEC, demanding that the subpoena's scope be narrowed. The SEC saw that the firm was serious in protecting itself and one of its own and told the four partners to get Ilan separate counsel, that the firm's interests were adverse to his. In that confrontation the SEC did a curious thing: the SEC staff told the Wachtell Lipton partners to ask Ilan about certain specified transactions. That was a signal that the SEC had more concrete information than anyone at Wachtell Lipton anticipated. And then the SEC staff told the partners that Robert Wilkis, a young investment banker who had previously been arrested, could confirm Levine's accusations against Ilan.

The Truth Squad, as Ilan named the four partners, called him in to talk on Monday morning, July 14, 1986. They had spoken to him just after he first received the subpoena, as part of their preparation of Wachtell Lipton's response. It was then that Ilan chose the name for the group, because of their probing questions. They were: Herbert Wachtell, Bernard Nussbaum, Lawrence Pedowitz, and Allan Martin. The first three were former assistant U.S. attorneys, federal prosecutors, and Allan Martin was formerly a trial attorney with the Enforcement Division of the SEC. As a deal strategist, Ilan was more than their equal, but he couldn't rival their tenacity or their analytic ability to use facts with precision, to find inconsistencies, and to reconstruct and order events into patterns that fully illuminated them. Each was older than Ilan, none a friend. Wachtell's mind was like a razor; nothing could deflect it. Nussbaum was warm and affable, but always astute; he would try to keep the hard edge of the inquiry from driving Ilan from the room. Martin had total command of the facts and all the intricacies of the deals involved. Pedowitz knew all the nuances of the rules. They advised Ilan at the start of the meeting on that Monday morning to get his own lawyer. Ilan knew that their commitment was to the firm and that they wouldn't give him the benefit of any doubt, but he told them he didn't need a lawyer. He felt that nothing he'd done would show up.

They spent the day with Ilan, doing good guy–bad guy routines. All of them left the room at some time, but one of them always remained with Ilan. The buffering of polite conversation couldn't conceal the deadly game at work. Ilan fully understood what they were doing, and denied wrongdoing. They had, however, something he didn't know they had: a list of deals provided to the SEC by Levine. Slowly they started narrowing the list, reviewing the cases. It was clear then that Levine had said he'd gotten information from Ilan in certain matters in which only Ilan would know such information. Ilan continued to deny, and they faced the question of whether they should actively encourage him to leave the conference room and get his own lawyer to deal with the SEC. If Ilan was guilty, they wanted to know: it was better for the firm, for everyone. But they advised him again that he could leave the room and that he had the right to consult with his own counsel.

He stayed in the room and denied everything for six hours. He ate no food, although sandwiches were available. He had a legal pad by him and doodled on it. The only information that reached him from the outside consisted of details about the status of the various moves in the takeover battle for control of NL Industries. Ilan was running that deal. He was the one person who knew all its aspects, and members of the Truth Squad fed him the information to get his reactions and suggestions. Those moments distracted him from his predicament, probably sustained him by renewing his sense of worth and command, and assured him that suspicions weren't deep enough to take the NL Industries matter away from him. Everyone in the room was impressed by his ability to concentrate on the takeover battle and not be distracted by the events in the room.

Why did Ilan submit to interrogation and then stay in the room? Believing in the wisdom of his original plan, he thought he could outwit them. An innocent man, however, would have been likely to walk out of the room, angered by the indignity of the interrogation. By staying and responding to the questions, he gave them information, raised doubts in his own mind about his legal position, and watched their confidence grow. After about six hours he understood that while he had relied on the fact that he had not taken money as the basis for deniability, they thought that they could prove the crime through the information passed. Some of the information Levine had traded on, they claimed, could have been known only by Ilan at the time. He now knew from them that someone, possibly Wilkis, could corroborate Levine's testimony about receiving inside information on certain Wachtell Lipton matters although Wilkis didn't know Ilan's name. Ilan recognized how damaging this corroboration was. At that point he asked to be given time to think matters through, giving no indication, however, of what he would do. They asked if he wanted them to leave, and he said no, they should stay. Ordinarily someone thinking through such matters would want to be by himself. Ilan, however, wanted to show them that he was doing all the thinking alone and wouldn't use the phone in the room to call outside. It was an assertion of his internal fortitude.

Sitting in the conference room, Ilan tore off the pages of doodles that were the product of his nervous energy, and on a clean sheet of paper tried to calculate whether he was caught. Again the pad became his external reference point, although it reflected only his point of view. He reasoned that over time they could possibly isolate a deal that only he knew about when the information was given to Levine. Wilkis would be credible because Levine had told him about Ilan long before Levine was caught, but Wilkis had only a description and not a name. From Ilan's perspective, it wasn't clear that they could snare him, although they claimed there was no doubt. But Ilan was exhausted from the strain of being hunted. Although he'd contemplated possible confrontation with investigators on his trip back from California, the reality was more demanding than he'd imagined and their tenacity more devastating. With the four partners sitting silently in the room, he listed for himself his logical alternatives: he could fight and continue to deny wrongdoing; he could commit suicide; or he could confess. For him, the list was rational and the range of choices confirmed its completeness. He didn't relish fighting, for he had already begun to experience its personal toll and he didn't have the economic resources for a sustained battle. He contemplated suicide with all its finality, ending deceit and pain. Confession would also end deceit and reintegrate his life, allow him to find equilibrium and reset his compass. Confession offered an avenue to a new life, but before he found a new life he would experience all the agony and horror of being pilloried, all the afflictions of retribution. But whatever the punishment, it wouldn't last forever. He could see a new life in five or more years. At least forty-five minutes passed as he wrote out his options and considered them. He took his time with each of the choices. The partners remained silent throughout. Finally, he decided to confess.

When he turned to the four partners in the conference room, he was crying. He'd already begun to experience the sickening distress of exposure. His crying was uncontrollable and heartrending. With a face wet from his grief, he confessed, telling them that he'd considered committing suicide. He told them he hated his life. He told them about how he had always lived under the shadow of his older brother and about how he'd become distant from his parents. He told them he was unhappy in his marriage. He sought and found, he believed, catharsis in confession. He cried again after baring everything, shaken by his own confession, and his personal misery. They called in Robert Morvillo, an able criminal lawyer, who had also represented Carlo Florentino on the firm's recommendation. Morvillo talked to Ilan and listened to his story and afterward said he'd never seen someone so distraught. He asked them to put on a suicide watch for Ilan.

Martin Lipton called me at home early in the evening and told me that Ilan had confessed. Lipton was shaken and told me that Ilan had apologized to him and to me, recognizing that he'd hurt us and hadn't meant to do so. Lipton told me that Larry Pedowitz was also concerned about Ilan committing suicide and that Ilan would stay at Pedowitz's home for the evening. Ilan, he said, wanted to speak to me and would call me. When I hung up the phone, I cried.

ILAN CALLED ME about 9 p.m. from Pedowitz's apartment, and we were on the phone for about three hours. He told me all that he had said to the Truth Squad. The confession was a moment of great despair, he told me, but in that despair he'd realized that he could, and would, start a new life. Diane was pregnant, and there would be a third child. But he was thinking of leaving his wife as a step in beginning his new life. I told him there was no such new life, there was just his old one, and he had to put that together again by seeing his wife and talking to her. If he couldn't talk to his wife, then he had to talk to his parents and make peace with them. The family would be hurt, and he had to deal with that hurt and seek comfort from them, because that would be the only comfort that he would get. I told him that most people outside of his family would be angry and want to see him punished, and that he had to be prepared to face that anger.

Our talk finished at midnight, and Ilan tried to telephone Diane at their summer house on Long Island, but the phone was either disconnected or off the hook. He then called his parents and told them what he'd done. They asked about Diane, and when he told them he couldn't reach her, they decided to drive to Long Island to the summer house and bring her home to New York. It was after 1 a.m. when they started out. Partway into the trip their car broke down. They wound up at an all-night Long Island gas station, where they were fortunate enough to find a lift to the summer house. Already shaken by the message they carried, they were further upset from the delay. They arrived at about 5 a.m. and woke Diane by tapping on the windows, frightening her. It was she, the person they had come to help, who ultimately comforted them and helped them back to the city. In helping each other, they were drawn closer together.

I wasn't able to sleep that night. Obsessively, I reviewed all I knew about Ilan. Nothing in his behavior had hinted at his deception. Even in retrospect, I couldn't find strange behavior. It was as if another person had betrayed our trust—not Ilan. I saw a fine person destroyed, losing his profession and forever marked. I thought of the firm. It had been hurt again at the partnership level: first Carlo, then Ilan. It was demeaning to have to face the fact that no other firm had experienced such significant breaches of trust by two partners. Could the firm withstand the revelations? I was confident that the firm would be able to ride out the rough time ahead. But how could it have happened and what if it happened again?

There was a troubling difference between most of the older partners and the young partners and associates, despite common background, common schools, and even common friends. The difference was more than one of age. The founders and most of the early members of the firm were largely committed to independence (and personal expression) in the formation of the firm. Monetary rewards were secondary, since their talents could usually command more at established firms than a fledgling organization could provide. The people who came later were often picked by the firm to preserve what had been developed, and they in turn were attracted by the success of the firm and the money that such success generated for the partners. Everyone in the firm was well off, but generally, in my view, the young partners seemed to want to own more things than many of their elders. Ilan, when he became a partner, promptly bought a brownstone on the West Side of Manhattan. Was this difference a source of the firm's problems with Carlo and now Ilan?

I was trained to pull together disparate facts and to try to predict events that the facts presage. I tried here, but I wasn't able to anticipate, from all I knew, the twists and turns that would follow Ilan's confession or its effect on the firm or on me.

THE PARTNERS HAD seen how the pain of confession had immobilized Carlo and rendered him incapable of defending himself, and for that reason the firm recommended a psychiatrist for Ilan to help him handle his pain and to prepare for his defense. We all thought there would be great suffering, and we were prepared for that. Ilan, however, was not like Carlo. Within a day of his confession Ilan called everyone he'd been working with in the firm, proposing lunch and asking about the status of the NL Industries transaction. This was unexpected, since Ilan was withdrawing from the firm and arrangements were under way to end his status as a partner. For Ilan to try to maintain friendships was also confusing. Many of the older partners, who had judged Ilan favorably at the time of his admission to partnership, felt deceived by him and remembered his arrogance. They experienced an unraveling of their feelings to those of an earlier time when they had first judged Ilan and found him wanting. Those younger than Ilan, for whom he'd been a mentor, were more willing to treat his deceit as aberrant and try to keep the friendship. Some people waited for the firm's official reaction to tell them how to act. That would not be forthcoming, because the differences of opinion among the partners were deep, unusual for the firm. Associates who had worked with Ilan and some young partners asked me if they could have lunch with him. I told them that they could. It was a positive step, I thought. Ilan hadn't, like Carlo, become crushed or turned on himself.

Within a few days complex issues emerged. It seemed that Ilan had recently withdrawn about $300,000 from the firm. There were no restrictions on a partner withdrawing money. The money, together with his other drawings from the firm, was slightly less than his anticipated pro rata share of firm income at that point in the year. Ilan used the funds to pay down the mortgage bearing a high interest rate on the brownstone he'd bought a year earlier. He'd made the arrangements to pay down the mortgage and withdraw the funds from the firm, plus arrangements for an additional borrowing of $125,000, from Chemical Bank on May 7, 1986, about five days before Levine was caught. The transaction was not effected until the end of the month, however, after Levine's indictment. Once Ilan confessed, the drawing of the large sum angered many at the firm, and they repeatedly described it to those people who still talked to Ilan as a scheming, manipulative act. They didn't know that Ilan's action had been initiated to reduce interest costs before there was a tangible threat of discovery.

Having Ilan's confession, the SEC then dealt with his lawyer over settlement matters. Ilan regularly visited his psychiatrist and his lawyer and grew restless, for he had little to do other than working around the house and taking care of the children. At his request I met him in front of the Plaza Hotel and shared lunch with him on a bench in Central Park, unaware then that I was following with him the same route he'd taken with Levine when he first gave him inside information. Ilan's selection of the meeting place was unconscious, or at least he never mentioned its significance to me.

He wanted to discuss his efforts to have the firm stand behind him and help him avoid prison. He was seeking the support Carlo had gotten, and was having difficulty in assessing the reaction of the firm to his requests. In the firm, there was more anger than sympathy, which he could now realize, for I was one of the few people who would have lunch with him. As a consequence, his window into the firm had been closed.

Ilan spent a lot of time speculating about how the various partners would act in terms of helping him. What he didn't understand was the degree of confusion. Lipton would ultimately determine the firm's point of view. At that moment Lipton was uncharacteristically ambivalent, sympathetic but prepared to embrace other points of view because he didn't want a division in the firm. Lipton had asked me, one day when I was in his office on another matter, if we were responsible. He took me by surprise because until then I didn't fully appreciate what had been troubling him. I had felt responsible for Ilan, but I thought my feelings were different from those of my partners because Ilan and I were close. Nevertheless, I had quickly answered: No. How could we be responsible? No one knew the rules better than Ilan, and no one had ever been more carefully instructed and nurtured. Lipton's concern was that we had raised Ilan as a lawyer and we were responsible for him. I could understand his disquiet, and my denial of our responsibility didn't resolve the question. It continued to trouble him and me and others for months.

The firm, still a relatively small, cohesive group, wasn't used to factionalism. While many wanted to be humane, there were strong feelings against forbearance or clemency. The members of the firm trusted each other's judgment in all working matters. Our language was abbreviated, a shorthand that was almost a code (which I discovered when I taught at law school and had to define all my terms). Molding objectives for the clients, partners anticipated each other's actions and solutions to problems. Now we disagreed over what to do with Ilan, and we discovered ranges of differences we'd never known. The resulting tensions and ambivalent feelings weren't easy to deal with. Every action taken by the firm was by consensus, and here, since there was none, the firm was stalled. Ilan, singularly seeking clemency, and used to quick decisions and decisive actions in the firm, couldn't appreciate the extent of the ambivalence. He treated the hesitancy as negative, which depressed him.

Sitting on the park bench, Ilan and I talked about his future, and I asked him if he wanted to teach. He wasn't interested in teaching. That was something I would do, but it wasn't for him. He would look for a position in business or investment banking. Enjoying the shelter from the summer heat provided by the park, we digressed and talked about a Walker Percy novel we'd both read. Discussing books was something we had done before. It was easy to fall into familiar patterns and he brought up the business of the firm and the deals we were in. But these were topics I refused to discuss because Ilan would never again be a part of the firm. Although I was meeting to help him ease his pain, in my refusal to share the firm's work with him, I became a reminder of his banishment. When I left him he started to walk to his psychiatrist, having time to waste.

THE SEC PLANNED to bring a criminal action against Ilan through the U.S. attorney. The only dispensation they offered was an agreement not to seek maximum penalties for Ilan's crime provided that he turned over all his money. The SEC was particularly harsh in defining what this meant: they demanded the capital in his pension plan, his capital in the firm, all his personal savings, and the entire interest in the brownstone and in the summer house, which included the recent drawings from the firm. The demand totaled approximately $1 million. The SEC took the position that Ilan was liable for all profits made from tips given by him whether or not he had received any of the profits. Unlike Levine, Ilan had nothing with which to bargain, and he was outraged because he'd never taken any money. His culpability, he felt, didn't justify their demands for money that he'd earned himself. The SEC had already retrieved all the ill-gotten gains from Levine. They were trying to collect twice. His counsel told him that the court was unlikely to impose such a heavy monetary penalty; fines would be minimal compared with what the SEC was trying to extract, and the court would mete out punishment through a jail sentence. His counsel also held out the hope that the jail sentence would be nominal or would be suspended.

The SEC's position contained a further threat, in addition to seeking maximum penalties. They stated that if Ilan didn't cooperate by settling on their terms, they would list in the official charges against him each of the deals in which he had passed on information to Levine. The period covered was about five years, and there were numerous matters involved. The complaint would show that his actions were not some slight momentary fall from grace, but a pattern of illegal activity. Ilan didn't want that displayed, because it would bring further embarrassment to himself and to the firm. And the firm worried about all the matters being recounted since a full listing could have the effect of encouraging people to bring civil claims against Wachtell Lipton. The firm also wanted Ilan to settle because it was felt that it would put the matter to rest. No one wanted the abuse of trust by a partner to be restated in the newspapers every time there was a motion made in his case, which could drag on for some time.

Although the firm's and Ilan's objectives were substantially the same, Ilan wanted a concession from the firm. He sought agreement or a tacit understanding that if he gave up his money, he'd be doing it for the firm's benefit, which meant that the firm would seek leniency in his sentencing and would give him money in settlement of his partnership interest after his conviction. He sought a letter from the firm and from key partners asking the court not to send him to jail, and wanted an agreement that he would be treated with the same compassion as Carlo Florentino. The firm wouldn't, and didn't, make any promises to him. He was told that he would be judged when the time came for judgment and he shouldn't have any illusions. However, he responded that he was helping the firm. Accordingly, he said, the firm had to be sensitive to the problems he faced and the concessions he'd made in light of the fact that his lawyer had advised him that he was better off fighting than conceding.

Finally, Ilan's lawyer negotiated a settlement in which Ilan agreed to pay the SEC $485,000. Ilan retained only his residence, the brownstone on the West Side of Manhattan. Diane, however, refused to accept the SEC settlement until they agreed to allow her to retain her one-half interest in their summer house. The SEC's complaint against Ilan mentioned his involvement in tipping on twelve matters and described only two of them with specificity. Later on, however, *The New York Times* and *The Wall Street Journal* reported on the deals that Dennis Levine had been involved in and mentioned the firm's representation of one of the participants, publicity that could not be controlled and was considered damaging.

THE MEMBERS OF the firm decided that there would be no official Wachtell Lipton letter written on behalf of Ilan, but that if any partner or associate wanted to write his own letter he could do it as a matter of conscience. Given the anger, and the fear of lawsuits against the firm, that was a substantial concession. It was an acknowledgment that there were people who cared for Ilan and that it would create an irreparable division in the firm if those feelings couldn't be expressed. I worked on a letter over one weekend and sent a copy to Lipton. My letter was an emotional plea for mercy, and after reading it, Lipton concluded he would join my letter, and encouraged clients to send letters also.

Ilan called several clients with whom he had worked and asked them to help him. On the advice of his lawyer, Robert Morvillo, Ilan also gave an interview to *The American Lawyer*. The article gave the facts of the insider trading and treated him like a brilliant but naïve prodigy. Since he'd taken no money and had given up everything, the article engendered sympathy from all quarters.

Although he had no control over its timing, the story on Ilan was published before his sentencing hearing, and it looked like it would be helpful. Also, after its publication a number of people came forward with offers for jobs of substance. People close to Ilan had already offered him employment, but others, now seeing Ilan portrayed in a sympathetic light, could appreciate his ability and believe that he would never break the law again. It seemed likely at this point that he could have a fruitful career in business. He wouldn't be able to act as a lawyer, but often the financial rewards are greater for those who act as principal or, like investment bankers, represent principals in their deals.

There was some reason for Ilan to hope that his sentencing would be light. David Brown, working at Goldman Sachs while part of the Levine ring, got only thirty days in prison, to be served on weekends. The most difficult hurdle Ilan faced was that he was the only practicing lawyer involved in the Levine scheme, and the court would take that into account.

At his sentencing Ilan made the following statement to the court:

> I pleaded guilty because I am guilty—guilty of criminal conduct, guilty of gross stupidity and guilty of betraying my family and my partners. I am making this statement not to excuse my conduct but to clear up what I did and to express my sorrow and remorse. I apologize to my family, my partners, and the firm's clients for my conduct, and stand ready to suffer the consequences of my actions.

Despite the numerous letters urging that Ilan not be sent to prison, Judge Robert Sweet felt compelled to sentence him to serve a year and a day. In his opinion of January 23, 1987, Judge Sweet, who hadn't sentenced any of the others involved in Levine's ring, said:

> If this sentence involved just you and your family, the outcome would be that you have suffered quite enough for the tormented acts you committed. But unfortunately, the sentence involves all of us and the strength of the laws of our society. Simply stated a breach of trust at this level with this effect requires a jail term as a deterrent, as a statement by our society that its rules must be obeyed and that personal integrity remain a paramount requirement of our society.

The court also concluded that Ilan was not motivated by greed or ambition, but by a need for friendship, and stated:

> Dennis Levine took you. He gave you that special feeling of belonging, as well as a sense of guilt because you knew what you did was not right, but wrong.

The conviction required under New York law that Ilan be disbarred. The law had been changed after Carlo's conviction. Judge Sweet addressed the issue by saying that he would personally back Ilan if he sought at a later date to be readmitted to the bar. The court was aware that his wife was pregnant and would be delivering within days of the decision. The court gave him two months after the birth of the baby to put his affairs in order before reporting to the federal prison camp at Danbury, Connecticut.

WHEN THE BABY was born, I visited Diane at New York Hospital. Ilan was home taking care of the other two boys since there was no one to help at home. Diane was in the maternity ward, with four beds in the room and little space for guests. Minimal privacy was provided by a curtain which did not draw completely around. Her mother was at her bedside keeping her company, comforting her. Capable and intelligent, Diane had accepted, without rancor, what had befallen them. She didn't criticize Ilan, in spite of knowing all that he'd said to others about their marriage. Seeing her with her mother, I felt that I was intruding. I stepped out to leave them alone, telling them I would look at the baby.

I met Ilan's parents while I was viewing the baby. They too had stepped out of the room to give the two women some privacy. The hall was better lighted and less cramped than the ward. Ilan's mother turned to me and asked why the judge had been so hard on Ilan. I gave the conventional answer: he felt he had to make an example of Ilan, who should have known better. It was an unusual moment, for there was little more that I could say, but we stood together observing the infant behind the glass, allowing time to pass, as if our thoughts were being shared. The infant was sleeping serenely, born unblemished. I looked at him with the knowledge that there is so much that can go wrong, despite a parent's best efforts. And then Ilan's mother looked into my eyes and asked me, pointedly: Why did Ilan do it?

It was a question that she had obviously asked of herself and others. She thought that perhaps I could tell her the answer, but I couldn't. All I could do was speculate, and sadly, one doesn't speculate about such things or discuss them with parents, however great their right to know.

I don't know, I said, and took her hand and kissed her cheek before I left.

A week later there was a bris, the ritual circumcision of the son at Ilan's home, which was a concession to the family. There was a good crowd, including some clients Ilan had represented, a number of the firm's associates, and family and friends. I was the only partner attending. I told Diane that I thought there was a good turnout and she told me, in an acerbic way, not as good as eighteen months before for the second son. But thus far Ilan had survived the ordeal in a way that Carlo Florentino had never been able to do. Being open about his disgrace, it was as if he were no longer disgraced. All the people there wished him well, and there was optimism for the future.

ILAN WAS PREPARING to go to prison. His chief concern was the money his family would need while he was away. He called me about three weeks before his sentence was to begin in March 1987 and asked me over the phone if I would lend him some money. I told him that we should have lunch and talk about it. About a week later we met at the Brasserie, in the Seagram's Building, and sat in a booth for two, facing each other. Floor-to-ceiling dividers between the booths gave a sense of privacy, and so separated, except for people seated with their backs to us at the adjacent counter (which curiously added a sense of remoteness), we could be open and direct. He looked tense, but as I examined him I saw that he'd retained his ability to relax, soften his features, and exude confidence. When he spoke, his voice was well modulated and resonant.

He told me that he wouldn't need money from me after all, that he intended to seek financial help from the firm to ease the burden of a year without income and the considerable expense of his legal bills. He had already asked Milton Gould, the senior partner of Shea & Gould, to represent him and present his interests to Wachtell Lipton. Ilan had chosen Milton Gould as a person whom the firm would respect and recognize as a wise man. Gould would be trying to get payment from the firm for Ilan's remaining partnership interest, in effect asking for Ilan to be treated like the partners who retire or leave the firm for other employment. In those instances there were varying amounts of the firm's receivables paid to them after their termination.

If there was any noise in the room, I didn't hear it. Although Ilan didn't see it, this action was likely to offend everyone. His asking a prominent New York lawyer to get in the middle of the firm's internal affairs would not be easy to accept. These were private matters to which no one on the outside had ever been given access.

I asked him: "Ilan, why did you do that?" I was aware of the tenseness in my voice, although I tried to control it.

When he answered, he harked back to October 1986 when the settlement with the SEC was being discussed. He was explicit then in stating that someday the firm should expect him to come back asking for financial help. There was a tautness in his voice when he spoke, revealing the pressure of his imminent prison term.

"Where are you getting your money from now?" I asked. Although disconcerted by his actions, I had a line of questions previously thought through because he'd asked me for a loan. This was the first of the questions I was going to ask him, all designed to explore whether he needed to borrow money.

"My father is giving me money," he said. His voice was less strained now. "But my father is borrowing against his real estate investments. His investments are illiquid. It's very hard on him."

"How much equity do you have in your house?" I asked.

"Five hundred thousand dollars," he said without hesitation, knowing precisely what he was worth.

I paused to evaluate his answer, thinking he was a bit optimistic in his assessment of value (assuming in my calculations that it was worth $300,000, about what he'd taken out of the firm to pay down the mortgage), but it was an honest response, which took into account all the equity, and favored the direction of my questions.

"How much do you need to live for a year?"

"About one hundred thousand dollars," he said, seeing where all this was leading, but directly responding.

"Then sell the house," I said. He couldn't borrow against the house because he had no job and his employment prospects were, at best, cloudy.

"I won't sell the house. We need a place to live," he said firmly. That response attempted to dismiss my conclusion, as if the equity in his house didn't exist. He wiped some bread crumbs from the table.

"You don't need to live in a brownstone in Manhattan. You can rent a house in the suburbs," I said, taking him back to the point.

Ilan said, "I don't want to live in the suburbs." His tone was even, but he was annoyed with my statements, telling me by the irritated curl of his lip that I should know him well enough not to suggest that.

"It's not you that's going to be living in the suburbs. And if Diane wants to be in Manhattan, rent an apartment." I wouldn't let it drop, despite his frowning.

"I'm not going to sell the house," he said, the tautness back in his voice to end the discussion. What he didn't say, and what I found out only later, was that he and Diane didn't relish the thought of uprooting the family, especially when Ilan wouldn't be available to help in the transition. The house was their only anchor to the life they had, and with the birth of the third child, change was too much.

"You feel guilty," I said, "because you're hurting your father, but there's no reason to do that to him. You can take care of yourself."

"The firm knows that I need financial help," he said, "and no one objected when I said I would come back for help." He was full of conviction. One of his hands on the table closed tightly.

"No promises were made. And sentiment has changed."

"Gould has made an appointment to see George Katz tomorrow," Ilan said. "I wanted you to know about the meeting. I didn't want you to feel that I had blindsided you, and so I held it off until I could see you." His voice was sincere, expressing his concern that I shouldn't be adversely affected in the firm by his actions.

"Does George Katz know the reason for the meeting?" I asked.

"No," he said. "Gould didn't tell him."

"I have to tell him."

"That's fine," he said, nodding, anticipating that I would have to do that.

"You won't get anything, Ilan," I said.

"That's up to Milton Gould," he said, his voice rising.

Someone turned from the counter to look at us, and I waited until the person turned away. Ilan believed that he had acted in the firm's interest in settling with the SEC. He had gotten very little out of the settlement, other than avoiding costly litigation. The devastating result to him from the penalties imposed, including a prison term, seemed to foster his belief that he'd sacrificed himself for the firm. Carlo never had to surrender his savings or serve time in prison.

"There's only one way you could have gotten money," I said, sidestepping confrontation. "You had to ask Lipton. No one else would be sympathetic."

"I thought about it," he said. "I thought a lot about it." His hand spread out on the table and he slowly drew a series of circles as if following the pattern over and over again, showing the degree to which he had thought about it. "I can't ask Lipton. When I wrote to him to ask him for a letter to the judge, I said I wouldn't ask him for any more favors. I meant that, and still do. But I cleared the path in October for a request for money from the firm when I told Bernie Nussbaum, and he told everyone, that I would be coming back with a request for financial help. Do you see my situation?" He paused and looked at me to see if I could appreciate the course he'd followed and where it all led. "But the SEC took all my money away. I earned that money. I wasn't like the others," he said, referring to the larger circle of inside traders, which in his mind included Carlo. "I never took any money. They took bagfuls of money."

There was no doubt that he'd never taken any money. Judge Sweet thought that he was hungry for friendship, and thus was seduced by Levine, who offered friendship. Sweet concluded that Ilan's motives weren't greed or ambition. But Carlo had never taken any money either (although he had ready access to it and might have ultimately taken it), and he wasn't twisted by a co-conspirator. What was it, then, that drove them over the edge? In my mind the link between Carlo and Ilan was their fear of failure. They both experienced it early and were driven by it. If success eluded them, they would seek money to cushion the loss. While their histories and actions were different, they responded to the same fear. Ironically, the firm offered both of them success, the antidote to their fear. For Carlo, it was too late because he'd already experienced failure at Davis Polk. From the start Ilan hadn't trusted the firm to make him a partner, and he gave away inside information shortly after he began working, well before he had any serious problems in the firm. By not touching the money, each sought to keep his integrity intact. Carlo kept the money within his grasp. For Ilan, the money was outside his control, almost not real, and he took inordinate care to assure himself that his professional advice was not tainted. In different ways, but with significant similarities, they tried to control their demons. The human heart has multiple chambers. But they can't be kept separate; each affects the other.

"Taking money wasn't the crime," I said.

"But I have nothing," he said. "I gave all my money away. I tried to protect the firm. Now I need money for my family so they can live. I have to pursue this matter."

He didn't turn away from me when he finished, leaving no doubt of his sincere belief that, given the circumstances, he'd acted honorably.

"No one will treat you like a partner," I said. He saw some connection left between him and the firm, entitling him to consideration like a member of the family. His financial burden could easily be lightened by the firm. But now that he'd been sentenced, everyone saw the cord as cut, all ties severed. "If you'd been honest at the time you were promoted to partner, you wouldn't have been a partner." My voice was strong, expressing the firm's position.

"I did those deals that earned the money for the firm," he said. "I earned the money." After sentencing, he had been offered loans by at least two clients of the firm to help him while he was in prison, but had turned them down. He didn't want to be beholden to them when it came to deciding on his new career. In his mind he was seeking money from the firm to help him begin his new life. He saw this aid as the fitting way to end the relationship.

"Ilan, you hurt everyone. The damage is irreparable," I said. "That's all anyone sees or cares about."

In the firm, there had been numerous attempts at explanations. Everyone always asked the same questions. Why did Ilan do it? First Carlo, then Ilan. Why did it happen to us again? The explanations led nowhere. None had predictive value, including mine. The firm continued to hire young people, but all the care taken in assessing them was no guarantee against future breaches of trust. Moreover, in the name of prudence, it was easy to exclude good people. Would the firm now be prepared to hire the young John Hunt, an honorable man with a conscience and good heart, who had taken temporary employment in a laborer's job to buy a suit to start work and may not have been entirely forthcoming about his intentions. Could we now credit his ambition and smile, as I had ten years before, at the story of the old gent's annoying cross-examination at the time of the Character Committee interview? It was easy to lose your confidence and trust in people, all to your detriment. But as I watched Ilan, I saw him preparing to devastate my argument that the firm had been deeply hurt.

"First, the firm's business hasn't been affected. Second, there have been no lawsuits against the firm. And third, if there were, there is no possibility of recovery," he said with fierce legal logic, which was probably correct on each point. For him, there was no harm. His conclusions buoyed his sense that he should get help from the firm.

What was strange was that no one would think that he'd do anything wrong again, but they would think, because of Carlo and then him, that it could happen to the firm again. For that reason alone the firm was tarnished.

"Loss of business and lawsuits are not the measure of the harm. The firm is not the same, even if all the points were conceded," I said, not describing for him the anger that was felt in the firm. All deals were now discussed only on a need-to-know basis. The easy intimacy was gone, and my relationship with the people who worked with me was more distant. Of all the emotional wounds, betrayal tears the deepest and takes the longest to heal.

"No one will ever feel that he owes you anything," I said.

"We'll see," he said, meaning that Milton Gould would make his case.

That was the last time I saw him before he went to prison.

▼

GEORGE KATZ MET Milton Gould over lunch. George was the most accessible of the founding partners, warm and easygoing, which was the reason Gould set the appointment with him. George was the firm's historian, and in many respects its conscience. He came to the meeting as an advocate for the firm. Gould knew all this about George, and he asked George to tell him the firm's side of the story. Gould had been intrigued by Ilan and his story, but hadn't agreed to represent him until he heard both sides. Gould, one of the country's foremost trial lawyers, was a formidable man of vast experience and at least twenty years older than George, then in his mid-fifties. Gould would make up his own mind. They fully discussed the issues, and it was a long lunch.

After the meeting Milton Gould advised Ilan not to pursue the matter, and Ilan agreed. Gould had seen the anger that had built up in the firm against Ilan. All the sensibilities in the firm had coalesced: Ilan was no longer part of the firm, and the firm wasn't responsible for him or obligated to him.

Ilan and I had one last conversation before prison. I called him the day before he left.

"I'd like to get you some books to take with you," I said. We'd talked about my making up a reading list of novels and plays and various texts that would entertain and occupy him.

"They won't let you take anything with you," he said.

"Oh," I said, surprised. Then I understood. That was the beginning of the punishment. Everything personal was taken away. The barrenness of it was appalling. In that statement, said matter-of-factly, was the loneliness of life without family or friends.

"Is there a prison library?" I asked.

"A good one," he said firmly. He'd thought through all I was thinking, and knew what he was facing. He didn't ask for a list.

"Do you know your address?" I asked.

"Not yet," he said.

"Write to me and I'll send you a book list."

"Yes," he said. It was a polite response, not meant as an affirmative, signaling the end of the conversation. I knew then that he was looking to find his new life and we would go our separate ways.

THE GOLD STANDARD

▼

"Predators don't have to justify their hunger."

"**B**oone Pickens is like a barking dog chasing a bus. What's he going to do if he catches it?" asked Gordon Parker, the chairman of Newmont Mining Corporation. He didn't expect an answer, but paused anyway to give himself a moment to vent his irritation. T. Boone Pickens, the source of his annoyance, had acquired a large block of stock in Newmont, 9.95 percent (an investment of over $500 million), showing serious intent. Indeed, many companies large enough to be traded on the New York Stock Exchange could be purchased outright for less. But Gordon Parker was expressing his incredulity that Pickens, whose hostile takeover bids had been limited to oil companies, could have any real interest in acquiring Newmont, one of the largest gold-mining companies in North America.

Gordon Parker was a tall, reserved man, whose appearance and urbane manner, reminiscent of Cary Grant, offered abundant charm and suggested quiet command. Parker was a South African, in his mid-forties, running an American company whose largest stockholder was an English company, Consolidated Gold Fields, which in turn had as its largest stockholder a South African company called Minorco, itself controlled by the gold and diamond billionaire, Harry Oppenheimer. Newmont had opposed Gold Fields' acquiring its stock interest and Gold Fields had opposed Minorco's acquiring its position. Neither was pleased with its largest stockholder and the potential threat to its independence. Boone Pickens, the menace of the oil patch who had forced the sale of such giants as Gulf Oil and Cities Service, now had to be factored into the situation, affecting delicate balances.

Gordon Parker didn't want to take any rash action merely because Pickens was on the scene. Like many corporate executives, Parker had become a student of takeovers. It was the summer of 1987 and acquisition activity was still intense and vigorous, confirming takeovers as indigenous to corporate life. The contests often required the target company, in defending itself, to take on staggering debt and sell valued assets to finance massive dividends to shareholders. Newmont was secure in its size and it would take strong and convincing provocation by Pickens before Gordon Parker would take any action.

We were in Newmont's boardroom, but even in his own quarters Gordon Parker showed noticeable detachment. This was my first meeting with him. I'd been called earlier in the day by Newmont's financial adviser, Goldman, Sachs & Co., to come to the meeting in the boardroom and had been introduced, before the meeting, to Richard Leather, general counsel and executive vice president of Newmont. Leather was a fair-skinned, clear-eyed man, very direct in his speech, precise and highly intellectual. He was a master chess player and attacked all problems by analyzing fully the logical moves, the resulting changes of position, and the forces at work. He'd been trained at a large Wall Street law firm much like White & Case, the firm that represented Newmont. The White & Case lawyers were present in force. William F. Wynne, Jr., was their merger specialist. He was young, but was already a knowledgeable and astute strategist. In addition, Leather had Goldman Sachs hire as their legal counsel Cleary, Gottlieb, Steen & Hamilton, and in particular a partner in that firm with whom he had worked before, so that he benefited from the advice of lawyers whom he knew and trusted. We were brought into the matter for our experience with Boone Pickens and because we were known to be able to work well with other lawyers.

Leather set out to brief me and my partner, Bernie Nussbaum, whom I'd brought with me to act as a lead litigator on the matter. I'd chosen Bernie because I valued his judgment. It's unusual to have litigators participate in the boardroom. Ordinarily, their advocacy skills are saved for court, but it had become my practice to have them involved because familiarity with all the steps taken made them more effective in court. With Bernie present, I also had a foil who would contribute a sense of how the court would see our actions, and someone to share the emotional burden of the tough decisions.

I had met Pickens when he bid to acquire Imperial American Energy in 1977. Since then he had become an accomplished raider. Bernie was familiar with Pickens's corporate warfare techniques. He'd opposed Pickens when he tried to take over Phillips Petroleum, and his knowledge was gained from months of skirmishes and the taking of Pickens's deposition. In takeovers, as in modern warfare, adversaries are often only a presence, rarely seen in person, and known mainly by their actions. Litigating lawyers, however, confront them face to face in trial preparation or in court. Bernie had been able to ask Pickens some hard questions on deposition and had gotten a chance to take his measure by baiting him. In the legal challenge, Phillips Petroleum had alleged that Pickens had given members of his Amarillo, Texas, country club inside information about his proposed takeover bid, so Bernie had questioned Pickens about his relationship to the other club members. In a pause in the deposition, while everyone was taking a break, Pickens, who had been very careful and guarded in all his testimony, invited Bernie to visit the Amarillo club. Bernie replied, "From what I've learned about the club, the membership probably wouldn't let me in." That was meant, off the record, to suggest restrictive admission practices to Pickens, a man of some political ambition. But it was said without apparent animus and with a smile and chiding humor. Pickens, in a measured response, said, "No, Mr. Nussbaum, we'd let you in. There's no issue about that." And then, free from any snare, he paused and, while smiling back and catching Bernie's tone, teasingly said, "But once in, we might not let you out." Bernie couldn't prove his case and came away from the deposition knowing Pickens to be a wily, formidable opponent.

In his briefing, Leather told us about the history of Newmont's relationship with Gold Fields and about Pickens's maneuvers. Gold Fields had acquired approximately 26 percent of Newmont in 1981, and Newmont had sued to prevent Gold Fields from attempting to get control. Gold Fields settled the legal action by agreeing to "stand still," limiting its stock purchases. As part of the arrangement, Gold Fields elected two directors of its choosing, one of whom was Rudolph Agnew, the chief executive officer of Gold Fields, a suave, cultivated man, readily likable. The arrangement was initially to last three years and in 1983 was extended to ten years, but it could be terminated earlier if anyone acquired more than 9.9 percent of Newmont's shares. For the last six years under the agreement, Gold Fields had honored all its terms, but Pickens had cleverly changed the balance by buying 9.95 percent of the Newmont shares in the open market, thus freeing Gold Fields from the standstill agreement.

Pickens's takeover vehicle was called Ivanhoe Partners, showing his humor and sense of himself by suggesting courtly times and rescuing knights. His strategy was to separate Gold Fields from Newmont and to induce Gold Fields to join with him, now that he'd freed them. Pickens, in an adroit letter to Gold Fields, which he publicly disclosed, offered to discuss various investment alternatives, including Gold Fields' swapping its stock for some of Newmont's mining assets or participating in Newmont as a minority shareholder when Pickens took control. In any event, the carcass of Newmont would be laid out and stripped.

There remained, however, an ambiguity about Pickens's motives. Pickens hadn't crossed the 10 percent threshold. If he bought over 10 percent of Newmont, he'd be subject to short-swing-profit rules and wouldn't be able to sell his stock for six months without forfeiting all profits. Thus his carefully calibrated purchases, more than 9.9 percent, to break the "standstill," and less than 10 percent, so as not to lose profits on short-term sales, suggested that he was rattling his knightly Ivanhoe saber to induce Newmont or Gold Fields to buy his stock at a premium price. This practice is known as greenmail. Supporting the theory that greenmail was Pickens's true motive was the cost of acquiring Newmont, $6 billion or more, a lot of money to raise in a venture in which Pickens had no apparent expertise.

Gold Fields, although now free of the standstill agreement, had informed Pickens publicly that it didn't intend, at this time, to disavow the agreement's terms. The statement was supposed to be a rejection of Pickens, but the qualification "at this time" left open the possibility that Gold Fields could change its mind at any time. The next move was up to Pickens, unless Newmont or Gold Fields wanted to approach Pickens about buying him out and was willing to pay greenmail.

In Newmont's boardroom after Richard Leather's briefing, Gordon Parker immediately made the point that there was no reason for Newmont to buy out Pickens. The boardroom, set up in an oval configuration, was now filled with lawyers from White & Case and Cleary Gottlieb, investment bankers from Goldman Sachs and Kidder Peabody (also acting as financial advisers), and the executive management of Newmont. Gordon Parker was flanked by Richard Leather and Ed Fontaine, his chief financial officer, a tall and lean bookish man. Leather and Fontaine supplied him with legal and financial information and together they made the business decisions.

"Buying out Pickens is probably something we can't do anyway," Bernie said.

"Why not?" Richard Leather asked.

"Pickens won't take greenmail payments. He'll take only what the other shareholders get, and nothing more," Bernie said, expressing his knowledge of Pickens. In Bernie's view, Pickens was now a national figure, and the image he projected of himself, defender of the shareholders against entrenched management, constrained his behavior and limited a quick solution like greenmail, although it would give him a substantial profit.

"What does he want, then?" Ed Fontaine asked, with irritation in his voice.

"Gold," Bernie answered, and chuckled. "You know the desire better than I do. It's the ultimate commodity."

"If we can't buy him out, then there's nothing for us to do,"

Leather said, steadfast, expressing management's resolve not to change the company. Gordon Parker had been trained as a mining engineer and had risen through the ranks by operating the mines. From his hands-on experience, he knew the disruption that change would cause in the organization.

"What's stopping Gold Fields from buying control of the company now that Pickens has freed them?" I asked.

"They're smaller than us," Fontaine said. "Their bank credit line currently limits them to $500 million, which is not enough to buy another 25 percent. They might have been able to do it a few months ago, but not now. They'll need at least another $700 million for that." The Newmont stock price, in the mid-50s, before Pickens's announcement of his stock position, had risen to the low 80s.

Leather spoke up to emphasize Gold Fields' limitations. "They regard their rejection of Pickens's invitation to do business with them as enough of a reaction to make Pickens go away and sell his stock." Leather smiled and raised his hands in a gesture which said: I don't understand how they can believe that the statement was firm enough. Seeing that we all understood his gesture, he said, "They're not being much of a big brother in this fight, and it's hard to say what they'll do if Pickens increases the pressure."

"Has Minorco spoken?" I asked.

"They're ready to help if we ask them, but Gold Fields objects to Minorco taking any kind of a position in Newmont," Leather said. "Each of the parties is jockeying for position, and with every move the alternatives narrow."

It was something like a chess game, but more involved. Here there were multiple players, with different resources, and none of their motives were known. Besides, it was no game; and as with most things in real life, there would be no rematch.

I turned to the investment bankers. "What economic actions stop Pickens?" I didn't expect a solution, but I wanted to understand their thinking. It would tell us what was making Gordon Parker balk.

"If we gave shareholders a major dividend, that would deliver value to them and deplete our liquidity. That could stop him," Tom Mendell said. Mendell was with the mergers and acquisitions department of Goldman Sachs and was an astute financial analyst.

His ready answer indicated that he'd probably spent considerable time presenting it before the management.

"How do we do that?" I asked.

"The company can raise over $2 billion in cash by borrowing against its assets," Mendell responded. "If we distributed the money to the shareholders in a dividend, about $30 per share, all our cash would be gone and it would be very hard for Pickens to raise money to buy the company." From Mendell's flat delivery, it was easy to see that the suggestion had been rejected.

"That just makes Newmont smaller and helps him," Ed Fontaine, the chief financial officer, said, making known to us his (and Gordon Parker's) distaste for the approach. "We give him money" (about $200 million for his roughly 10 percent of the stock in a $2 billion dividend) "and lower the price of our stock by the amount of the dividend. If the dividend's $30 per share, we lower the price per share by that amount. What we've done is help finance Pickens's acquisition."

"By itself, it may not be a winner," Mendell said defensively. "But if we also substantially increased gold production and told the market so, that might move the stock price up. The combination could work. Once the stock price is high and the cash is out of the company, there's nothing left to interest Pickens and he'll sell his shares." Mendell was pointing out the standard reason companies become targets: low stock price, with assets worth more. If you reversed the situation, pushed up the stock price and distributed the valuable liquid assets to shareholders, you would have the antidote. Standard formulas only work, however, in conventional situations.

"It's not certain," Leather said, expressing management's view.

"No, it's not certain," Mendell admitted.

"We're radically changing the company if we take those steps," Leather said. "It's a $6 billion bus that he's chasing. To declare a massive dividend is to throw money at him." He paused, satisfied with the reasons for management's inertia, but added, "And Gold Fields is not prepared to do anything. There's nothing we should do—or need do," ending the meeting on that note.

"They're not ready yet," I said to Bernie after leaving the meeting. We were walking up Park Avenue from the Pan Am Building, the site of Newmont's headquarters, to our offices.

"They don't want to act too soon," Bernie said. He then asked me technical questions about alternatives. Litigators don't spend sufficient time in boardrooms to develop technical financial expertise, but once immersed in a problem, they can quickly learn all its aspects. In response to his query as to our alternatives, I said, "My feeling is that Tom Mendell of Goldman Sachs is right. Some form of large dividend is going to be required," which made action painful.

"This is difficult," he said, "a mess."

"When isn't it a mess?" I said.

We tried to fathom the motives of all the players as we walked up Park Avenue. We were disturbed by the shadowy figures of Gold Fields and Minorco. Their positions could take any form. Gesturing and arguing as if alone, we were a strange sight, two middle-aged men totally absorbed in our problems, expressing our passions publicly. Realizing our exposure, we became self-conscious, which dampened our animation, but not our concern.

"Don't get busy on something else," I cautioned.

"I'll get us some more help," he said, giving me his assurance that he was involved.

"Let's figure it out first. More people will just get in the way."

If no one was prepared to act until Pickens moved again, we concluded, then there was nothing to do but wait for him. As a consequence, we would see a fine strategist at work.

The wait wasn't long: within a week Pickens sent a letter to each of the Newmont directors offering to buy the company for $95 per share in cash. This type of letter, known as a "bear hug," was coercive, but not lethal because the letter left it up to the discretion of the Newmont board of directors whether to accept or reject the offer. Pickens, however, had now set a price for Newmont, a substantial premium over the trading price, indicating that he was willing to acquire Newmont. On the New York Stock Exchange, Newmont's stock price moved up to the high 80s, a barometer of the pressure. However, Goldman Sachs and Kidder Peabody, acting as financial advisers to the board, were prepared to tell the board members that the price was inadequate, based on their assessment of what the company could bring if sold, which was in the range of $107 to $110 per share. On that advice, Newmont could reject the Pickens initiative and not take any further action. Although feeling the pressure, Gordon Parker resisted being bullied into taking drastic action, for Pickens's motives were still not clear. Pickens had kept his stock position at precisely 9.95 percent and hadn't made any financial commitments to raise the billions needed to buy the company, leading everyone to believe that Pickens might not have an interest in acquiring the company and was simply trying to panic the management.

After three days of silence in response to his letter, Pickens further turned the screw by beginning a tender offer at $95 cash per share for a majority of the shares, which he claimed would be followed by a merger in which the minority shares would be bought out. Pickens made no commitments as to the buyout price, which could be less than the $95 offered, making the offer coercive, to induce shareholders to get the money while they could. The tender offer was a lethal move, and the Newmont stock price advanced into the low 90s, leaving no doubt that in twenty business days, the time period for the tender offer, Pickens would acquire control of Newmont unless Newmont, Gold Fields, or Minorco took some defensive action. While Pickens's bid was subject to financing, his investment bankers, Drexel Burnham, stated that they were highly confident that the financing would be completed. Any bid of this size needed Milken's capacity to raise money. In this case, Milken and Pickens were a natural pair, master takeover entrepreneur and master financier. The marketplace, acknowledging Pickens's determination and knowing the capacity of Milken to raise staggering sums, treated the bid as if the money were in place, substantially increasing the trading volume in the stock. Long-term shareholders were being replaced by arbitrageurs and market professionals, eroding management's constituency and encouraging Pickens. It looked like very little would dissuade him.

In one of our innumerable walks to Newmont's offices, I told Bernie that we should bring a lawsuit against Pickens challenging his tender offer as defective because he didn't have the $3 billion in hand to acquire the majority of the shares he sought in his tender offer.

"You lost that one last year," he said to me, referring to a case brought in Connecticut, defending Warnaco, the apparel company.

"It didn't get fully briefed," I said, meaning that the issue was a small part of a larger case.

"What's your complaint against Pickens?" he asked, making a stern face as if he were the judge.

"He doesn't have the money," I said.

"Counsel, if you believe he won't succeed in getting the money, why are you seeking relief? His tender offer will fail," Bernie responded in high judicial style. "Don't waste the time of the court."

"You're tough," I said. His argument was devastating.

"It's the judge who's tough," he said.

"Let me change the argument," I said. "If he doesn't put up the money until the last minute, we don't know who's buying the company. He could be a front for a lot of strange people. Gold is a strategic material."

"There's nobody behind him," Bernie said.

"How do you know? There could be. He shouldn't be able to begin a tender offer until he tells where he's getting the money from. The issue is: Who is buying America?"

"This is not a good case to win that argument," Bernie said.

"It's the case we've got," I said.

"Even if we win, it won't stop him. He'll just disclose."

"He'll have to pay commitment fees to Milken and the bank lenders for the extension of credit. That's at least $30 to $40 million," I said. "That will tell us if he's serious." I spoke loudly. It was my best point.

"What's the SEC's position?" Bernie asked.

"The SEC has been trying to encourage tender offers and has tolerated this nondisclosure. Yet it's counter to its disclosure philosophy."

"You want me to bring this case?" he asked, not particularly eager. Milken had invented the highly confident letter that served as a substitute for putting up the money at the outset. It had become standard procedure for all bankers.

"Yes," I said.

"We're not only attacking Pickens, we're challenging Milken's method of doing business," he said. That realization gave him pause. He saw a fierce response to any attack we made.

"It should be brought," I said.

"Where?" he asked.

"Newmont's mines are in Nevada. Let's try the federal court in Nevada and take it away from the East to some western judges. We may get a more sympathetic hearing."

"Let's talk to the client," Bernie said when we reached Newmont's offices.

We spoke to Gordon Parker and Richard Leather, who both liked the approach. It fit in with their view that Pickens might still be trying to bully Newmont into doing something, that Pickens didn't really intend to buy the company. The Federal District Court in Nevada would be able to hear the case promptly because it was a purely legal question, without factual issues. No one had any hope, including me, that the case would go anywhere, but it had some emotional appeal and was worth a try.

"It's a warning shot across Pickens's bow," Richard Leather said. "Maybe Milken will get worried."

"That won't stop them," Bernie said.

Gordon Parker and Richard Leather went to England to talk to Gold Fields and, while in London, had talks with Minorco. Gordon Parker had been elected a member of the Gold Fields board shortly after Gold Fields had acquired its 26 percent position in Newmont, but these meetings were outside the boardroom. The English weren't participating in Newmont's board meetings now, and Gordon Parker wasn't invited to Gold Fields' meetings, all to avoid conflicts of interest. Unfortunately, the arrangements, while necessary, accentuated the conflicts. Parker and Leather were in Europe about a week, and on their return we all met in the Newmont boardroom. The travel and meetings had been wearing on them and they looked tired.

Parker reported that Gold Fields had stated that if Newmont approached Minorco for help, Gold Fields would feel free to act unilaterally to protect its position. But Gold Fields claimed that it didn't have sufficient cash to buy another 25 percent of Newmont.

Instead Gold Fields offered to sell Newmont one of its assets, a mining company, for $1.2 billion, which would then give Gold Fields the needed funds. As part of the terms of the sale of the mining company, Gold Fields was willing to agree to "stand still" at the purchase of 49 percent of Newmont's stock and to elect only a minority of the directors. The plan offered Newmont the opportunity to keep control of its destiny for another ten years, a reasonably long period by corporate standards. But the problem with the proffered solution was that the mining company to be sold was worth far less than the $1.2 billion that Gold Fields was asking for it. Gordon Parker rightfully bristled at the scheme, and said that he was prepared to reject it, even though it was the only proposal Gold Fields had made after some professed soul-searching. Minorco again said it would help, but Newmont faced Gold Fields' resistance. Thus it seemed that there was no help to be had from the large stockholders.

We had bad news from Nevada. The SEC had intervened against us, and the judge, relying on the SEC's expertise, had ruled against us. We told the group that we were appealing the case to the Federal Court of Appeals in California. The court would give us an expedited appeal, but considering the SEC's opposition, we didn't hold out much hope for the case.

There weren't many options left. Newmont could act on its own to defend itself by competing with Pickens to buy its own shares. But shares that Newmont repurchased could not be voted and would have to be canceled. For the repurchases to effectively repulse Pickens, Newmont would have to make a tender offer for slightly less than 50 percent of the outstanding shares, about 34 million shares, which would reduce the number of outstanding shares and raise Gold Fields' percentage of the stock up to almost 50 percent from its 26 percent position. The cost, at $100 a share (the price necessary to compete with the $95 Pickens tender offer), would be about $3.4 billion. That was more than the Newmont management was prepared to borrow. And if Pickens raised his price it would defeat Newmont's offer.

Interestingly, Boone Pickens was prepared to borrow almost twice that amount against Newmont's assets and radically change the company to help pay off the debt. With Milken behind him, he was encouraged to leverage the company. Milken usually promised that if a company got into trouble because of its debt structure, he would help reorganize it and work out the problems. The decision on the purchase price, however, was for Pickens to make. Pickens had been trained as a geologist, but it was unclear whether he understood all the effects the necessary changes would have on the company. Those changes, which management had been loath to contemplate, included selling its lead, zinc, copper, nickel, and cobalt mines in the United States, Canada, and South Africa, as well as Newmont's interest in Peabody Coal. In addition, the gold company would have to increase its gold production substantially to service the debt. Increasing production, to the degree contemplated by Pickens, wasted assets because recovery of gold was less efficient. Moreover, dedication to paying down massive debt meant abandoning exploration efforts and renewal of the enterprise, which were necessary to keep a mining organization intact. In effect, the company was being liquidated, with the termination of its existence in sight. Such a result was resisted by the mining engineers, including Gordon Parker.

"Pickens has already made at least $100 million on his stock. Isn't that enough?" Ed Fontaine observed.

"Predators don't have to justify their hunger," Bernie answered, directing us all not to look for faults in Pickens's scheme but to seek solutions.

Of all the alternatives, offering value to the shareholders and draining the liquidity of the company by paying a $2 billion dividend started to look like the most acceptable course. The $2 billion was approximately the value that could be raised from selling the non-gold-mining assets, which would make the company solely a gold-mining company. Psychologically, the management and the board had come a long way, prepared to change the company, but the problem with the dividend was that it wasn't certain to stop Pickens. We all sat in the room turning the problem over. Everyone was tense and tired. The four barren walls offered no horizon or windows to provide an avenue for a drifting mind. The dreariness of the room made you think that you had heard or thought of everything before, without a sense of resolution. Moreover, large groups rarely come up with a point of view that will displease anybody, and thus insight is discouraged. Contemplating a problem without a solution is enervating. Finally, however, the frustration conditioned everyone to be receptive to some harsh judgments, which Bernie began to express.

"Gold Fields is being very difficult," Bernie commented. "Offering to sell assets at prices in excess of their value is not a very constructive approach. Are they really interested in buying at these prices or have they become sellers, looking for an excuse to do a deal with Pickens?" He addressed his question to everyone in the room, but it was meant for management.

"They don't want to sell out to Pickens," Richard Leather said. Gordon Parker took out a cigar, which he carefully lit, while Leather continued. "All their other mining interests are in South Africa, and if they lose Newmont, it will seriously affect the value of their stock in the London market and their prestige as an international mining company. Rudolph Agnew told us that he is prepared to do whatever is necessary to retain Gold Fields' investment in Newmont."

"Then why would he try something so one-sided as to sell assets to us at a price well over their value?" Bernie asked, seeking to understand a complex situation. Now that Gordon Parker had started to smoke, Bernie took out a cigar and began chewing on it.

"Maybe he doesn't see it that way," Ed Fontaine responded. But from his voice I could tell that he wasn't convinced.

"He's using the threat of Pickens to get a bargain," Nussbaum said. This was the first suggestion of his point of view, and he got everyone's attention.

"That's probably part of it," Fontaine said. "He's a clever man." But his statement was a grudging acknowledgment, accepting Agnew's business acumen, and nothing more.

Agnew served on the Newmont board of directors, and it was a long time since he had been an adversary.

"But why isn't he more reasonable and evenhanded? If you assume he doesn't want to lose Newmont to Pickens, you would expect him to be more sensible." Bernie attacked the problem that Gold Fields posed by making management face it. Letting them think about what he said, he lit his cigar.

"Maybe he doesn't feel the pressure management does," someone said.

"He's aware, like the rest of us, that the time is short," one of the bankers answered.

"Then why is he waiting?" a White & Case litigator asked, turning the question back on the banker.

"He expects that management will be more pliant and give him what he wants," Bernie said. We looked at Gordon Parker, and he shook his head, indicating that he wouldn't be coerced into doing something foolish.

"He could lose everything, then," Ed Fontaine said.

"He knows it's a gamble," Leather said, "which means that he must have another card to play, an alternative." Leather recognized Agnew as an adversary.

"What could that be?" a banker asked.

"I'm assuming self-interest," Bernie said softly, waving the cigar like a baton, gathering everyone's attention.

Gordon Parker nodded.

We had all come to the point of being prepared to see beneath the surface congeniality and friendliness that Agnew always managed to convey. "In his public statement rejecting Pickens," Bernie said, "Agnew reserved the right, at a later time, to use his release from the standstill. That annoyed all of us because it weakened the rejection, making it look like he might do a deal with Pickens." Bernie paused to give everyone time to follow where he was headed. The cigar was now a pointer, punctuating his sentences. "Then Agnew threatened us by saying that he would act unilaterally if we dealt with Minorco. Which means he's up to something. Otherwise, his actions make no sense and his threat would be empty." Bernie found eye contact with Gordon Parker, then with Richard Leather and Ed Fontaine, and took a shallow puff on his cigar, before continuing. "It comes down to this: if he wants to keep his investment in Newmont secure, he must be contemplating making hostile purchases of Newmont's shares. That explains the threat—and everything."

"How effective could those purchases be?" Fontaine asked, interested in this turn in perspective.

"Gold Fields could buy 25 percent of the shares in the open

market in no more than two days, and then take control. That's why Agnew has time."

"Gold Fields doesn't have enough money," Ed Fontaine curtly reminded the group. Fontaine, as financial officer, always kept his eye on the money.

"If Gold Fields took control of Newmont, they could immediately force Newmont to declare a $2 billion dividend," I said, taking over from Bernie to cover the financial aspects of Gold Fields' strategy. "With Gold Fields then holding half the stock, their share of the dividend would be $1 billion, which would be enough at current prices, along with the $500 million they already have on hand, to more than pay for the stock. They would only need a temporary loan for a few days to be able to do that, and their banks would readily finance them."

"It's efficient," Fontaine acknowledged, "and economically more resourceful than our buying our own stock for over $3 billion."

"It's the path of least resistance, if we're not prepared to give them a bargain by overpaying for their mining company," I said. "Unless, of course, they're prepared to sell out to Pickens."

"That's very aggressive for them," someone in the group said, resisting the idea. "They would have to act hostilely."

"They were never invited to be Newmont's stockholders in the first place," Leather responded. "They were very aggressive six years ago. Six years of peace doesn't make them lambs."

"They've been known to be aggressive," someone said in an understated way that drew a laugh.

"Besides," I said, to dispel any residual disbelief about Gold Fields being hostile, "Joe Perrella of First Boston is their investment banker. He's definitely thought of acquiring control of Newmont, and probably counseled Rudolph Agnew to do it." They all knew Perrella, a tall, thin man, bald, with a well-trimmed beard that made him look like a Renaissance prince. Perrella was known to be aggressive and to counsel quick, affirmative action. It was easy to project the manipulative scheme on Perrella's persona, diffusing any remaining doubt.

"First Boston would probably finance Gold Fields' purchase of stock," Tom Mendell said.

"If we don't act soon, they'll have little other alternative," Bernie said. He put aside his cigar.

"Can they just go into the market and buy the shares against Boone Pickens's tender offer?" Richard Leather asked of all the lawyers.

"That's known as 'sweeping the street,' " I said. "It means that you buy all the shares held by the Wall Street professionals, the arbitrageurs. You pay the tender-offer price, even less if it's clear that the sweep will win. It's effective because you're buying large blocks of stock from people who know their business. The SEC has proposed rules against street sweeps, but those proposals haven't been adopted, which means that it's allowed."

"What about the courts?" Leather asked.

"In the two cases where the SEC has taken the position that street sweeps are illegal, the federal courts have ruled against the SEC. At the moment, the action is legal. Do you agree?" Bernie asked a White & Case litigator for the benefit of the group.

"Gold Fields would win that case," the litigator said. "It's a winning strategy."

"What does this all mean for our idea of declaring a large dividend to drain our liquidity?" Leather asked. His question contained a perceptive observation about Gold Fields.

"If you accept the premise that Gold Fields is intent on getting control of Newmont," I said, "then you have to rethink whether Newmont declares the $2 billion dividend." In declaring the dividend, Newmont was financing Gold Fields, and in effect handing Gold Fields the money necessary to take control. Before Gold Fields' deception had been pierced, everyone had been looking at the effect of the dividend on Pickens, but not on Gold Fields. Newmont didn't want to lose control to either Pickens or Gold Fields.

"Then it doesn't work," someone said, expressing disappointment.

"But Newmont need not give up control, if Gold Fields signs a new standstill arrangement agreeing not to take control," I said. "Gold Fields can buy shares away from Pickens, and Gold Fields can still be kept in a minority position."

"And Pickens can't counter Gold Fields' open-market purchases by doing the same thing," Leather said, "because he hasn't yet raised the necessary money." We all smiled at the irony.

Everyone now saw that we had the seeds of a solution. The question was whether Gold Fields would enter into a new standstill agreement, this time at the 49 percent level, and also agree to take only a minority of the seats on the Newmont board of directors. The arrangement offered Gold Fields the financing it needed, and dovetailed with its plans, but also clipped its wings. We were sure, however, that Gold Fields would go along with the standstill because Newmont's cooperation took away the risks it ran if Newmont opposed its purchases of shares and sided with Pickens or sought help from Minorco.

Before talking to Gold Fields, we related the plan to the board of directors for their information during one of many status report meetings. The intricacy of the maneuvers made the directors nervous. It was agreed to hire independent counsel for the directors to review all aspects of the plan, which was likely to add a conservative gloss to any action approved by the board. Meredith Brown of Debevoise & Plimpton was hired. We now had another firm of lawyers acting, which made, with local counsel in Delaware where Newmont was incorporated, five firms for Newmont alone, slowing rather than helping the process.

When presented with an outline of the proposal, Gold Fields quarreled with many of the technical aspects and found the standstill constraining now that it wasn't getting the benefit of selling Newmont its mining company. There was more work to be done.

Meanwhile, the Federal Court of Appeals in California ruled against our claim to thwart Pickens. Rather than disheartening us, it had the opposite effect. One of the three judges in the case dissented and strongly criticized the SEC for encouraging nondisclosure about the people buying up America. Ordinarily the next step in the appeal process was the U.S. Supreme Court, but the Supreme Court, even if it was interested in the case, wouldn't be able to act soon enough. Bernie chose to have the case argued before all eleven judges of the Federal Appeals Court. On the basis of the dissenting opinion, the judges decided to hear the case. The SEC was now being forced to carefully examine its articulated reasons for its rules. We knew we had little chance of winning, but getting one strong-minded judge to side with us enhanced, in the Newmont directors' eyes, our legal acumen, which would help us when we asked them to make some hard decisions. Everyone was pleased that Pickens and Milken had an unexpected fight on their hands.

There was one last chance to deflect Pickens, and Newmont took the opportunity. On the basis of the work that Goldman Sachs and Kidder Peabody had done in valuing the company, Newmont publicly rejected the Pickens bid of $95 a share as inadequate. At the same time Newmont also announced that it had obtained a $2.2 billion line of credit from a consortium of banks. The announcement indicated that Newmont was in a position to defend itself, and was a signal to Pickens that if he wanted to talk about selling his shares the money was readily available and he could call Newmont.

Boone Pickens had an uncanny sense of timing. Just as the plans seemed about to coalesce, but before we could implement them, he raised the price of his tender offer to $105 a share, sending everything into disarray. The anticipated action of the Newmont board in declaring a $2 billion dividend was to be justified because Pickens's $95 bid was inadequate in relation to the value of the company. At the higher price, however, the adequacy of the Pickens offer had to be fully reassessed. In addition, by raising the price, Pickens reopened the question of whether Gold Fields was a buyer or a seller. In the stock market, Newmont's stock price moved up a full $10 to well over $101 a share, and the trading volume increased, putting more stock in the hands of professionals. Wall Street traders now almost held control of Newmont. Pickens's entire strategy had been to separate Gold Fields and Newmont; at some price that would happen. To effectuate that strategy, Pickens had bid against his own $95 offer, something few bidders are willing to do. How firm was Gold Fields' resolve?

Everything that Gordon Parker and management wanted to avoid they were now having to face. Newmont would have to borrow more than the $2 billion originally contemplated, and not only would it have to devote itself solely to gold mining but annual gold production would also have to be sharply increased to service the larger debt. If Gordon Parker and the Newmont management didn't act, either Gold Fields or Pickens—or Gold Fields and Pickens together—would acquire Newmont using Newmont's own assets. In other words, either Newmont management sold assets and leveraged Newmont themselves or Gold Fields or Pickens would do it for them. And Minorco, not approached by anybody, would probably sit on the sidelines and watch.

Gold Fields was still committed to its investment in Newmont, even at $105 a share, expressing irritation, however, that they hadn't acted earlier, since, with each escalation of the price, purchases of shares would be that much more expensive. Goldman Sachs made another evaluation for the Newmont board and found the $105 offer for a majority of the shares inadequate.

We again went through a complete assessment of whether the plan would work after Gold Fields finally agreed to a standstill arrangement. The mechanics of the plan operated in the following way: Newmont would declare a dividend of approximately $2 billion, of which Gold Fields would get, as a 26 percent stockholder, approximately $500 million. If Gold Fields promptly purchased in the market an additional 24 percent of Newmont's shares, it would get an additional $500 million from the dividend that went with the shares that were purchased. The billion dollars it received from the dividend and the $500 million that it had from its own line of credit would help finance the purchases of the shares.

William Wynne, the White & Case partner, felt that it was best not to require Gold Fields to buy shares after Newmont declared the $2 billion dividend, but merely to give Gold Fields the opportunity to do so. It was a clever and sensible tactical move. Gold Fields would then be acting totally voluntarily and in a manner consistent with Newmont's contention that Gold Fields would otherwise seize control. The problem from Newmont's perspective was that it left it entirely to Gold Fields' discretion whether to buy additional shares. None of the business people liked the idea of not controlling Gold Fields' purchases. They saw it as a "no win" suggestion. They all saw that Gold Fields could take the dividend money and run, or Gold Fields could have a change of heart and deal with Pickens. Those were the risks. The lawyers saw the suggestion as brilliant, and it was adopted. Mike Overlock, the head of mergers and acquisitions at Goldman Sachs, and Tom Mendell spent four hours with me going over all the ramifications to see if it would work.

"Our case is that they'll buy the stock anyway," I told them. "Let's not tamper with it." Overlock, very experienced, didn't like leaving control in other people's hands. He explored all the alternatives. Ultimately, he and the others accepted the arrangement. When we presented the plan to Gordon Parker, he also was uneasy about a situation in which Newmont declared the dividend and was left to watch what happened.

"It's not all watching," I said. "There are going to be legal challenges to the dividend and the purchases in both the federal and state courts."

"It's going to be very fast, though," Leather said. "The dividend is paid out in ten days."

"Fast, but thorough," Bernie said. "In ten days you can litigate and get a judicial decision on the validity of the Apocrypha."

"What are our chances of winning?" Management wanted to know.

"There are always great risks in litigation," Bernie said, giving his customary admonition. "In Pickens we have a resourceful and determined adversary. We've spent a month analyzing this situation, and so has Pickens. The judge won't have that kind of time. In this type of a case, first impressions can often color the outcome."

"What does that all mean?" Leather asked, cutting through the cant.

"We believe we'll win," Bernie said in a cautious tone. "Otherwise, no one would be suggesting this course of action." The caution in his voice indicated that his conclusion was reasoned, and that there was no firm assurance of success. "The steps that we're taking, the declaration of the dividend, entering into the standstill agreement, and Gold Fields' purchase of shares in the open market, are each legal, valid steps. But if you put all of them together, you get something different. The judge may not like the result. You must appreciate that the court may not see our choices the way we see them, given the result, the defeat of a tender offer which offers shareholders $105 a share."

"We understand," Richard Leather said.

No action of this novelty or magnitude could be taken without touching all the bases. We had to clear it with the independent counsel for the directors who had been appointed to review our actions. Meredith Brown, acting for the directors, had gone over each step. Meredith was the son of the literary critic John Mason Brown and in his own right a scholarly and thoughtful man. Meredith understood the tension between effective defensive action and protecting the directors from responsibility for actions that would be judged too aggressive. Totally familiar with the plan, he approved it. Bernie and I consulted with Lipton, who thought that we were taking a great risk with a street sweep since its legality was the subject of debate at the SEC. He thought the size of the street sweep could color the court's thinking against us. But the street sweep was a critical part of the strategy; otherwise Pickens would buy control before Gold Fields could block him. Thus we told him there was no choice: we had to assume the risk.

Then the board reviewed it with great care. We reported all the risks. The outside directors were all business people, used to taking risks. They were familiar with the plan and all its variations and had gotten comfortable with it. They approved it knowing that if anything went wrong they would be held responsible.

We thought that Gold Fields' response would be immediate once the dividend was declared. We expected Gold Fields to plunge directly into the market. Following the morning announcement of the dividend, Boone Pickens lowered his $105 tender-offer price by the amount of the $33 per share dividend to $72 per share, but Gold Fields didn't begin buying shares on the Exchange. I called Gold Fields' lawyers at Paul Weiss Rifkind Wharton & Garrison, and was told that they were still filing forms. It seemed a lame response, and the game that was supposed to play itself was not in progress. At the same time Pickens was attacking. His lowering of the tender-offer price to $72 and continuing the offer indicated that the dividend, which drained liquidity, wouldn't dissuade him. Had Gold Fields lost its nerve? Was Gold Fields talking to Pickens? There was no way to know. None of us had anticipated our sense of estrangement.

At the end of the first day, Gold Fields went into the market and purchased about 190,000 shares of the additional 16 million shares needed. At that rate it would take them three months to make the purchases, and Pickens would win. Word drifted back to Goldman Sachs that purchases would begin in earnest the following day. But now we all had doubts about their resolve, and by 9:30 a.m., before the stock market opened, Pickens had already brought a lawsuit in the Chancery Court in Wilmington, Delaware, to enjoin purchases by Gold Fields of any stock in the open market. Pickens sought emergency relief, and a hearing was set by Vice Chancellor Jack B. Jacobs for 2 p.m. to hear the application for a restraining order prohibiting purchases.

Although Pickens's legal action was designed to chill Gold Fields' desire to make purchases, the suit galvanized Joe Perrella of First Boston Corporation, Gold Fields' banker, into action. First Boston began to buy all the available stock from arbitrageurs and market professionals. The purchases were made on the New York Stock Exchange for Gold Fields' account, and as the volume of purchases rose, brokers joined in the sales. First Boston was intent on purchasing the 16 million shares that morning. The trading was so intense that at various times the Exchange had to close down trading to maintain an orderly market. By 1:30 p.m. Gold Fields, through First Boston, had purchased all the shares needed, 23.7 percent of the outstanding shares, at a cost of $1.6 billion (an average price of $98 a share), bringing Gold Fields' position to 49.9 percent of the outstanding shares. Never had so much stock of one company been purchased in so short a period. Since all the sales were on the New York Stock Exchange, the sales would not settle for five days, leaving Pickens the opportunity to invalidate the sales and block the closings. It was in that posture that the case came to the chancellor at 2 p.m.

In preparing for the litigation, I went over various questions and answers with Bernie. Finally, I playfully asked him, "What are you going to say when the chancellor, knowing about our fees, says that your presentation was not a million-dollar performance."

"Your honor," Bernie snapped back, "my wife has the same complaint." He was prepared. Bernie would be working with a first-rate team of White & Case litigators and Delaware counsel as well.

In court, Bernie's prediction proved entirely accurate: the chancellor had two hours to try to understand what had happened in the last month and then figure out what to do about it. Pickens's lawyers emphasized the flagrant purchases of stock for over $1.6 billion, made after the legal action was filed but before the court could get to hear the matter. Counsel's challenge in the courtroom was to explain what had been done and not make it sound devious. The chancellor's total focus was on whether he could enjoin the trades from closing on the Exchange and therefore put the matter back to where it was at 9:30 a.m., when Pickens had first filed his application with the court. All at once the issue changed from whether there had been any wrongdoing to whether judicial relief could be granted. It was as if everything had been done wrong.

Somehow the litigators had to deflect the chancellor's desire to give prompt relief, and the human need to have a simple static situation to examine. Newmont's courtroom lawyers and the counsel for Gold Fields pointed out to the chancellor that to enjoin the purchases would be affecting not only those trades but all the trades made in reliance on those trades. Billions of dollars had to be accounted for, invested in innumerable securities. The enormity of the consequences of an injunction was presented to him, and he was told that since there were five days before the trades closed, the decision didn't have to be made hastily. The issues should be fully briefed and time allowed for argument. The chancellor was a careful and thoughtful man, used to reading cogent arguments; without papers before him he realized that he was adrift and set up a briefing schedule and hearing date. He allowed two days for briefing and set the hearing for the third day.

Once the matter had to be briefed, focus would shift from the remedy to the actions taken, and the decision process would be more rational. What we saw as also helping the case was that as each day passed there were sales and purchases of stock, all relying on the sale of the Newmont shares on the New York Stock Exchange. The warp and woof of these trades made a very tight fabric that couldn't be torn easily. Given the additional time, the New York Stock Exchange intervened in the case to tell the court that the consequences of trying to break the trades would devastate the Exchange. As Bernie said, "What's done can't be undone."

But that pronouncement, as comforting as it seemed, didn't end the case. Pickens resourcefully shifted his request for a remedy, turning the issue away from disruption of the trading markets. The court, Pickens suggested, could require Gold Fields to rescind the purchases by allowing the sellers to buy the stock back from Gold Fields and then let them tender the shares to Pickens or let the sellers instruct Gold Fields to tender the shares to Pickens. Pickens was offering $105 ($72 per share plus the $33 dividend) when Gold Fields had paid an average of $98 in the market. If the court forced Gold Fields to release the shares, they would flow into Pickens's hands, giving the sellers the benefit of the higher price without affecting the trading markets. In this manner, the real issues became the focus of the litigation and Chancellor Jacobs could ask: What happened, and why had it happened? The parties then had to prepare their best case, and began by seeking discovery of each other's case.

There is something remarkable about the discovery process in litigation. Everyone has to disgorge his papers, lay them out in the bright light for examination, and be available for testimony. The details of the conflicting designs can be brought into focus and perspective. With all the information before you, there is a sense of omniscience, for then you learn some of the most secret thoughts of the parties and get answers to questions that in daily life you would never be able to ask. Benign appearances give way to manipulative realities.

What did it all show? Pickens wanted Newmont. There was no doubt about that. Indeed, he thought it was undervalued and that gold production could be increased significantly. Gold Fields wanted, more than anything else, to hold on to its investment in Newmont and to increase that investment so that no one could take it away. Rudolph Agnew had gotten Gold Fields' board, reported in its board minutes, to approve a hostile bid for Newmont to gain control of the company. Once it had control, Gold Fields would cause Newmont to declare a $2 billion dividend, which would pay out the banks for temporary loans to carry out the purchases of Newmont shares. Agnew had already signed the papers and delivered them to his lawyers to put the plan into effect. It was all just waiting for his word. Agnew hesitated to act, testing Pickens's credibility. For Gold Fields, this revelation of its dirty fingernails under its elegant gloves was embarrassing. But for Newmont, the disclosure showed that it hadn't been paranoid: all the threats were real.

By the time Pickens's case came before Chancellor Jacobs for the preliminary injunction, however, he was able to remark that he had extensive briefs on all issues, over 400 pages of argument from twelve different law firms. Reason had overtaken action and the court would be able to properly deliberate. Newmont's case was solid. It was able to show that it was being threatened on the right and the left. What it did was defeat a tender offer at an inadequate price, as well as constrain Gold Fields, so that for at least another ten years Newmont could independently conduct its own business. Chancellor Jacobs found for Newmont, and the Delaware Supreme Court also approved Newmont's actions. The Supreme Court's opinion is a high-water mark in sanctioning complex actions taken to defend against an inadequate takeover offer.

We all met in Newmont's boardroom again after the Delaware court cases were decided. We had finally lost the case in California, but that didn't affect the victory over Pickens. The SEC, however, forced to think through its rules, changed them anyway to require disclosures of sources of funds (and names of investors) at least five business days before shares were purchased in a tender offer. While the SEC still allowed Milken and others to start tender offers without all the necessary funds, bidders couldn't buy without full disclosure of the financing sources.

Our gathering in the boardroom was to recapitulate the battle. Discussion was helped by the glow of victory, and our weariness was satisfying.

"Pickens's mistake was in freeing Gold Fields. Rather than gaining an ally, he wound up with an enemy, and that did him in," someone said.

"That was the risk he took," I said, meaning that it was knowing and calculated.

Gordon Parker, seeing that I had raised a point of contention, said, "He misjudged the English. In the war in the Falkland Islands, it took the English ships three weeks to get from Plymouth Harbor to the Falkland Islands. When they got there, they did the job. It took the English about four weeks this time, but they did the job."

We all smiled. Everyone was appreciative of Gold Fields.

The company had its work cut out for it. It now had a lot of debt and would have to sell assets. The sense of the work ahead kept the meeting short.

As Bernie Nussbaum and I were riding down in the elevator, we had a conversation that only lawyers can have, free from the emotional points of view of those personally involved. He said, "You don't think Pickens made a mistake?"

"He played it very well," I said. "He always faced the threat that Gold Fields would defeat his offer. Gold Fields was the largest stockholder to begin with and he knew that if they bought shares they would be able to defeat him."

"But Pickens freed them to do that," he said.

"In this situation," I answered, "Newmont was always able to free Gold Fields to buy shares. By freeing Gold Fields himself, Pickens gave them the opportunity to talk to him, an opportunity that they otherwise wouldn't have had. That was the right move."

"You're saying he was clever."

"Adept at what he does. And Gold Fields waited too long," I added, commenting on the cost to them.

"But everyone, including Newmont, got the satisfaction of knowing that there was no other choice. That's not insignificant."

As the elevator reached the ground floor, I put my arm fondly around his shoulder and said in mock reproach, "You led your witnesses, counsellor," referring to his questioning technique in the boardroom. "And, using the cigar, almost went too far."

"The boardroom allows for that," he responded and, teasing, said, "It's not as demanding as the courtroom."

"You think so?" I asked.

"There's no judge," he said. "And most of the time you're telling the directors what they want to hear."

"Every time I want to do something serious, they hire another set of lawyers to judge me."

"Not the same thing," he said. "No one's arguing against you."

"When I lose, it's a case I shaped. When you lose, it's a case I gave you to argue," I countered.

"That's true," he said, laughing. "You have trouble getting it right." And then seriously: "But I always remember the losses more than the victories. The losses seem to get etched in my mind, and the victories become unimportant."

"For me as well," I said. "Does that make you less willing to take up the next case and risk defeat?"

"No," he said.

"Good," I said, "because I need you."

"Something permanent came out of all this, where we least expected it," Bernie remarked.

"What?" I asked, curious to see what he saw.

"We got the SEC to change the disclosure rules," Bernie said. "Less opportunity for duplicity."

"We added another rule," I said, "which is not so good. We compounded the difficulty of doing deals."

"Good," Bernie said. "Then we'll both be needed."

A MATTER
OF PERCEPTION

▼

The devil has the most appealing face,
and the most persuasive arguments.

Ned Evans, chairman of Macmillan, introduced Henry Kravis to the board with a flair that suggested the raising of a genie from a bottle. With Henry beside him, Ned told everyone that Henry's firm was offering to buy Macmillan for $85 a share, an aggregate price of about $2.3 billion. Ned and his three senior managers would hold about 20 percent of the equity of the company after the buyout. There seemed little doubt that the price was compelling and would end the six-month takeover battle for the company, a fight in which the board had been severely criticized. As the board contemplated peace with honor, Ned adroitly turned the meeting over to Henry.

Henry needed no introduction. In the decade since Henry had participated in founding Kohlberg, Kravis & Roberts and made his first leveraged buyout, he'd purchased over thirty companies for $35 billion and become a legend. Upon entering the Macmillan boardroom, Henry had worked the room, while his staff waited behind him. With a bright smile he acknowledged everyone he knew, warmly shaking hands, individually addressing each person. I felt his graciousness at the opposite end of the board table as he caught my eye and said hello to me by name. It was a moment in which the business community, and the people I knew, seemed to have matured and taken on all the assurance and command of prosperous middle age. Henry currently had available to him a fund of over $5.6 billion for equity investments, which provided over $55 billion of capital to make purchases of companies when leveraged with bank and other borrowings. Sitting a few feet away from Henry was Bruce Wasserstein, engaged by the board to evaluate Henry's proposal. Bruce had become, in the past decade, one of the preeminent investment bankers in America, the head of his own firm, Wasserstein, Perrella & Co., a top-tier banking firm. In the same period Ned Evans had emerged as a major business figure and helped Macmillan grow from an enterprise with a market value of less than $200 million to one in excess of $2.3 billion.

On this Monday morning, September 12, 1988, everyone was poised for success. Optimism could clearly be treated as realistic, since Robert Maxwell, the British entrepreneur and publisher, had finally been outbid by Henry. Maxwell, a large man, grandly self-made to mirror his own physical proportions, had previously tried to extend his publishing empire in the United States by mounting unsuccessful takeovers of Harcourt Brace Jovanovich and Bell & Howell. His frustrations had made him tenacious in the contest for control of Macmillan. In business matters he was determined and without sentiment. But Maxwell seemed to have uncharacteristically set the basis for the contest now coming to an end.

As usual, the board meeting had begun precisely on time. It was to be a two-hour meeting, and after the meeting there would be lunch for the directors in the commodious Macmillan dining rooms. The agenda, definitively set, would be adhered to strictly. Before Henry's entrance, Ned Evans had brought the board up to date on the auction process for the company. There had been six bidders, McGraw-Hill, Gulf & Western, Rupert Murdoch (through News America Corp.), Robert Bass, Robert Maxwell, and Henry Kravis, the most recent entrant. On Thursday, September 8, Bruce

Wasserstein had called all the potential players and told them that "the matter seems to be drawing to a close" and asked them to submit their best bid by 5:30 p.m. on Friday, September 9. Only Henry and Maxwell were expected to bid.

Maxwell was making a hostile tender offer for the company at $80 a share (which was his initial bid that had put the company in play), and that price had set the floor bid, dissuading all others, except Henry. In response to Bruce's request for final bids, Maxwell submitted a further bid of $84, topping his own bid by $120 million, designed to be high enough to end the auction for the company. With the bid, he sent a letter, one of the most remarkable letters that any of us had ever seen. It said simply, but in quaint terms, that if the board got an offer of over $84 that was fully financed, he'd withdraw his offer. It was both peevish and arrogant, and was saying: This is what the company is worth; if you can get a higher price, take it; it's not worth my chasing it at more than $84. Of course, he thought his bid was preemptive and didn't expect anybody to be willing to pay more. But that remained to be seen, and nothing in his proposal prevented the seeking of higher bids. Thereafter, Ned, in direct discussions with Henry, who had been studying Macmillan and watching the contest for weeks, persuaded Henry to offer $85. A year after the market crash of October 1987, with mergers still in full swing, there seemed to be no price limits. It was Maxwell's averring his limit that was the final inducement to Henry to declare himself. Henry was in the enviable position of being able to flex his economic muscle, avoid an auction, and get the prize with certainty.

Each director had in front of him Maxwell's letter, and everyone asked whether he meant what he said. The only reasonable response was: If he didn't mean it, why did he bother to say it? Could he change his mind? Yes, but why would he corner himself, only to look foolish and indecisive if he were to change his mind? No, he meant what he said. Yes or no, it all came out in the same place: at $85 Maxwell should withdraw. Ned and Henry believed that. Besides, everyone in the room knew that Henry was going to try to turn the screw on Maxwell with some request for a lockup arrangement that would make it more difficult, if not impossible, for Maxwell to bid further. The bidders were strong-willed men committed to success. That was the reason Henry was here and presenting the buyout proposal himself. One of my jobs, representing the board, was to keep the turning screw from pinching unreasonably.

According to the agenda, after Henry's presentation, Ned and the management involved in the buyout would step out of the room with Henry, and the independent directors would meet to discuss the transaction. Bruce Wasserstein would evaluate the bid for the board and then the board would take a vote. It was fascinating watching Henry go through his polished routine. He was a man used to winning bidding contests and he'd stretched to offer $85 to buy the company. Henry would soon begin angling for an advantage over Maxwell to ensure his victory.

THIS MEETING, NOMINALLY dealing with the sale of Macmillan, was a celebration of Ned Evans. Everyone had looked to Ned to understand the company's value and prospects. And Henry was relying on Ned's assurance that after paying such a high price he'd be able to continue the company's growth. The success of Macmillan was a direct outgrowth of Ned's effort to distinguish himself from his father, Thomas Mellon Evans. For much of his career he'd worked with his father—first at Evans & Co., the old man's investment vehicle, then at H. K. Porter, the cornerstone of the industrial empire. His participation alongside the old man in the hostile takeovers of Missouri Portland Cement and Fansteel (a manufacturer of mining tools) created the impression in the business community that the world would have to suffer another Evans.

Physically, the two men were different. Ned, much taller than Tom, was described by *Fortune* magazine as a stocky George Hamilton. But over time the family likenesses, always mildly present, became more pronounced. As Ned matured, he became heavier, his face became round, and then his body also proportionately rounded, leading almost inevitably to his becoming a larger version of the old man. He even had Tom's temper, which sparked and then flashed like his father's. Nothing set him apart, and working closely with the old man made any deviation difficult.

If Ned wanted to distinguish himself and not bear his father's baggage, he would have to fundamentally depart from his father's business style. In 1979, at age thirty-seven, Ned hadn't set out to achieve independence through buying control of Macmillan. He had more modest aims—mainly to turn a quick profit from 5 or 10 percent of the stock of the company. With the stock trading at about $10 a share, and the book value at $16, the company fit within Tom Evans's criteria, a company with good earnings potential selling well below the book value of its assets. By 1979 such companies were already hard to find; most companies were trading in the market at a premium to book value, and it was easy for Ned to convince Tom to overlook the fact that the assets were largely intangibles, such as contract rights rather than manufacturing facilities. The Macmillan stock had gone from a high of $51 in 1967 to a low of $3.00 in the mid-1970s, reflecting severe operating problems. Ned had done his homework in finding Macmillan as a target, and had properly diagnosed its ills: a series of poor acquisitions in the early 1970s made by Raymond Hagel, the sixty-three-year-old chief executive officer. Hagel hadn't acted fast enough to correct his mistakes. Substantial pruning of a number of the businesses would have to be effected (a polite way of saying they would have to be sold or liquidated). Stripped down, there would remain a core publishing business and, at that time, an education business through the Berlitz language schools and the Katharine Gibbs secretarial schools, making the stock a good investment. The old man agreed to the stock purchases, and this endeavor became, at age seventy, Tom Evans's last major hostile acquisition.

When H. K. Porter acquired over 5 percent of Macmillan in March 1979, the board reacted to Tom Evans's reputation as a corporate raider by immediately beginning to look for a White Knight. Ned was interested in profiting from a sale and showed the necessary patience during the spring and most of the summer of 1979 while the Macmillan board continued to conduct a reasonable search for a buyer. At the end of August, Mattel, diversifying from Barbie dolls and other toys, offered a deal that included cash, stock, and some debentures, worth an estimated $24.50 a share. Within a week after the announcement, ABC, the television network, made a counterproposal to acquire Macmillan. The ABC bid at $25 only marginally topped the Mattel bid, but its securities were of better quality, making it the superior buyer. In arbitraging the transaction, Ned increased his position slightly, remaining under 10 percent so that he had the flexibility to sell without being subject to limitations on short-swing profits.

ABC, however, was suffering from internal politics, and there was clear resistance to the transaction from a number of important officers in the company. The deal collapsed at the end of November 1979, leaving Ned disappointed and with an important and tough decision to make. Should he sell or merely hold his position? Or should he buy? The stock, as high as $21 in anticipation of the deal, had dropped to about $13.50, reflecting few prospects for another deal. The market was confused about what would happen to Macmillan and there was a lot of stock for sale. Confusion carries opportunity. Ned began buying until he held about 15 percent of the company. He told the old man that with the large stock position they would be in a better position to influence management and work out the company's problems, including selling the poor businesses. Macmillan, still looking to avoid being acquired by Tom Evans and face the dismantling of the company, tried to patch up the deal with Mattel, the rejected suitor. Mattel declined, and Macmillan was damaged goods.

With the stock declining, all the disappointments of the large stockholders on the board came to the fore. Knowing that the management had consistently miscalculated the company's prospects, the board didn't have faith in the commitment of the management to revitalize the company. Tom and Ned had more at stake than anyone, and the board agreed to meet with Ned. Totally versed in the business, Ned explained to the members where the business had gone wrong, and told them that he was ready to make the necessary corrections, which were too deep and painful for the management to make. The board members recognized that they had found someone who understood the business and was committed to it. Ned was appointed to the board, and the board was restructured.

In the change, Ned was made the head of the powerful Executive Committee, which ran the company. Within a short time Hagel resigned and Ned took his place as chief executive officer. In that transition, Ned was able to politely step off his father's ship, H. K. Porter, and take command of his own vessel, which, although in trouble, could be guided again into full and promising service. That step away from his father's command was an important one toward total independence, and seemed gracefully executed, without squabble or outward rancor. As he made the move, he committed Porter to further investments, increasing Porter's position to 20 percent of the outstanding shares.

Ned's instincts were correct in buying additional shares of Macmillan when the price of the stock was down, for it assured control and was a good investment. But as soon as he began selling the poor businesses, the old man wanted to realize on his investment by selling his stock. Publishing and education weren't the kinds of businesses that the old man was interested in being in for the long term. All the worth of Macmillan was in goodwill, contract rights, know-how, and other intangibles, things that he was uncomfortable with and found difficult to value. Hard assets like plant, equipment, and real estate can be sold when businesses are not performing, but with soft assets there is no such market underpinning, and the businesses either have to work well or suffer losses. With the old man interested in selling, it was clear that, although Ned was the chief executive officer, the old man controlled the company. If he sold his block of stock, there would be a new owner and Ned would be dismissed, and he'd be working again for his father. It was as simple as that, and the old man had relatively little patience: he'd sell, and soon.

In June 1982, less than two years after Ned took over control, Macmillan repurchased Tom Evans's stake in the company, paying him about $50 million for stock for which he'd paid about $37 million, giving him his desired profit. The stock purchased by the company was canceled, severing the business connection between the two men, and Ned lost the security of a 20 percent shareholder.

Macmillan became Ned's life and it changed his life. In the eight or so years that he ran Macmillan, he made sixty-five acquisitions, all negotiated, none hostile. Each was small, but incrementally they created, from the starting embryo, three major enterprises under the name Macmillan: an information company, an education company, and a publishing company. There was a personal cost to this strategy because Ned wasn't comfortable negotiating. He had neither the affability nor the winsome ease necessary to cajole concessions. But where the old man would respond to an emotional seller by being dictatorial, Ned would find enough flexibility to get the deal done. For Ned, the prize was worth the game, and in making that effort he showed more control over himself than the old man.

The constraints Ned imposed on himself he imposed on others. Most of all, he needed to assert control, like the old man. But there was a difference between the two: if the old man was in charge, he was never fastidious about it; Ned governed through sustained control. Nothing happened at Macmillan without his knowing about it. Meetings were always short, with a strict agenda. Brief meetings were governable and without surprises. Ned had seen enough meetings disrupted, especially by his father, to be wary. Brevity suited him, for he was basically a man of very few words. When he spoke, it was thoughtful. Most of the time he listened.

His concentration and effort in those eight years made Macmillan one of the ten best-performing companies on the New York Stock Exchange, with record growth rates each year. Not only was the performance exceptional, the vision was also remarkable and quite different from his father's. If the old man had held on to his investment in Macmillan, it would have been worth about $500 million, more than his entire net worth. Ned had decidedly found his own path, well away from smokestacks and bent metal, and had broken new ground. But being a public company is like being a white leopard, Ned told me. Everybody wants you and there's no way of keeping free.

HENRY'S BUYOUT PRESENTATION in the boardroom had two parts. The first was to give absolute assurance about his firm's ability to effect the transaction. While this transaction was sizable, it was small relative to the amount of capital to which Henry had access. In addition, he had in attendance bankers from Drexel Burnham and Merrill Lynch to give assurances that there would be no problem in placing the bonds necessary to do the transaction. Their presence was to satisfy Maxwell's condition in his letter that the money for the bid was readily available. Then Henry told the board how impressed he was with the management of Macmillan, Ned and his team. All the words of praise justified the 20 percent equity participation of the management.

In short order, Henry began the second part of his agenda, angling for fees and his expenses if Maxwell made a higher bid. His estimated expenses, largely for paying commitment fees to lenders to raise $2 billion in capital, came to $40 million, about $1.30 a share. In addition, he asked for a fee of $29 million for his firm if Maxwell raised his bid over $85, which translated into approximately another $1.00 a share. Thus, if Maxwell bid $86, then Henry would get $69 million from the company, or about $2.30 a share, and Maxwell would have to pay the equivalent of $88.30, even though the shareholders were getting $86. Henry's fees and expenses created a significant hurdle for Maxwell. If Maxwell had second thoughts, they would have to include the company's paying Henry $69 million.

Henry was leaving nothing to chance, for he then additionally asked for what is known as a crown jewel option. As its name implied, he wanted to be able to buy the best pieces, in this case about $1 billion of selected assets from the information side of the business, in the event that Maxwell raised his bid to $86 and got control of the company. Maxwell would then be in the unenviable position of having to sell Henry the crown jewels, largely unique assets, that he'd just bought. Even if the option was at a fair price meant to compensate the Macmillan treasury for the assets sold, in reality it would not do so. The taxes on the gain from the sale would be significant, and even if similar assets could be purchased, there wouldn't be enough cash remaining to buy them. Maxwell wouldn't buy under such circumstances. Thus, the grant of the option to Henry would be an absolute bar to further bidding by Maxwell, even if the $69 million in fees and expenses was not.

Ordinarily, boards don't grant crown jewel options and end the auction process. If there was a time, however, when a crown jewel option could be fairly contemplated by the board, it was at this juncture, because Maxwell had indicated that if his bid was topped, he wouldn't bid again anyway. It would be totally reasonable for the board to grant it. The problem with granting the option was that it ended the takeover battle definitively, leaving no opportunity for Maxwell to have second thoughts.

This was the most important decision for all of us to make. It was now time for Ned to leave the room, but he lingered longer than he should have according to his agenda, knowing that once he left the room, unguided discussion would occur. But as planned and prescribed, he finally got up and said, "The management will leave now," smiling as he left his seat in the center of the board table, with his staff following. It was as if he were leaving his only child alone with strangers.

NED FOUND HIMSELF in the position of abandoning his fate to the will of others because Macmillan had to be put up for sale. The early-warning signal of a possible takeover of Macmillan came when Robert Maxwell made a bid to acquire Harcourt Brace Jovanovich about two years before. Attention had now been focused on publishing and information companies. Worse, Maxwell wasn't able to achieve his objective, and Ned reasoned that Maxwell would eventually turn to Macmillan. Ned began at that point to have Charlie McCurdy, his financial officer, prepare business plans for recapitalizing Macmillan. His objective was to keep the company public, if he could, but in any event to acquire control of the company in a recapitalization. In all his various plans Ned and his team wound up with control of at least a majority of the shares. It was a strategy that he would keep on the shelf in case it was needed. In March 1988, Robert M. Bass acquired a stock position in Macmillan of about 8 percent, which he claimed he was holding for investment. Slowly, Bass increased his position to just under 10 percent, leaving himself free to take short-swing profits if they became available. Ned had been given less than six years to foster the company's growth after he'd cut himself free from his father.

In June 1988, Robert Bass sent a letter to Ned offering to acquire the company for $64 a share. The company was then trading in the $50 range. In preparing to respond, Ned engaged me and my firm to represent the independent directors. He then proposed a recapitalization plan to the board, the one he had on the shelf. After we met with him and the board, the board approved a plan that was much more modest than anything Ned had contemplated. Macmillan was to be split into two businesses, publishing and information services, and Ned's (and the management's) interest was to be concentrated principally in the information company, which was continuing to grow. As a group, Ned and the management would hold about 38 percent of the equity of that segment, and agree not to increase their stock position for at least three years. The recapitalization was worth about $64.50 to the shareholders, slightly more than Bass's proposal. However, the public shareholders would retain a significant equity interest in both segments, rather than being cashed out, making the plan more attractive to them than the Bass buyout proposal.

Ned and I met with Bass following the announcement of the recapitalization in an attempt to induce him to go along with the plan. Robert Bass was about forty years old, slightly younger than Ned, and very pale, with gray hair that was fast becoming white. He was slim, almost frail, and didn't look like he had the energy to wield the billions of dollars that he had at his command. Ned had prepared himself thoroughly for the meeting. He'd gone through all of Bass's deals and was prepared to compliment him on the transactions, which was all preparatory to Ned's trying to convince Bass to take his profit and allow the recapitalization to be completed. Bass was curt and didn't take well to compliments, aware that they were manipulative. Ned had a simple message, which he'd worked out in the anguish of trying to find common ground for the meeting, which was: "If you start out hostile, you'll never again do a negotiated transaction." Ned tried to explain to Bass that he'd abandoned the hostile route for Macmillan because it was very costly and left no assurance that you would get what you were seeking. Ned tried to explain how hard it was to put the image of the hostile raider behind him and how rewarding it had been for Macmillan to do only negotiated, friendly transactions. Bass was not interested in Ned's commentary. It was all beside the point. He acted as if he were waiting for the national anthem to finish and for the ball game to begin.

"What are you seeking?" I asked Bass.

"I want the company," he said.

"What do you bring to the party?" I asked.

"What do you mean?" he asked.

"What is it that you think you can provide that is different from what's being done or that can be done better?"

"I think the company's a good buy," he said. "I'm prepared to pay value for it." He had a benign smile that belied his indifference to anyone else's interests and used that mask of politeness to avoid addressing any of the issues.

"There is no good reason to sell it," I said, making my point directly to pierce the smile. "It has good management and the shareholders are still participating in the growing company." Even as I spoke, I saw him stiffen at the suggestion that he should have second thoughts, and his eyes became impenetrable. I said, "There's every reason to resist selling it."

"It's a public company, which means it's for sale. And as shareholders, we don't like the recapitalization arrangements," he said, refusing to justify his actions. From Bass's perspective, one that I first fully understood from Tom Evans, he was entitled to take a profit wherever he found it, without considering the effects on a flourishing company.

The meeting was a failure, and promptly thereafter Bass made a tender offer for the company at $73.50. In addition, he brought a lawsuit in Delaware, where Macmillan was incorporated, to enjoin the recapitalization. The Bass bid to buy the company sparked Maxwell's interest and he bid $80 in a tender offer. Here was an opportunity that Maxwell didn't want to lose: to buy a major publishing and information services company. The Delaware Chancery Court, Chancellor Jack Jacobs presiding, faced with a bid of $80 against a recapitalization valued at $64.50, enjoined the arrangement and criticized the board for being too permissive with management in allowing them to take 38 percent of one segment of the company, which the court saw as a controlling interest. Chancellor Jacobs treated the recapitalization like a sale, refusing to follow the precedent of the South Carolina court in the Multimedia case. The court's criticism made the board and all of us sensitive about acting in any way that appeared to favor management.

Ned, seeing that it was likely that Maxwell would purchase the

company, searched for other buyers. He decided to sell to Robert
Bass or Henry Kravis, not concerned that Bass had triggered the
takeover process. Either group would give him and his team an
equity stake in Macmillan. He invited Bass to bid again, but the
$82 to $83 range was as high as Bass would go, and Ned figured
$83 would probably be topped by Maxwell. Henry Kravis, Ned
decided, had the capability to be the highest bidder. In the meantime, the board sought bids from all other interested buyers, but
as the prices escalated in the contest it became obvious that only
Henry Kravis would compete with Maxwell.

ONCE NED AND his team left the room, the board discussed the issues.
The question was whether you believed Maxwell's letter. If you
believed it, then it didn't matter what you gave Henry. You might
as well give him what he asked for and not antagonize him. But if
you believed that Maxwell might change his mind, then the board's
obligation to the stockholders was not to terminate the auction.
Bruce told the board that Henry could be given half of what he
wanted, the fees and expenses. At $69 million, they came out to
only 2.5 percent of the total transaction costs, which wasn't a
crippling tax to impose on the transaction to induce Henry's bid.
There was, however, no rational basis for stopping the auction with
a crown jewel option if there was the possibility of an additional
bid by Maxwell, unless Henry wouldn't bid at all without it. The
court's criticism of the recapitalization plan and Bruce's lecture
hardened the board to deny the crown jewel option, leaving it up
to Henry to insist that there was no deal without it.

We called Ned back into the boardroom for the full board meeting, and I told him the decision of the independent directors. They
had approved the transaction but couldn't approve the crown jewel
option. The question now was whether Henry was prepared to go
forward with the deal on that basis.

"Henry has placed only one deal on the table," Ned said. "The
option is part of it."

"It's not acceptable the way it is," I said.

Ned didn't argue and, understanding the sensitivities of the
board, accepted the result rather graciously. He left the room to

talk to Henry. Within a few minutes he came back and told us that Henry would make the deal without the crown jewel option. Finally, it had been done: Maxwell had been outbid at $85 a share, and an elegant solution, with honor, had been achieved. Buoyant goodwill was everywhere present in the room. The meeting was adjourned for the board to eat lunch.

WITHIN A DAY, and despite his letter, Maxwell increased his tender offer to $86.80 a share in cash, $1.80 per share more than the $85 face value of the KKR bid, and Maxwell was prepared to absorb the $69 million that Henry would get on top of all that. There was going to be another round of bidding, if Henry could be convinced to go higher. But Henry wasn't going to be tractable this time. Given the higher bid, the board directed its financial advisers, Wasserstein Perrella and Lazard, to contact the interested bidders. On Friday, September 23, Bruce Wasserstein called all six potential bidders and told them that if they were interested in participating, the bids should be submitted by 5:30 p.m. on Monday, September 26, 1988. This was meant to be the final round.

Everybody knew that he was in an endgame and each move would be examined. Maxwell's financial adviser was Robert Pirie, head of Rothschild's U.S. operations. Pirie had been a partner at Skadden Arps, the firm that acted as Maxwell's lawyers, and an adversary of mine on a number of occasions. He was a mature, battle-scarred veteran with the personality to advise and stand up to Maxwell. Pirie had said to Wasserstein that the process favored Henry's firm, KKR. Keeping that accusation in mind, we made sure that all our steps were carefully thought through. Pirie wanted an open-bidding procedure, as at an auction house, where he could know the other bids and could bid against them. KKR wanted to have one final round of blind, or sealed, bids and was again requesting a crown jewel option in the event its bid was accepted, which would enforce the one-round procedure.

The board had to encourage KKR; otherwise there wouldn't be another round. The board, therefore, had to entertain the request for a crown jewel option, the grant of which would assure that there would be a last round and not a series of anticlimaxes that would discourage KKR. While one final round would most likely extract the highest price, it played into Pirie's contention that KKR would be tipped or otherwise advantaged. To make the best record, Bruce Wasserstein prepared a script which was to be read by him and Steve Gollub of Lazard to Maxwell's representatives and to KKR's representatives on the telephone. The script was straightforward, but very detailed, beginning with the salutation "Hi" and, in retrospect, the ironically inaccurate phrase of Bruce's that "the matter appears to be drawing to a close." Each bidder was then advised that bids should be submitted by 5:30 p.m. on Monday, September 26, and was told to put in his best bid, stating all conditions.

Maxwell and KKR both bid. Maxwell's bid was $89 per share in cash for all the shares, $5 a share (or over $150 million) more than the $84 he'd said was the highest price he'd be willing to pay. KKR's bid had a face amount of $89.50 per share, and although higher than Maxwell's by a nominal $0.50, KKR's bid was deemed worth approximately $89.05 to $89.10 when the securities were evaluated. Ned was informed of the bids.

While the one-round strategy had worked and the prices were in the stratosphere, the bids were too close to declare a winner. A situation like this was often resolved like a tie, by holding another round. But in this case, in addition to annoying the competing bidders already tortured by the ratcheting process, there was a further problem in requesting another round. KKR had added to its bid what is known as a "no-shop clause," which meant that its bid could not be disclosed to anybody in any manner. In requesting another round of bidding and telling people the bids were too close to call, we would in effect be violating the no-shop clause. After talking to Bruce Wasserstein, I advised him that choosing one bidder over the other in a tie was more disruptive than another round, and we should override the no-shop clause. Also, we didn't have to address KKR's request for a crown jewel option by holding another round.

We all met at Bruce Wasserstein's office at about 7:30 p.m. on that Monday and prepared another script just as detailed as the first (with the same introduction of Bruce's about the matter drawing to a close). In an artful attempt not to conflict with KKR's no-shop provision, Bruce and Steve Gollub were to say the following: "We are not in a position at this time to recommend any bid. If you would like to increase your price, let us know by 10 p.m." That was code for: The bids are substantially the same and we're compelled to hold another round. Both parties were to be told the same thing. In addition, KKR was to be told that if its bid included a lockup proposal, it should focus on price. The statement was meant to say that a crown jewel option would be granted only if the bid was reasonably higher than the competing bid. It took us about fifteen or twenty minutes to work out the script to everyone's satisfaction. Shortly after 8 p.m., having made all necessary arrangements, we were in a position to call Pirie, who was acting for Maxwell, and to call Mike Tokarz, a partner of Henry's at KKR.

We thought we were in total control of the auction at that time. What we didn't know was that Ned Evans had already called Henry and reached Tokarz. Also on the call with Ned was Bill Reilly, the president of Macmillan, and Evans's personal lawyer. Ned told Tokarz that Maxwell had bid $89 all cash. Tokarz responded, "Great. We've won." After an awkward silence Reilly told Tokarz, "Well, it's a little close." At that point Tokarz realized the call wasn't an official communication of the results of the auction, and he quickly ended the conversation.

The official call to Tokarz was made at 8:20 p.m. by Bruce, who assiduously followed the script. The first thing Tokarz said was: "Aren't you violating our no-shop arrangement?" Bruce told him that we didn't think we were doing that, and if we were, we had no choice. There was a long pause, as if he was trying to figure out whether there was any way he could enforce it. His choice was either to withdraw or to bid again. In that hesitancy, not knowing what he knew, we saw him suggesting to us that it was possible for him to withdraw and that it was being seriously considered.

"What are you telling Maxwell?" he asked.

"The same thing we told you," Bruce said.

"Exactly the same thing?" His inquiry was harsh and suspicious. Clearly, he was disturbed that there was to be yet another round, for he was hoping to end the auction without having to pay more money.

"Exactly the same thing," Bruce said.

We told him he had until 10 p.m. to respond, and Bruce then called Pirie at about 8:30. Pirie told us that he was going out to dinner and mentioned a new Manhattan hot spot on the West Side. For his client in London, it was 3:30 a.m., and he asked us if he could be given additional time, until midnight in New York, to reach Maxwell. The difference between 3:30 a.m. and 5:30 a.m. might allow Maxwell to awaken at his normal time, and would give Pirie time for dinner. After that conversation we got back to Tokarz and told him that the deadline had now been extended until midnight.

I left Bruce's offices to go to dinner myself and then to go home. The arrangement I had with Bruce was that he could call me if he needed to talk to me. He would accept bids until midnight, and if there was any problem I would be told about it. At 10:30 that evening, Pirie called Bruce to ask if Macmillan had received a bid higher than Maxwell's. He said, "If you have a higher bid, then please inform us of that bid and we will tell you promptly whether we will raise our bid to top the bid. If you don't have a higher bid, then regard this as our highest bid." After a pause, he asked, "Will you get back to us?" His statement was stilted, fodder for his anticipated legal case.

Bruce responded, "We've gotten back to you. If you have anything further to say, tell us by midnight."

Bruce knew that he hadn't directly answered Pirie, but he felt he had no other choice; otherwise he'd be shopping KKR's bid. That would risk KKR's bid being withdrawn, leaving Maxwell as the only bidder. Bruce called me and I told him that Pirie was trying to set us up. "I know," he said. We both pondered the inevitable collision if KKR bid again. We felt that as long as Pirie was given every opportunity to bid and we were careful, the appropriateness of the procedures we were following would be upheld in court. I told Bruce that he should call Pirie back (so there would be no misunderstanding) and tell him that Macmillan wasn't in a position to inform him which bid was higher and that Pirie should call in his highest bid by midnight. Bruce called Pirie back and conveyed that information to him.

Pirie didn't submit a bid. The strategy of not bidding left two chances to win. If he already had the high bid, he would take the company; if not, he would take his case to court based on arguments detailing unfair procedures. Once before, Pirie had won a company, SCM, by challenging the mechanics.

Before midnight KKR submitted a bid of $90, face amount, which we valued at about $89.80. To be accepted, the bid required that KKR be granted a crown jewel option. Since KKR's was the high bid, we continued to negotiate with the firm (without telling KKR the amount of Maxwell's bid) and got it to raise its bid by another nickel to $90.05. We also continued to negotiate with Skadden Arps, Maxwell's lawyers, over the terms of the merger agreement with Maxwell in the event that KKR for one reason or another withdrew its bid.

The Macmillan board met at 9 a.m. on Tuesday, September 27, to consider both bids. At that time, Maxwell publicly announced, for the opening of trading on the New York Stock Exchange, that he'd bid $89 cash. The announcement was meant to put pressure on the board to accept the all-cash bid. The tack taken by Maxwell was consistent with his position that all bids should be announced. Public disclosure, however, put Maxwell in a position to be topped by Henry, if Henry hadn't already done so.

The boardroom was crowded. Not only were the board members there, they were surrounded by investment banking advisers (three firms: Wasserstein Perrella; Lazard; and First Boston) and legal counsel (four legal firms: Wachtell Lipton and Delaware counsel for the board; Weil Gotshal and Kirkpatrick Lockhart for the management).

Henry Kravis appeared and made a presentation telling us that the granting of a crown jewel option to KKR was an essential part of his bid. Without the option there was no bid. It was clear from his presentation that he regretted not insisting on it when he'd bid $85 a share.

After Henry left the room, the board was concerned about whether we had to ask Maxwell if he wanted to bid again, since he'd stood firm at $89. We told the board that if we asked Maxwell whether he wanted to bid again we would be violating the rules we'd set out for the bidding and would lose KKR's bid. If KKR dropped, then Maxwell wouldn't be induced to raise his bid. He could even lower his bid. Everyone knew that Macmillan had once failed to be sold because a bidder, Mattel, had been disdained.

I explained our dilemma to the board. If we accepted $89 in cash, the board wouldn't be subject to any criticism. As a matter of business judgment, an all-cash bid at these bidding levels could be preferred. If we accepted the higher KKR bid with the crown jewel option, and thus stopped the auction, we could be open to criticism—if Maxwell subsequently raised his bid, subject to the court's striking down the crown jewel option. But the only way to get Maxwell to raise his bid was to accept the $89.80 that KKR offered.

I told the board that if the court found, after Maxwell raised over $90, that the option was an improper impediment to the auction, then the court would also find that the auction hadn't been fairly conducted. In such a finding, the board would be subject to criticism and probably so would the advisers. Making the picture darker was my assessment that a crown jewel option had never been sustained in the face of a higher bid. The courts have always been result-oriented. If Maxwell raised his bid, he had a good chance of winning. The bidding contest presented difficult decisions. The good news was that the shareholders were benefiting. After my bleak statement of the situation, I asked Ned Evans to leave the room.

When Ned was out of the room, the board members asked Bruce and me, as advisers, whether we felt that the procedures that had been followed were fair. That was the right question. We told them that we'd been careful and followed equitable procedures. We described them at length, the details showing that Maxwell had every opportunity to top the bid if he wanted to do so. With Ned back in the room, we outlined our conclusion that the procedures were fair. None of us knew about Ned's conversation with Henry's partner, Mike Tokarz. The board approved the transaction with the option, and we announced it, leaving Maxwell to decide whether to bid again.

MAXWELL PROMPTLY BID $90.25 in cash and challenged the crown jewel option in court as having been illegally granted. Interestingly,

Robert Bass joined Maxwell in bringing the court action. Bass stood to make about $80 million (or about $30 a share on his 10 percent stock position) whoever won, but he was looking without sentiment for the extra profit of about $0.25 a share. His actions in this whole affair were always entirely consistent.

Although Bass had joined Maxwell, we were confident of winning, until we found out that Ned had called Henry. The information was given to us while we were preparing a report to the SEC on the transaction. KKR, which had to file a similar report, informed us that they had been told at approximately 8 p.m. on the 26th about Maxwell's bid. The question was whether Ned's call was material to the bidding and should be disclosed. I thought the call made no real difference, since Maxwell had soon thereafter been told that there was a tie and even announced his bid the next day. But I knew that once the legal challenge started, Maxwell's lawyers would probably find out about the call, and if it was not disclosed in the filing it would look like we were hiding something. Any hint of a cover-up would make the information look more powerful than it was. We decided to disclose the call before Maxwell's lawyers began their discovery routines.

Knowing that there would be a major confrontation in court, I sat down with my litigation partner, Bernie Nussbaum, to work out a strategy for the defense. Bernie had been involved in the matter from the outset and already knew all the ins and outs of the situation. He told me this was a case that should be argued by our Delaware counsel, Gil Sparks. Sparks had been in the board-room for most of the critical meetings and knew the lengths to which we had gone in trying to make the auction fair. Importantly, Sparks was one of the preeminent Delaware lawyers, the one whom the state had looked to as its advocate when it defended the validity of its anti-takeover legislation in the federal courts. Bernie knew that Sparks's presence in the courtroom would assure the court of fair-minded intentions.

Bernie and I went through all the bidding steps with Sparks and showed him that by 8:30 p.m. the information that KKR had been given was totally canceled out by our calls to Maxwell. In our view, the board had acted in good faith throughout, aiming to benefit the shareholders. The board hadn't favored Evans. Indeed, the board pushed the price to the limits. None of the board members should be tarred by the telephone call. Neither should KKR be punished.

"We should have another board meeting," Sparks said. He looked troubled.

"What for?" Bernie asked.

"To give the board a chance to decide, knowing what they know now, whether they would have voted for KKR's deal over Maxwell's."

"There was no $90.25 offer on the table when they reviewed those contracts," I said.

"I know that," Sparks said firmly.

"KKR's offer was the highest," I said.

"I'm not asking you to change the facts," Sparks said.

"Then the result will be the same," I said.

"We can't know that. It's their decision. And we'll have a much stronger case," Sparks said, "if everyone has all the facts and a chance to discuss the decision, whatever the result."

"This is not going to be an easy meeting to hold," I said. "Ned is going to have to be out of the room entirely." Looking at Sparks, I saw that he was committed. The board had to be given another opportunity. "Ned is not going to want another meeting," I said.

"It doesn't matter what Ned wants," Bernie said. "This is what we have to do."

There was shrewdness in reconsidering the matter, but it was like whitewashing a crack: it wouldn't erase the flaw. The meeting, however, would be a reprimand to Ned, and the more he fought it, and I knew he would, the greater the reprimand.

I called Ned and told him that I wanted him to call a meeting of the board of directors in which he wouldn't participate. There was hesitation at his end, and I heard the catching of his breath, which was like a click on the phone.

"Why do we need a board meeting?" he asked sharply.

I explained it to him, knowing that his view was that the high bid, Maxwell's, would win in court. For him, the high always won. Cobbling reasons to justify a lower bid was sense gone awry.

"It's not necessary," he said acidly. "That meeting doesn't make any sense." His tone was belittling, all his personal defenses now in place.

"We've decided it has to be held," I said. "It's a meeting of the independent directors."

"I'm not going to call it," he said definitively.

"Then I'll call it," I said, "and have it in our offices." What I was saying had to horrify him.

"It's my board," he said.

"The directors have to meet," I answered. "We have to act to avoid criticism of the board. There's no choice, Ned. It's either at our offices or at your offices." I paused, waiting for him to challenge me. He was breathing shallowly, very upset. I wanted more than anything then to close the conversation and get off the phone. I said, "That's the only issue. The meeting should be held tomorrow." He hung up on me.

Within a few minutes, Beverly Chell, the company general counsel, called to ask me why I felt we should have a meeting. It was always startling to realize that Beverly was one of Ned's closest legal advisers. Tom Evans would never talk to a woman lawyer, yet Beverly had Ned's confidence. I went over the whole matter with her, told her that there would be a meeting and that it was probably much more reasonable for Ned to call it and have it at his offices so that it didn't look like the meeting was being called for the sole purpose of ganging up on him. That was the only way he could ameliorate its effect. She told me that they would call the meeting.

Ned appeared at the meeting as if the gathering was his idea and an opportunity for him to bring the board current on all events. He told the Board of his call to Mike Tokarz and explained that under the terms of the original contract with KKR (signed when they bid $85) he was obligated to inform KKR of the bid. He hadn't realized that there would be a further round of bidding that evening. After he finished speaking there was a long, uncomfortable silence. No one spoke or moved; everyone was waiting for him to leave. His well-tailored suit looked rumpled and his shirt was damp and wilted. When he left, he looked very tired.

After the door was shut, there was a long, contemplative silence.

"From what you now know, would you do anything differently?" I told the members that they could rescind the contract with KKR, if they wanted to do so. I then described the events as we knew them, including management's arrangements. Ned's stock and options and other payments would amount to upward of $90 million on the sale of the company. Abe Gitlow, one of the original members of the Executive Committee that had appointed Ned to the board and a former dean of the NYU Business School, asked a series of questions. Abe, with a teacher's perspective, had a way of defusing personal animosity while sharpening sensitivity. Slowly, all the questions were aired. No one tried to explain or justify Ned's behavior. Everyone knew the case would be heard by Chancellor Jacobs, who had criticized the board's recapitalization plan. These were proud, sensible business people who realized that their reputations were at stake and that, while they were a jury for the moment, they in turn would be judged. Always present in the room was the thought that if they acted now in favor of Maxwell, they could avoid the legal challenge. They were given every opportunity to rule against Ned, but concluded that they wouldn't have done anything differently, and were bound by what they had done. Of all the possible decisions, that was the one that put them at risk for personal criticism. Gil Sparks and Bernie Nussbaum were sitting on either side of me when I told the board that it was a reasonable decision to make and we would defend it.

BEFORE THE COURT hearing, KKR and Ned Evans tried to settle with Maxwell, offering him some of the educational and information services businesses. He wasn't interested. He wanted more businesses than they were prepared to offer. From the way he was acting it was inevitable that this would be a test case.

The Chancery Court in Delaware considered all of Maxwell and Pirie's arguments about the lack of fairness in the auction. Gil Sparks argued the case for the company, standing up to all the accusations. The court, after reviewing all aspects of Ned's call, concluded that Messrs. Pirie and Maxwell were highly sophisticated businessmen experienced in the corporate takeover field and knew that to win the auction they would have to submit the highest bid by the close of bidding. No complex auction procedure is ever perfect. Whatever its defects, the auction procedure afforded Maxwell his chance to submit his best offer. On that basis, the Chancery Court found for KKR and thus vindicated the Macmillan board.

Maxwell appealed, seeking the Olympian point of view of the Delaware Supreme Court. Everyone knew that no matter how the Chancery Court had decided, the Delaware Supreme Court would express its own opinion.

We urged everyone to settle. There was enough for everybody. Maxwell could take a large part of the company, and KKR could take another part of the company. Each would be able to get sufficient assets to make a difference to them. There were at least three substantial businesses: the publishing business, the educational business, and the information services business. Whoever bought the whole company would still be selling substantial assets, and there was no reason why the parties shouldn't be able to get together. But the decision of the lower court had affected the psychology of the situation. KKR felt that it had the edge, while Maxwell was still willing to gamble—and he felt he was right: he believed that favoritism had destroyed his chances. Moreover, on a business level, Maxwell seemed to have a refined sense of indifference about the purchase, which was present at the negotiating table. If he didn't get exactly what he wanted, he was prepared to walk away. It is very hard to negotiate with someone in that frame of mind. I concluded that a deal between the parties was unlikely.

Up to a half hour before oral argument, the parties continued to try to resolve their differences. I was asked by members of management to estimate how much time after the argument they would have to continue negotiating before the opinion came down. I told them the opinion would probably come down that same day or the next. But I added that in argument the justices might signal, by their questions, their point of view, which would tilt and likely destroy the negotiations.

Having won in the court below, Macmillan's and KKR's lawyers were confident. The confidence remained until Gil Sparks began his presentation. Sparks rose and addressed the court: "If it please the court, I am counsel for the outside directors."

Justice Moore immediately broke in from the bench: "As counsel for the outside directors, are you and your clients disturbed that senior management of this company tipped the bid?"

Sparks: "My clients were disturbed. And in part—"

Not giving Sparks time to complete his answer, Justice Moore leaned over the bench and demanded, "Why didn't they fire them?"

Sparks: "Fire them?" Sparks was incredulous.

Before Sparks could recover, Justice Moore said, "Yes. It seems to me that if it was such a breach of duty . . ." And then Sparks tried to argue, but never got a chance. In the Manichaean world of Justice Moore, where dark and light are at war with each other, Sparks was the devil that day. The devil has the most appealing face, and the most persuasive arguments. And Justice Moore, controlling the courtroom, wouldn't listen to them. He found that the board had been misled. Ned Evans hadn't told the board that he'd intervened in the process. As a consequence, the board didn't have adequate information at the appropriate time, tainting everything from the beginning. Moreover, the board had been too pliant, and the advisers, the lawyers and bankers, should never have allowed Evans and his management to participate in or be informed about the status of the bidding.

There was no way to answer those contentions because the court's word was final, without appeal. The only thing worse than hearing a damning opinion of the court, edged with outrage, is having to explain it to your clients, who had agonized over the same issues.

I visited Ned just before he closed up his office. Incredibly, everything that had filled his life for years had to be sorted into boxes.

ABOUT A MONTH after the court decision, I was in Bernie's office when he told me he had a confession to make about Macmillan.

"What brings this up?" I asked.

"I've been thinking about it," he said.

Macmillan had been on my mind too, and for a moment I turned my gaze to look out the large window of his corner office onto the East River, the Fifty-ninth Street Bridge, and, in the clearness of the day, north to Connecticut.

"I made a deal with God," he said, catching my eye. "My deal was that if I can win only one case, let it be my cousin's case."

I looked at him and saw that he was in earnest. His cousin, an aide to Donald Manes in Queens, had been accused of bribing a public official. Bernie had worked on the defense and helped support the family. The cousin was convicted by the jury at trial and sentenced to three years in jail. On the appeal, which ran concurrently with the Macmillan cases, the court reversed the conviction for insufficient evidence and freed the cousin.

"How did you make this deal?" I asked.

He looked at me, his face flushed with the sincerity of his confession. "By praying," he said.

"You're not supposed to make deals with God."

"I know," he said, smiling, almost like a young boy caught leaving school early.

"Also, it was a poor deal. There were two Macmillan cases—the recapitalization, challenged by Bass, and the sale, challenged by Maxwell. If you had traded only one of them for your cousin's vindication, and I wouldn't have cared which one, you would have had a good result in both situations. Next time you're going to make one of those deals, please consult a lawyer."

"You'd represent me?" he asked.

"Why not," I said. "It would be an interesting opportunity."

"You realize," he said, "when you're really under pressure, the importance of your family."

"There's nothing like a sense of perspective," I said.

"Do you have any thoughts on what happened in the courtroom?" he asked.

"The court was responding to excesses," I said. "The excesses of leverage of companies, the high fees that the advisers get, and our visibility. The court can't control the economy or the size of the deals or the greed of the parties, all the vectors that make deals happen. But it can control the people that come before it. It's demanding that we make everything perfect."

"These deals can't be perfect," Bernie said. "They're too complicated and there are too many people involved."

"There'll always be deals. The pace and size will depend on the economy. The court told us all to be careful. We'll be careful, very careful."

"What's going to happen to Ned?" he asked.

"Ned will start again," I said. "He's resilient. And his success with Macmillan assures him of all the opportunities that he wants."

"I didn't make a bad deal for myself," Bernie said.

"You're a sensible man."

A WASTELAND

▼

*Clint Murcheson was supposed to have
said that a man is worth two times what he
owes, which made him a visionary in some quarters.*

"**Y**ou should leave, and give us a
chance to talk." Joe Lanier, chairman of West Point–Pepperell,
was speaking to Tom Foley, chairman of Bib, a small sheet manufacturer. Anger made his words a command. Rarely did Joe Lanier
lose his temper, but now his eyes hardened and his mouth twisted,
holding back an eruption. It was 2 a.m., and Lanier and Foley had
been sitting opposite each other in the conference room for at least
fourteen hours, trying to reach an agreement. This was their second
day at it, and they were close. If they could contain their bitter
feelings, they could adjourn until the morning and begin again
after some sleep. Tom Foley, much younger than Lanier, but no
less weary, stood up stiffly, followed by his chief financial officer
and his two lawyers, leaving without a word to wait in the adjoining
conference room.

"We've come so far," Joe said after they had closed the door.
"We shouldn't have to quit now."

"There's no way we'll ever make a deal with him on these points,"
Clay Sauers said. Clay was West Point–Pepperell's chief financial

officer. He spoke slowly and deliberately, reflecting his habitual caution. Joe always listened to him.

"We don't have to agree on everything," Joe said. "We have most of a deal. Tom Foley's agreed to buy J. P. Stevens's institutional sheet and towel business for $122 million. That's what we've asked him to do. That's all that we have to settle tonight."

"We found out a lot about him tonight, Joe," Clay said, reminding Joe that they had just spent over two hours arguing to the point of impasse.

"That we have," Joe acknowledged.

"He's a very tough man, Joe," Clay said.

"That's no surprise," Joe responded. "He's a good businessman. Remember, we haven't been able to find anybody else."

That was true. West Point–Pepperell and its investment banker, Merrill Lynch, had called everyone in the industry to find someone to buy a portion of the sheet and towel business of J. P. Stevens. Tom Foley, who ran Bib, was the only one interested enough to talk, but he wanted every advantage.

The situation at that late hour came to this. West Point–Pepperell was about to make a tender offer to acquire J. P. Stevens, a direct competitor in the sheet and towel business. Ordinarily West Point's bid would be barred as anticompetitive unless it could show that it had a reputable purchaser of a sizable portion of Stevens's sheet and towel business, approximately 20 percent of the sheets and about 50 percent of the towels. Only a sale to that degree would reduce West Point's market share to a level acceptable to the antitrust authorities. Wrestling with selling a large share of a business West Point didn't yet own, and hadn't been permitted to examine, was novel and not easy. Tom Foley would wait until Joe figured out how to proceed, secure in the knowledge that despite his anger Joe would offer up a reasonable compromise. None of us realized that we were embarked on a course of action that would signal the end of the merger wave of the 1980s and of indiscriminate leveraging of companies.

While Tom Foley waited outside, everyone turned to Joe Lanier. There was nothing on the surface about Joe Lanier that expressed his determination or uncommon ability. If you asked him, he'd tell you that there was nothing particularly special about him. He was down-home. He was a Southerner who lived simply, spending his time with his family. Of little more than average size and full-bodied, he looked soft at every turn, his face full and round, and his figure that of a man who lingered at the dinner table with hearty pleasure. He was now in his mid-fifties, and middle-age spread had been part of his life for at least twenty years. He was comfortable with himself: there was never a suggestion that, like many men of his station, he'd commit himself to some diet or fad that would change the way he looked. That sense of ease and acceptance carried over to his personal and business dealings. He always listened, giving everyone time to make their case, whatever it was. By asking questions, he'd get to understand the matter, however intricate and however convoluted the speaker's motives. Layer on layer of complexity would be slowly peeled apart like towels in a stack, each examined and then pulled back to reveal the next, in an attempt to uncover the crux. If the meaning was worth understanding Joe would try to find it and express it himself. His words were simple and direct and always stated with a slight hint of a question: have I gotten it right? If he hadn't, he'd listen again.

Four generations of Laniers had run West Point–Pepperell, from about 1880, and Joe had worked in the company for about thirty years. The company was headquartered in West Point, Georgia, about an hour's drive from Atlanta, next to the Alabama border. The family owned very little stock, less than 1 percent, and management responsibility came from being involved in the business. In this acquisition, he was pursuing his vision of making the company the leading bed and bath company in America. During his tenure, the company had changed significantly, with emphasis shifting from manufacturing to marketing. What differentiated the products was marketing efforts to replace the clean, white hospital look. By making bedrooms cozy and baths intimate, sheets and towels ceased to be commodities and became an expression of the personality of the house. Highly styled products, cast as unique, offer better profit margins than their utilitarian counterparts and benefit from elasticity in personal budgets. West Point's sophisticated designs had made significant marketing inroads, increasing the firm's market share. Those gains hadn't come about by following a well-tracked path that had been laid down by Joe's forebears.

Business had extended Joe, forcing him to meet and best the competition.

West Point had never done a hostile deal and the thought of doing one made Joe uncomfortable. The closest he'd come to the hostile arena was the acquisition of Cluett Peabody, an apparel manufacturer, in which West Point had been a White Knight. He was aware of the stresses involved in hostile transactions and had acted decisively to buy the company against all bidders. That arena held no lure for him, and he had no particular desire to expand West Point by acquisition. But in mid-February 1988, Whitney Stevens, chairman of J. P. Stevens, announced the management buyout of J. P. Stevens for $38 in cash plus a $5.00 debenture, an aggregate price of $43 per share. The announcement of a proposed sale of J. P. Stevens prodded Joe to reevaluate his thinking about acquisitions. He began to consider buying the company.

Five generations of Stevenses had run J. P. Stevens since its founding prior to the Civil War. The company's headquarters were in New York, but its textile factories were located in the South, like West Point's. Whit Stevens, the chairman, was a soft-spoken, quiet man, more bookish than outgoing, conscious that the history of his family was entwined with the development of the United States. His father had been Secretary of the Army under Eisenhower, and like him, Whit Stevens was used to command. But there was nothing harsh in his manner, and he was accessible. Although the family name was on the door, the family owned very little stock in the company, like the Laniers, less than 1 percent. Although chairman, Whit Stevens had little to do with the operations of the company, but he wanted to keep the company independent or at least to control it. Twice in the last few years the company had paid greenmail to buy out raiders who had accumulated sizable stock positions in the company. The company paid premium prices for this stock, eroding its equity, subjecting itself to further coercion. Being at the mercy of bullies and extortionists is no way to run a business. Whit Stevens's experiences weren't unique, nor was his distaste for paying greenmail. Like others, he thought about doing a leveraged buyout. An idea like that grows over time, but most often is dismissed for a number of reasons: the stock price is too high, making a buyout too expensive; there are too many likely bidders once a company is put into play; business prospects are cloudy; and the risks of leverage are too great. All these reasons are substantial and truly discouraging.

On October 19, 1987, the stock market crashed and along with it so did J. P. Stevens stock. For almost everyone the crash was a sobering experience. In the ensuing weeks everyone watched the stock market's trading activity as a recognizable early warning of drastic changes in the economy. Few were willing to take any risks, and even if they wanted to make a corporate acquisition while the prices were low, the banks were wary. But many executives found that while the market had crashed, their businesses hadn't. Companies were induced to buy their own stock because the prices were low, and in that environment, leveraged buyouts became thinkable again. With the J. P. Stevens stock trading in the 20s, it was possible to offer a huge premium for the company and still pay substantially less than it would have cost six months before.

Whit Stevens again took up the idea of buying out his company and contacted Bankers Trust to act as his investment banker. The planning took time, and by the beginning of the year, in January 1988, the merger and acquisition market showed signs that it would be as frenetic as ever. Stock prices, however, hadn't rebounded, making a buyout still look desirable. But there were a thousand judgments that had to be made before announcing a bid, and all the risks had to be measured and understood. With so much at stake, it was important to be careful. And the most important decision was the offering price. Not until February was the decision finally made, and then $43 was chosen—a significant premium over the trading price, which was still in the 20s.

On the announcement of the buyout of J. P. Stevens, the New York Stock Exchange halted trading in its stock during dissemination of the information, and when the stock again opened for trading, the market price was at $48 a share, $5.00 above the bid by Whit Stevens for the company. The market had found Whit Stevens's offer to be a low-ball bid and was betting against his buying the company at any price under $50. The expectation was that if Whit Stevens didn't raise his bid, then others would offer to buy J. P. Stevens at a much higher price. The players were arbitrageurs who were speculating, but they were a highly informed lot, and their pricing was a sharp criticism of Whit Stevens and his advisers. The reaction of the market professionals was almost immediate. Every day that the stock traded the arbitrageurs held more of it at prices higher than Whit Stevens had thought to offer, which meant that he'd probably have to raise his price.

Not only was Whit Stevens's bid undistinguished; nothing in his situation differentiated him from Bill Stokely when Stokely attempted an unsuccessful buyout of Stokely–Van Camp. Indeed, Whit Stevens had much less stock than Bill Stokely controlled and lacked Stokely's claim to hands-on leadership. Stevens looked like he was seizing an opportunity, taking advantage of the depressed market. If the seismic reverberations of the crash didn't frighten everyone, his bid was an invitation to an auction. And the J. P. Stevens board would have little choice but to orchestrate one.

Whit Stevens's buyout announcement was a total surprise to Joe, and was received the way one views self-immolation. "Does he understand what he's doing?" Joe asked. He paused after he said that, letting the question hang in the air. Whit Stevens had guaranteed that his company would be put up for auction by making an unreasonably low bid. Joe concluded that Whit Stevens had lost his bearings, and Joe remarked, "He's not close to the smoke-stacks," referring to Whit's permanent residence in New York, far from the company's operations in the South. To Joe, that said everything.

Joe understood the pressures of the marketplace and the imperatives of family control. Whatever Whit had gone over in his mind, Joe Lanier had gone over in his. Joe's interest was in running West Point and keeping it independent, knowing that it was a target company, bound to be attractive to a raider. Like Whit Stevens, he'd seen the appeal of a leveraged buyout: it took the company out of the takeover cycle. But as a practical businessman, Joe didn't like the debt burden that a buyout would bring. Its weight required more than discipline; it made you cut corners and make do with old equipment rather than replace it, which ultimately affected safety, production, and even innovation. But there was some level of debt that he could live with, a reasonable trade-off for the benefit of controlling his company. He more than toyed with the idea: he went through financial plans to see what it would take to buy the company and concluded that nothing justified a leveraged buyout unless you were directly threatened by a hostile takeover.

"We should buy J. P. Stevens," Joe said. "Someone's going to buy it, and it ought to be us."

"It'll be perceived as hostile, Joe," I said.

"It's for sale," he said. "The shareholders are supposed to get the best price. The arbitrageurs are already bidding against him. There's no reason why we shouldn't put in a cash bid."

"Whit Stevens will see it as hostile," I said.

"No doubt," Joe said. "But the company isn't his private preserve, and he's put it into play."

Joe was committed. He knew Whit and his wife socially and knew that one of the consequences of the bid would be that they wouldn't talk to him again. There was nothing he could do about that outcome. More was at stake than merely the possible breakup of someone's leveraged buyout. A vision had made itself clear to Joe, which he would follow.

Putting the two companies together would create the premier company in the bed and bath markets. J. P. Stevens had licenses for the Ralph Lauren and Laura Ashley brands among others, which presented extraordinary marketing opportunities. What was more exciting, Stevens had profit margins of about 10 percent of sales, compared with West Point's of upwards of 15 percent. Operating efficiencies would help to improve the Stevens margins if Stevens was combined with West Point. That kind of built-in profit growth would permit West Point to pay more than almost anyone else for the business. And acquiring Stevens would significantly increase West Point's debt, at least until it was able to dispose of many of the unwanted businesses. About two years would be required to rationalize the businesses and sell off those that were unrelated, which would make West Point largely takeover-proof during the period. Moreover, after it emerged from redoing itself, it would have at least a third of the market for bed and bath products in the United States, which would entitle it to a higher multiple of earnings in the marketplace, substantially increasing its stock price. Conservatively viewed, the acquisition would help Joe maintain the more than 20 percent compound growth rate the West Point stock had experienced in the last three years, which again would make West Point more difficult for a raider to acquire. This opportunity of buying J. P. Stevens wasn't to be missed. Accordingly, West Point sent a letter to the directors of J. P. Stevens indicating that it was interested in submitting a bid.

Before the bidding started, Joe Lanier tried to talk to Whit Stevens. The approach was not only to confront the human elements of the contest on a man-to-man basis but also to offer a rational economic deal that could satisfy both of them. Whit Stevens wouldn't talk to Joe, and the economic message was delivered for him through intermediaries representing Whit Stevens's acquisition vehicle, called Palmetto. The representatives were told that West Point was prepared to buy the bed and bath businesses and sell everything else to Whit Stevens. In effect, Whit would be able to retain the carpet and apparel businesses, among others (representing almost two-thirds of the assets of J. P. Stevens), on an assured basis. It was better than half a loaf and should be seriously considered. The rejection by Whit Stevens was almost immediate. After the bidding started, the same proposal was again made and rejected again. After each rejection we tried to determine what would convince Whit Stevens that it was in his interest to join forces with us rather than compete. At first he probably thought he could outbid us, and then he must have looked upon the antitrust barriers as insuperable. The personal acrimony couldn't be bridged.

The committee of independent directors of J. P. Stevens sent out a notice of the auction procedure to be followed, which included blind bids, and invited offers from all interested parties. As always, there was lively interest shown by financially oriented buyers in getting the bidding package, but we thought that few parties would participate. West Point's first bid was $56, against the market price of about $48, which was meant to preempt the field. Whit Stevens, however, made a bid, consisting of cash and paper, that nominally looked like $55. Finding the offers close, the committee called for another round.

In this further round West Point bid $61, again to make a preemptive bid and clear the field of competitors. The bids were taken in on a Friday, and a day after the auction I was called by John Golden, the partner at Goldman Sachs representing J. P.

Stevens, and told that our bid had been leaked to the next-highest bidder of $60 cash, which wasn't Whit Stevens, but an unnamed financially oriented buyer seeking to do a leveraged buyout. We chose not to challenge the failure in the procedure because West Point was given a chance to bid again. The interested party, we found out later, was Odyssey Partners, a group formed to do leveraged transactions. In that round Whit Stevens had thrown his lot in with Odyssey. He could no longer compete and felt that if Odyssey bought the company, the firm would retain the current management.

There was going to be another round, and Joe decided to raise again, from the $61 bid to $62.50, seeking once more to distance West Point from its competitors. At this point, he felt that he'd stretched farther than he thought he'd have to go. Although West Point had the high bid, the committee chose Odyssey at $61.50 because the firm didn't have an antitrust problem. Only after the auction was over, when it could no longer be taken into account for bidding, did we find out that a discount of $2.50 was being applied to West Point's bid to reflect uncertainty of completion based on antitrust considerations. The discounting action was consistent with other barriers imposed, for the committee wouldn't delay the bidding until after West Point cleared its antitrust obstacles, which would have taken about thirty days. Once Odyssey emerged as the victor in the auction by announcing a merger contract with J. P. Stevens, including a breakup fee of $1.00 a share (worth $18 million) if its offering price was topped by West Point, the only way West Point could compete was to commence a countertender at $62.50, the price it had bid in the auction. Since it was a dollar better than Odyssey's bid, the marketplace would choose West Point's tender unless the antitrust authorities indicated that they would block the deal.

Although the Reagan administration had considerably relaxed antitrust enforcement, which permitted many domestic competitors to merge, antitrust authorities still carefully watched acquisitions where there were only a few industry leaders. In those cases, the best way to overcome antitrust obstacles was to buy the company sought and then divest those parts that, according to federal guidelines, would lessen competition. Once the acquirer began operating

the business, the necessary divestitures could be precisely calibrated and effected. The government, however, wouldn't go along
with buying and then divesting, and favored a procedure known
as "fix it first," which involved selling the offending assets (or
making arrangements to sell them) before buying any of them. The
reason for the government's harsh position was that it had found
that companies rarely fixed it after they bought it, or if they did,
they were dilatory in doing so. The government didn't have the
manpower or necessary funds to monitor activity after the
acquisition.

The problem that West Point–Pepperell faced was that it was
buying a business which it had never physically examined. J. P.
Stevens wouldn't let West Point personnel on the premises. To
allow an inspection of assets, the company was requiring that West
Point agree to stand still and not make a bid except on terms
approved by J. P. Stevens. I counseled against signing the agreement. Accordingly, West Point was in the position of contracting
to sell assets that it had never seen. Considering the federal guidelines, we estimated that divestitures of 20 percent of the sheet and
50 percent of the towel business would have to be made. West Point
wanted to retain the designer products and sell the institutional
product business. The revenue stream of the institutional business
was known and the task was to find a purchaser at a reasonable
price, approximately $122 million, game enough to buy the insti-
tutional sheet and towel business sight unseen. Among the pitfalls
faced in such a purchase was not knowing the condition of plant
and equipment, which affected future capital costs and the cost of
production. Neither West Point nor Merrill Lynch could find such
a buyer until Tom Foley called Joe, having read of Joe's interest
in Stevens in the newspapers.

Tom Foley had acquired Bib in 1984 when he was little more
than thirty years old. After Harvard College and Business School,
Foley worked for McKinsey & Co., a management consulting firm,
and then moved to Citibank's venture capital organization. It was
there that he found Bib and bought it by putting up $5 million of
equity (part his own money and the largest part from friends) and
$95 million borrowed from Citibank. He left the bank to run the
company and within one year he'd paid down a substantial portion

of the debt, partially through selling assets and partially from cost reductions and improved earnings. By the time he'd come to see Joe, after controlling Bib for about four years, Bib's debt had been substantially worked down and it was in a position to make the acquisition. To make this deal, Tom Foley would be betting much that he'd made. Citibank would want Bib to co-sign the loans now that Foley had a successful company.

We all met to sell something that we couldn't describe in concrete terms. The differentiation of the products by end users was conceptual, and didn't necessarily accord with the way they were manufactured. Facilities that made institutional products also made brand-name products, and there was no way to begin to separate, without physical inspection and discussions with Whit Stevens's managers, the different businesses. The only way to make headway was to create an abstract model of a business, the way mathematicians would proceed, which was intimidating for business lawyers and businessmen used to dealing with tangible reality. After J. P. Stevens was acquired, we'd then put together a physical business in a manner most reasonably approximating the model.

Foley was a difficult negotiator. He told Joe right out he was doing West Point a favor, that he was necessary for the transaction, and that without him Joe couldn't proceed. While Joe Lanier was heavyset, Foley was all angles, lean and stringy, sharp edges at the knees and elbows and chin. As the discussions wore on, it became clear that West Point was taking all the risks. The last argument was over the liabilities of the institutional business. Attached to these J. P. Stevens plants would be liabilities, mortgages and other liens, as much a part of the physical aspects of the facilities as the operating fixtures. Foley wanted to be assured that in buying the institutional sheet and towel businesses he wouldn't be taking on any of the liabilities, that West Point would assume all of those. Foley's position was that he had to have a deal that was bankable: in other words, he was borrowing all the money to buy the business, and the bank had to know that there would be at least $122 million of assets (at book value) and matching revenue, without any offsetting liabilities. If West Point couldn't give those assurances, then Foley wouldn't play. Joe Lanier clenched his teeth and asked Foley to leave the room.

"That's one hell of a deal," Clay Sauers said. His words reflected the weariness of making concession after concession.

"He's the right man at the right time," Joe said.

"He never meets you halfway," Clay said, shaking his head.

"He doesn't have to," Joe said, "and he knows it."

"We've given him a near-perfect business," Clay said, "when no business is perfect."

"There'll be warts," Joe said. "The warts are in the leverage. He's going to have to run it to pay down the debt."

"He's young, Joe," Clay said. "He's used to living with all that debt."

Joe paused as if asking himself what would happen if negotiations failed that evening. He couldn't accept or countenance failure. This was a mission, he told me, to save his company and make it grow. He was a regular churchgoer and he'd prayed and promised to devote all his energy to this task and withstand all the pain of dealing with greed, petty peevishness, anger, and exhaustion.

"Being used to it doesn't make it any easier. He'll have to run it," Joe said, appreciating all the operating difficulties never reflected in the financial statements.

"The mortgages and liens that are on the plants go with the plants," Clay said. "He's got to take some bad with all the good he's getting."

"The reason that he's so difficult," Joe said, "is that he's become like us. He may have started out willing to bet everything, but he's built something in Bib and doesn't want to lose it. Let's call him back in to see if we can make a deal." Joe sighed. "Everything always costs a little more than you first thought. But you're right, let's protect ourselves."

Once a deal was struck with Tom Foley, antitrust clearance was in the hands of Jack Izard of King & Spalding, West Point's Atlanta law firm. Jack was a tall, courtly Southerner with impeccable manners which belied his commitment and political acumen. He had to guide the transaction through the Federal Trade Commission in fifteen calendar days, the initial period for antitrust review, and not a day longer. If the commission made a request for additional information, quite usual for a transaction between competitors, the period of time for review would be extended by at least ten calendar days, which would totally kill the credibility of West Point's offer and push the time for acceptance of shares well past Odyssey's closing date. On that basis, the market would choose the Odyssey bid, although a dollar less. It was the likely possibility of delay that had been the committee's basis for discounting the West Point bid and for favoring Odyssey. West Point was now put to the test of showing that it could clear the antitrust hurdle.

Knowing Jack to be tough and clever, it was still hard to imagine this soft-spoken gentleman ramming the transaction through the commission and its staff in record time. His major tactical weapon was the agreement with Foley that showed that the offending assets would be sold to someone who would be able to manage them and be an effective competitor. But it wasn't a perfect answer, and there would have to be some horse trading with the staff. All the offered concessions wouldn't be seen as enough, and they would try to extract some additional divestitures. Any changes would mean further negotiations with Tom Foley, which would be my responsibility.

Joe gave Jack a free hand to make the decisions as he saw fit. There really weren't enough hours in a day to accommodate all that had to be done, and a lot of the work Jack had to do ran around the clock. Each day I'd get a report, after encounters with all the commissioners and the staff members, filled with storm warnings and the effects of local squalls, averaging individual temperatures and pressure readings. Most days it seemed hopeless, but Jack persisted. Even on the fifteenth day it wasn't clear whether we'd get approved. In fact, at 5 p.m., the ordinary close of business, the commission put out a news release that they had requested additional information, which would mean the crippling of our bid by the additional ten days of review. With that announcement, Odyssey thought it had won. Twenty minutes later, however, the commission cleared West Point. The request for information had been made for the record, without requiring that additional information be produced, to accord with the policy that in acquisitions involving competitors such requests were always made. Immediately Odyssey raised its bid to $64. Since both bidders were now able to acquire J. P. Stevens, price would determine the winner.

In the same way that we'd approached Whit Stevens, Joe called

Odyssey to see if we could make a deal, rather than bid up the price for the company. After the call, Joe concluded that Odyssey's price thinking was way out of line. It wanted to sell the bed and bath businesses at a price practically equal to the price West Point thought it would have to pay for the whole of J. P. Stevens. Not only was it senseless, it was also offensive. Joe was dealing with a competitor that had an inflated estimate of the value of the businesses. The only way for him to get what he wanted was to compete directly by bidding again, but it began to seem hopeless. Odyssey's price thinking permitted it to continue to keep raising. On the final round, Odyssey bid $68.50 against West Point's $67. Odyssey was now at a price beyond which Joe wasn't prepared to raise.

Joe felt that Odyssey had bid itself into a corner, for it would be next to impossible for it to get the kinds of prices it thought it should get from breaking up the company. To confirm his thinking, Joe made an analysis of Odyssey's position. If the new owner of J. P. Stevens sold the bed and bath business, the oldest of the J. P. Stevens businesses with a low tax basis, there would be a profit realized significantly above its tax basis, which would attract a very substantial tax. The tax was punitive in amount and soured the whole deal. The only sensible tax strategy would be to sell the other, more recently acquired carpet and apparel businesses with tax bases close to their current fair value, and retain the bed and bath business. But Odyssey, at the prices bid, was expecting to sell the bed and bath business. Joe concluded that, in the heat of the auction, Odyssey had lost sight of the values (and tax strategy) and would be left with an insurmountable problem if West Point didn't raise its bid. Joe informed the Odyssey partners of his tax analysis, letting them know that he thought they were out on a limb. They realized then that Joe would walk away, and it didn't take long for them to acknowledge their problem. They proposed that West Point swap places with them, which meant that West Point would also bid $68.50 and be allowed to buy all stock tendered. Once West Point acquired Stevens, Odyssey would buy the other J. P. Stevens businesses from West Point. It was a strange situation, one that had never occurred before. Finally someone was acknowledging that it was possible to bid too much.

We were then able to sit down with Odyssey to negotiate the

prices for all the other J. P. Stevens businesses. West Point, however, was in a powerful bargaining position and wouldn't bid $68.50 until it was satisfied with the prices to be paid for the businesses Odyssey wanted. What was clear from the outset was that Whit Stevens was no longer a party to the discussions and that J. P. Stevens would be broken up without any of the Stevens senior management participating. It was more complicated than a mere swap of positions. There had to be a three-way split of J. P. Stevens. Foley and West Point would take the bed and bath businesses, and Odyssey Partners the other textile businesses. (Little more than a year later Odyssey Partners was to feel the effect of the heavy acquisition debt incurred to buy those textile businesses and ultimately put the businesses into bankruptcy to rationalize the debt structure, taking the losses from bidding up the price of the businesses.)

None of us had contemplated an immediate carve-up of J. P. Stevens at the closing. The thinking had been that it would take a year or two to make the dispositions of all the unwanted businesses. The auction, however, had flushed out all the interested buyers. The disposition of the J. P. Stevens businesses to Odyssey and Foley at the closing was an efficient vehicle for keeping West Point from being burdened with cumbersome and unwanted debt. Most of the money that would have been borrowed to buy the whole company (and then repaid from the sale of the parts) didn't have to be borrowed, and West Point's purchase obligations were limited to only those businesses that it would be running directly. Management was able to get on with the job of integrating the acquired sheet and towel brands without operating what would have been the corporate equivalent of a used-car lot, selling textile assets, such as apparel and carpet businesses. Dashed was the hope, however, that putting the two companies together would dissuade others from being interested in acquiring West Point. In many respects West Point looked more attractive now than it had before the acquisition. It possessed a unique market position in bed and bath products, with the largest market share of any company and most attractive margins.

No more than six months passed before there were intimations that a takeover bid would be made to acquire West Point. In

October 1988, William Farley, through his company, Farley Industries, offered to acquire West Point at $48 a share, for an
aggregate price of about $1.5 billion. Who was William Farley and
what was the source of his interest? When I found out, it was as
if all the avoidance actions we'd taken had led West Point inevitably
into Farley's orbit.

The information available on William Farley was a hodgepodge.
Most obvious was the public figure, the man who had thrown his
hat in the ring in early 1988 as a Democratic candidate for the
United States presidency. In preparation, he'd hired Jack Albertine, one of Senator Lloyd Bentsen's speechwriters, and made him
vice chairman of his company. Albertine scripted a series of national television spots, costing about $2.5 million, in which Farley
talked earnestly in locker rooms and other sports settings about
the benefits of teamwork and good management. One of them had
him standing alongside a swimming pool saying, "Just imagine being
a diver for a coach who pushes you to do a lot of dives as fast as
you can, instead of one perfect dive. Is putting quantity before
quality any way to win?" In personal appearances in Iowa, he
pledged that he'd reduce the federal deficit, neglecting to mention
that his whole business structure was supported by massive borrowings. His candidacy fizzled early in the Iowa caucuses, but the
public persona was still on display. He dated a recent Miss America
and promoted Fruit of the Loom products on television while shown
pumping iron in the ads. Handsome, physically fit, with high-status
women on his arm, he cultivated the image of the all-American
male from a humble background. He'd grown up in Pawtucket,
Rhode Island, where his father had been a postman.

His business success, unlike his image, was spotty. He was an
early believer in leverage, embracing the concept of financing with
debt as only the undercapitalized can. Though trained as a lawyer,
Farley never practiced law. He worked as a financial analyst in
mergers and acquisitions at NL Industries (the old National Lead)
and then as an investment banker at Lehman Brothers in Chicago.
He did his first negotiated deal in 1976 when he was twenty-nine
years old, putting up $25,000 of his own money to buy a metals
company from his old employer NL for $1.7 million. Until 1984 all
his deals were negotiated acquisitions in which he risked everything

he'd earned to keep growing larger. In 1984 he paid $135 million for Condec, using $10 million in equity, outbidding the company's management for control of the company. The acquisition was a financial disaster. The company experienced significant cumulative losses, upwards of $100 million, until settlements were made with the creditors in 1988. But in the merger marketplace, Farley was seen as a success because he'd won an auction. In 1985, before the effects of the operating difficulties at Condec were felt, Drexel Burnham backed Farley against Don Kelly of Esmark in his bid for Northwest Industries, which became Farley Industries. The acquisition price for Northwest was $1.4 billion, a tenfold increase in acquisition size for Farley in little more than a year, engineered largely through Drexel Burnham's junk bonds. In that acquisition Farley sold off all the businesses except Fruit of the Loom, the crown jewel, which continued to grow with the help of professional managers already in place at the company. That billion-dollar acquisition, with the operating success of Fruit of the Loom, gave Farley national business prominence and allowed him to raise money for further deals and settle up the mistakes made in the Condec acquisition.

In February 1988, Farley Industries raised $500 million from junk-bond sales sponsored by Drexel Burnham, $300 million of which would be a war chest to make acquisitions. The bondholders left the target to Farley and Mike Milken, who had placed the bonds with them. Farley's successful management team was at Fruit of the Loom, so he was looking closely at textile and apparel companies. The timing of the raising of the money coincided with Whit Stevens's announcement of the buyout of J. P. Stevens. Once West Point bid, Whit Stevens contacted Farley and had him look at the company and its prospects, in the hope that Farley would serve as a White Knight. Farley did a study of J. P. Stevens and became familiar with its business, but declined to bid. Stevens alone wasn't an inviting target for him. But half a year later Farley hadn't found a target, and West Point and Stevens together became a very interesting acquisition opportunity.

The $500 million of junk bonds issued by Farley Industries bore annual interest of from 14.6 to 15.6 percent, costing about $80 million a year. There weren't sufficient earnings in Farley Indus-

tries (including the earnings from Fruit of the Loom) to come anywhere near to covering those carrying costs. The proceeds of the
bonds, which were meant to be the acquisition war chest, were
being used to cover the interest, and Farley Industries showed
negative net worth on its financial statements. Everyone knew that
Farley had to make an acquisition; otherwise the bonds would
bankrupt him. The theory was that if a good acquisition was made,
the excess assets of the acquired business could be sold to pay down
a fair portion of the debt and the earning assets could be polished
and squeezed to service the remaining debt. In practice, that theory
had always worked, for each year companies were worth more than
they had cost, especially good companies, and there was little or
no risk in the process of getting into a business and then getting
out of it. Everyone always sold businesses for more than they paid
for them, sometimes substantially more.

There was a corollary theory at work, which also encouraged
acquisitions: it wasn't possible to pay too much, at least in the long
term. If the business was a market leader and you paid too much
because anticipated earnings didn't match required payments, the
debt could be stretched out over a longer term to accommodate a
difference in the business cycle. In the period when delays in debt
payment might be required, then Mike Milken would be there to
help with the holders of the junk bonds, always able to swap the
debt securities of one kind for other securities that more easily
accommodated current needs. Ultimately, under this theory, the
value of the unique assets of the business would pay off. The one
thing that had been clear for as long as people could remember
was that equity compounded every year at a greater rate than even
interest on high-yield junk debt, and the longer you held on to the
entrepreneurial equity, the greater your reward, which meant that
the more you borrowed, the greater the winnings. Clint Murcheson,
the wildcat oilman, was supposed to have said that a man is worth
two times what he owes, which made him a visionary in some
quarters.

Bill Farley, backed by Drexel Burnham, was formidable. Indeed,
the adversary was Mike Milken, the power behind Drexel. Farley
might pick the target, but Drexel would supply the cash. The more
Farley paid, the greater Drexel's power, for the debt would control

the equity until it was substantially repaid. Given that relationship, there would be few restraints on Farley's bidding for West Point: Drexel was his safety net, always there to refinance the debt. There was another powerful incentive for Farley to ignore all customary bidding limits. The credit of his crown jewel, Fruit of the Loom, wasn't involved in the financing, nor was his personal equity interest in Fruit of the Loom. If he defaulted on the loans, his personal wealth was safe, unless he chose to commit it at some later time. For the first time, he'd taken a significant portion of his winnings out of the game.

Farley had a theme: superior managerial and marketing skill. He'd turned Fruit of the Loom around and substantially increased its profit margins. From his perspective, West Point's vision was faulty. Its game plan was to bring the Stevens assets up to West Point's margins, and those margins were their ceiling. Bill Farley felt that Joe Lanier had aimed too low. Also, he'd keep West Point largely in the bed and bath business, where he saw the most profit, and sell off all the apparel businesses, including Cluett Peabody, a recent West Point acquisition effected before West Point acquired J. P. Stevens. Bill Farley would be competing to buy West Point not only on the basis of cost cutting but also on the basis of more aggressive marketing, which meant he could pay more than anyone who didn't share his vision.

How could you stop someone so formidable? There was only one blocking move, and that was to challenge leverage itself. We brought a case in the Federal District Court in Atlanta, the court nearest West Point's headquarters, alleging that Farley's financing for the offer violated the federal margin rules. Those rules, part of the New Deal legislation correcting deficiencies in the financial system, were adopted after the stock market crash of 1929 to curb speculative buying of stocks largely with borrowed money. The margin rules require that at least half the purchase price of stock come from equity, the acquirer's own funds, and not from borrowed money. Paul Volcker, when he was chairman of the Federal Reserve, had expressed significant concern with highly leveraged merger transactions, especially hostile takeovers by shell companies financing acquisitions largely through the target's own assets. The Federal Reserve issued an interpretation of the margin regulations

meant to limit these highly leveraged transactions because they
could easily fail in an economic downturn and weaken the financial
system. Although unintended, the interpretation encouraged negotiated leveraged buyouts, since it set guidelines that could easily be
followed, in friendly transactions, without needing significant equity. Most hostile transactions did not remain so to the bitter end.
At some stage the parties commenced negotiations. To the extent
that a hostile transaction resulted in the target's finally agreeing to
be taken over at an acceptable price, the interpretation also facilitated the transaction at that time. But during the period of hostility
the interpretation could be used to defend against the leveraged
takeover bid. Relying on Volcker's regulations, we believed that we
had a clear-cut case to stop the takeover bid. Farley showed only
$300 million of equity out of transaction costs of $1.5 billion, and
the $300 million called equity came directly from the Drexel-placed
junk bonds. Thus, the bid was based solely on borrowed money.

Judge G. Ernest Tidwell in Atlanta concluded, however, that
there was no right of action by private parties to enforce the Federal
Reserve's rules, which meant that the court couldn't act on West
Point's complaint. If enforcement action was necessary, the court
found, it should be done by the federal regulatory agencies. The
court, however, stated that the "financing is substantially suspect
and may be a violation of the margin requirements," and asked
the Federal Reserve to look into the matter. Following the court's
lead, we wrote to the Federal Reserve, which asked for position
papers from both parties, much like briefs. Once the Federal Reserve decided the issue, it would have to be turned over to the
SEC, which enforced the margin rules. It was a curious split of
authority between the agencies, existing only because of historical
circumstances. We felt we were on fairly solid ground with the
SEC, as well as the Federal Reserve, since the former chairman of
the SEC, John Shad, had, like Volcker, given a number of speeches
expressing concern with the increased use of borrowed money to
make acquisitions.

Farley's claim was that Farley Industries was not a shell company
and therefore the rules didn't apply to his takeover bid. When
examined carefully, however, it was clear that he was proposing
to make an acquisition for about $1.5 billion using Farley Industries

as his equity. But Farley Industries had a negative net worth, its surplus earnings having been drained by bond interest. On that basis, we argued that there was a clear violation. Joe Lanier called all the congressmen and senators that West Point had dealt with over the years concerning all phases of its businesses, including tax policy and import duties. West Point was able to contact a broad group and got many of them to urge the commission and the Federal Reserve to enforce the rules. We told everyone that this was the perfect case to use to speak out against high leverage. Farley Industries was a failing company without the acquisition. All the acquisition did was impose the debt of a failing company on West Point, weakening it as a competitive company. A downturn in the economy would make a wasteland out of a fine company, costing numerous jobs, benefiting foreign competitors.

No one wanted to take up the debate in this case. The Federal Reserve took the position that where there was a holding company such as Farley Industries involved with a principal operating subsidiary such as Fruit of the Loom, a determination of whether excessive leverage was being used was a question of fact. The Federal Reserve stated that it wasn't a fact finder, merely an agency that expressed rules, and it would be up to the SEC to look into the facts of the matter. With that position, the Federal Reserve could ignore the fact that Fruit of the Loom's credit and earnings weren't standing behind Farley Industries and leave findings like that to the SEC. The SEC took the position that it hadn't been given any clear direction by the Federal Reserve and that it wasn't going to get into the midst of an ongoing takeover battle. At one level it was an internecine dispute between the two agencies, and at another it was a complete withdrawal by them from the responsibility of dealing with the issues. Nothing can be more frustrating to a lawyer than silly finger pointing. Joe expressed his anger: "Getting them to act is like trying to nail Jell-O to the wall." What we had learned was that no one wanted to intervene in a particular case and stop the merger music. The effect of such an intervention on the financial system and the economy was unpredictable, and contemplating calling a halt to leveraging paralyzed both agencies. They felt that it was up to Congress to add new rules, after debating the political and economic consequences, rather than themselves enforcing the old rules. But even Congress was wary of taking any action. In October 1987, congressional talk of limiting interest deductions in corporate acquisitions, which would deter leveraged deals, had been implicated as an important factor in the market crash of October 19. Thereafter, there had been few regulatory initiatives directly attacking leveraging.

Our failure with the agencies to stop his offer emboldened Farley, just as we'd run out of effective defenses. All other challenges to Farley's tender offer were simply delaying tactics. Early on in the fight Joe Lanier had said, "We'll fight him until hell freezes over, and then we'll fight him on the ice." It was a rallying cry that showed the spirit of the man, but he knew that if we couldn't stop the Farley bid on the basis of its leverage, West Point would be put up for auction. Once that happened, Joe would have to bid for the company, and West Point would end up being highly leveraged, devoted to servicing its debt, not anything like the company that Joe had helped build.

There was one hope in delay and that was that Drexel would fail and Farley's offer would then fall flat. By November 1988 everyone knew that Drexel was subject to criminal indictment for certain of its junk-bond and takeover activities. The indictments were the outgrowth of the SEC's insider-trading investigations based on the confessions of Dennis Levine in May 1986. What had started out as a small upsetting vibration with convictions of players such as Levine, Robert Wilkis, and Ilan Reich had become a sizable quake threatening the foundations of merger activity. The effects of imminent criminal action against Drexel and of investigations of Milken were already noticeable in the marketplace. When Henry Kravis had proposed to do the buyout of Macmillan, he'd appeared with Drexel, but had Merrill Lynch as a backup. If Drexel couldn't put the deal together, he told me, then Merrill would, indicating that even at that time there was some question by knowledgeable bidders about Drexel's financial muscle and long-term viability.

We could delay Farley until about February 1989—six months from his October 1988 starting date. For defense, we interposed the "poison pill" between Farley and West Point. The pill was so named because once adopted (in effect swallowed) it allowed the shareholders of the target company to buy shares of either the target company or the raider at half price. All shareholders had this right, proportionate to the shares they owned, except the raider. The pill became lethal when the raider crossed a predetermined threshold of share purchases in the target company, usually between 10 and 20 percent. The raider could request the board of the target company to "redeem" the pill (in effect rescinding it) to permit the raider's offer to be considered by shareholders. As fiduciaries, the board of the target company had to carefully consider the fairness of the offer. If the board rejected the raider's request for redemption (cancellation of the rights to acquire stock for half price), then the raider could take his case to the courts to consider whether the directors had acted properly or to the shareholders, requesting them to change the incumbent directors in favor of a slate proposed by the raider. The raider's slate would seek shareholder votes on the platform that they would "redeem" the pill, making way for the raider's offer. Imposing the pill in the face of an offer, at the least, usually bought time for the target, which otherwise would only have twenty business days in which to defend. The end point for West Point was its annual meeting, in February, when Farley could take his case to the shareholders. Farley's lawyers also understood that by the time of the annual meeting they would be able to present to the shareholders their proposal in the form of a proxy solicitation seeking removal of the West Point board of directors. West Point couldn't withstand that solicitation, which would pave the way for Farley's bid, and had to provide a financial alternative to Farley's tender. The question was whether Drexel would fail by then. If so, either Farley's bid would expire for lack of financing or he would be outbid.

Farley never faltered. He made the rounds of the Georgia and South Carolina state legislatures, introducing himself, acting like the new owner of West Point, promising people that if he controlled the assets, he'd expand the business. He might have to sell Cluett Peabody, he openly admitted, but he had no intention of selling other assets or changing the headquarters or the venue of operations. Wherever he went, he gave syrupy assurance, which played well, for West Point hadn't shown any ability to derail him and his audience was appreciative of his attention to them. Not until much later did he announce that he would sell all assets other than the bed and bath business.

Farley well understood the risks he ran from delay, but there was nothing that his lawyers or investment bankers could do to accelerate the process. He felt that if he could talk to Joe he'd be able to convince him to step aside. But Joe wouldn't talk to him, for there was nothing to say. Joe knew that Farley would just try to sell himself and wouldn't listen to what Joe had to say. Farley, however, persisted. Finally, in a move that I'd never seen before, he demanded to be allowed to attend Joe's deposition in the ongoing court case between the companies. It wasn't a sensible way for the two men to get together, but Farley was entitled as a matter of law to be present at the deposition of his adversary. Farley hoped that if he was in the same room with Joe, Joe would talk to him at some time.

Joe's deposition was taken in Atlanta at the offices of King & Spalding, and Farley sat quietly in the room waiting for an opportunity to talk to Joe. But Joe ignored him. Finally, during a break, Joe left the room to go to the bathroom, and Farley followed him. No one else went along, and Farley and Joe stood next to each other at adjacent urinals. When he came out Joe was asked what had transpired. "He introduced himself," Joe said, and then smiled in a cherubic Southern way and added, "and we politely acknowledged each other." Later Joe observed, "Ego's driving him. He won't stop."

In January, Drexel was indicted and settled with the government, agreeing to pay $650 million in fines and assorted damages. In that connection, Milken withdrew from the firm. But the payment of the huge sum and the loss of Milken didn't then seem to have weakened Drexel's vigor, and the admissions of wrongdoing didn't seem to have affected its ability to do business in the marketplace. It had been able during the past three months to place enormous quantities of junk bonds for the leveraged buyout of RJR Nabisco, first as a bridge loan and then in the form of permanent financing. There seemed to be some contraction of the market for junk bonds, but that was accounted for by the herculean effort of Drexel to place the RJR debt, which sopped up most funds available for junk debt. When it came to Farley's tender offer, Drexel continued to state that it was highly confident that it could finance the offer. What we didn't know was that Leon Black, acting as adviser to Farley at Drexel, was having trouble convincing the Drexel organization to "buy" West Point. It later came out in the press that Drexel traders in a "screaming match" with Black warned him against the deal, saying they would have trouble selling the junk bonds. Black was reputed to have castigated them by saying, "Since Mike left you're all lousy salesmen." Finally, through force of personality, Black was able to get the Drexel organization to work for the deal.

In February 1989, Joe announced that the company would be put up for auction and that a bidding package would be made available to all interested buyers. As expected, those interested were all financial buyers looking to compete against Drexel. Joe decided that he'd help anyone bid for the company against Farley, which was the most sensible strategy. Whoever outbid Farley could then make a deal with Joe Lanier and his management team.

A committee of independent directors was formed and they would structure the auction procedures and negotiate with all the bidders. We continued to represent the company and the directors. Joe withdrew from any participation in consideration of the bids and was treated like an outsider. Merrill Lynch, which had been the investment banker for the company, asked to withdraw from its representation in order to participate in putting together a group that would also make a bid. They thought that they had an excellent chance of winning and were committed to retaining the management. Goldman Sachs, which had been co-banker with them, would conduct the auction with the committee.

Everyone was told it would be a blind bidding procedure. Such a procedure was usually used in corporate auctions to maximize the bids. All bidders were told to bid cash. When the final sealed bids were opened, Farley had bid $58, making him the clear winner.

He was notified immediately. I then spoke to Joe and told him that Farley had won the auction.

"No one was going to beat him," Joe said. He paused, wanting to speak his mind. "But how is he going to make it work for him and pay down the debt? I don't see it."

Farley was eager to get his tender offer closed, and acted as a gracious winner in all respects. By the end of his offer, 95 percent of West Point's shares were tendered, and he bought them all.

Thereafter, Farley visited West Point, Georgia, and was received with a parade in his honor. The turnout was grand, and for the day the town was renamed "Farleyville," proclaimed in streaming, bright banners.

And then everything collapsed around Farley. This tender offer was the last deal that Drexel was able to finance as the stresses of the indictment and the loss of capital in fines began to show. Drexel wasn't able to support a weakening junk-bond market which began to fail as recessionary pressures in the economy slackened corporate revenues. And Farley was affected by the failures in the junk-bond market almost immediately. He'd anticipated selling Cluett Peabody, the apparel company, for about $600 million but finally was able to get only about $350 million, part in cash and part in notes. The buyer had also been relying on Drexel for financing, and when Drexel couldn't raise the money, the offering price was drastically cut. Farley took what he could get, but that sale practically wiped out the $300 million that Farley had put into the West Point acquisition. Other assets that he planned on selling couldn't be sold, leaving the debt piled higher and on more costly terms than had been thought possible. If the assets he couldn't sell were realistically priced, then the whole structure was insolvent.

The banks, weakened by failing acquisition loans, wouldn't lend Farley any more money and Drexel couldn't raise any more. As a result, the unthinkable happened. Farley wasn't able to buy the remaining 5 percent of West Point and replace all the temporary acquisition financing. There was no other case like this one. This was the high-water point in the merger tide, and as the financing sources withdrew, Farley was left high and dry, able only to pledge his Fruit of the Loom stock, putting everything at risk, to buy time in the hope that the market would come back soon enough for him.

And Joe Lanier, dismissed by Farley, joined an investment group to acquire Dan River, which he now runs and which competes against a debt-weakened West Point, the company he and his family helped build.

I remember Chief Justice Roger Traynor, for whom I'd been a

law clerk after law school, saying to me, over twenty years before these events, that "change hurts." It was an eye-opening statement to me then because I'd always benefited from change. And looking back, I know that I am a creature of change, for lawyers administer it and it's the source of our activity. I continue to welcome it and encourage it, but it isn't always for the best. And there are considerable costs.

EPILOGUE:
NOTHING PERSONAL

▼

"The Wall Street Journal doesn't print obituaries."

The tender offer was scheduled to start on my birthday but was foiled at the last minute by my client's business partner, who had a change of heart. Taken off guard by the precipitous withdrawal, my client couldn't cancel about $40,000 worth of space, one-third of a page in *The Wall Street Journal*, heralding the proposed offer. Experienced in these matters, the *Journal* was nimble enough to eliminate the announcement and wise enough not to leave blank space commemorating the misjudgment. Not surprisingly, it would fill that space with an advertisement noting the merits and services of the *Journal*, all at the client's expense, unless an alternative advertisement was promptly supplied. The client had no ready ad copy, but came up with a novel idea, as he pushed his chair away from his desk. "How about making it a birthday card?"

"What do you mean?" I asked, not quite fully grasping where he was headed.

"It's your birthday," he said, standing to explain. "Happy birthday," and his hands outlined a layout and made squiggle movements to show the message. "It's a wonderful tombstone. You'll keep it with your collection."

"Don't do that," I said, finding it intimidating.

"Why not?" he asked.

"It's too flamboyant for me," I said.

"Relax," he said, not listening to me. "It's fun."

And with that he picked up the phone, called the *Journal*, and told them the message. There was a long pause while he listened to the person at the paper, after which he belligerently said, "It's my space." There was a short pause, then he hung up in a huff.

Turning to me, he said, "No personals. The *Journal* doesn't print personals."

"It's the thought that counts," I said. Although pleased that he'd thought about me, I was relieved that I didn't have to bear the telephone calls that such a birthday card would provoke.

"Let me try again," he said, about to tackle this situation with the enthusiasm and energy he gave to everything. "I'll get the supervisor of the department."

"Please, don't do this for me," I said.

"I want to."

"Another call won't change anything," I said to discourage him. "The paper has a very precise and limited view of its role. It doesn't print obituaries, for example. That's for the *Times*."

That gave him pause. "You're right," he said. "But that's a failing too." He didn't take his hand away from the phone. "Businessmen aren't properly appreciated by the *Times* unless the social ingredients of their lives amount to something. And then the central part, their business, is left out or described only in broad strokes."

"The *Journal* doesn't see reporting businessmen's lives as part of its job," I said.

"What's the *Journal* trying to avoid?"

"Probably making judgments, showing the blessed and the ill-fated," I said.

"Where else does it show timidity?" he asked. "Our lives are entwined in our businesses. The *Journal* should understand that better than anybody else." He smiled self-consciously. "And few of us are social figures interesting enough for the *Times*."

"This is all a far cry from personals," I reminded him. My obituary example had gotten him off on a tangent, one in which he was far too emotionally involved.

"Another fault," he said, apparently irritated enough now to feel justified in making the further call.

Another relatively short conversation with the *Journal* ensued.

"He was a wise guy. You know what he said to me?"

"What?"

" 'Nothing personal.' That's how he turned me down. He said, 'Nothing personal,' and chuckled. Cute, he thinks he's clever. Probably used that line a hundred times."

Like many driven men, being thwarted angered him.

"It's the thought that counts," I said again.

"How old are you?" he asked.

I told him.

"You'll survive this," he said, smiling.

"There'll be other cards," I said.

"Not as neat," he said, sitting down behind his desk, still bothered. "He doesn't understand his own paper. Everything in there gets personal. Sometimes very personal. I wish I'd said that to him."

"You said enough."

"I'm not sure."

"Nothing you could say would convince them."

"Do you think we'll be able to put this deal back together?" he asked.

"It's hard to tell. The market's changed and your partner has lost his confidence."

"It's getting harder to hold things together," he mused. The effects of losing the deal were beginning to show. He seemed tired, no longer optimistic.

"This was a $750 million deal," he said. "Not so long ago I was doing $5 and $10 million deals. I may have to go back to doing smaller deals."

"Times change," I said.

"Faster than I can understand. And that's my point," he said, getting back to what was bothering him. "Birthdays help to mark change, make sense of things. And when people die, in their obituaries we see the ups and downs they experienced, the changes they lived through." He pushed the phone back on the desk as if it were useless. "That's history. That's substance. And it makes sense of the news." He paused, somewhat deflated. "I couldn't say that to him," he said. "But it's well worth thinking about."

"Not only when people die."

"He should pay half for the space," he said abruptly, referring to his former partner. "Even more than that."

"He owes you for half," I said.

"Nothing's in writing."

"Doesn't matter."

"Good," he said, relaxing. "Are you working on any other deals?" he asked.

"A couple."

"I'll have another one soon," he said with assurance, as if telling me would help it along.

"There's no end to deals," I said. Deal making, I'd learned, is as fundamental to business as change is to our society.

"Good," he said. "I know something will happen."

AUTHOR'S NOTE AND
ACKNOWLDGMENTS

This is a work of memory. The events described cover more than twenty years and were experienced without any intention of writing about them. Only after most of the period was past did I perceive the significance of the time and the events.

Working from memory requires reconstruction. My commitment was to accuracy. The task I set for myself was to discuss only illustrative transactions and events, to be as unobtrusive as possible in the lives of the people described, and not to disclose any confidences or privileged matters. Where persons who were clients were described in more than a superficial way, I furnished the material to them and discussed it with them and, if requested, with their advisors. It should be understood that no client waived in any manner the lawyer-client privilege, or any other privilege, with respect to any matters covered. The process of reviewing the material with others was helpful to me. The events took on more depth as other perspectives were considered, and factual accuracy was enhanced. The point of view presented is my own, and it almost goes without saying that any mistakes are mine. I appreciate the cooperation I received and want especially to thank Ilan Reich, who was willing to relive, in exhausting detail, a dark period of his life. Ilan's personal strength is evident. He has renewed his marriage, grown his family to four children, and extended his skills working as a business executive in Manhattan.

The events covered are often related as stories with scenes and dialogue. That is the way I experienced them and think about them. The dialogue should not be considered as a verbatim report. The dialogue set out in this book is a reconstruction of what I remember the persons said or rendition of their point of view in the situations described.

This work took over four years to write. No undertaking for such an extended period can be carried out without the encouragement of others. I am most appreciative of Kitty Hawks's love and affection. Her Hawk eye always seeks and finds the elegant structure and the simple solution. Kitty also understands people and knows how to get things done. Kitty found Kathy Robbins, my literary agent, for me. Kathy was as committed as I was, sometimes more so (which is a tribute to her, given my own determination). Kathy is smart and wise and as good a counselor as I have ever met. Kathy brought me to my editor, Linda Healey. Linda is astute, thoughtful, and perceptive. Her diligence astounded me and it was no surprise to find that she understood the cases as well as I did. From first to last, my secretary, Monica Alessi, saw me through every step. She was my first reader, and the first reader always holds a very special place in a writer's heart. Even the birth of her son Vincent didn't interfere with her delivery of the manuscript. With all that support, the four years did not seem long.

INDEX